SINAI AND ZION

New Voices in Biblical Studies

edited by

Adela Yarbro Collins

and

John J. Collins

SINAI & ZION

An Entry into the Jewish Bible

by Jon D. Levenson

HarperOne
An Imprint of HarperCollinsPublishers

HarperOne

HarperCollins books may be purchased for educational, business, or sales promotional use. For information please write: Special Markets Department, HarperCollins Publishers, 10 East 53rd Street, New York, NY 10022.

HarperCollins Web site: http://www.harpercollins.com

HarperCollins®, ♛®, and HarperOne™ are trademarks of HarperCollins Publishers.

FIRST HARPERCOLLINS PAPERBACK EDITION PUBLISHED IN 1987

Library of Congress Cataloging-in-Publication Data

Levenson, Jon Douglas.
    Sinai and Zion.

    Includes bibliographical references and index.
    1. Bible. O.T.—Theology.   2. Covenants (Theology)—Biblical teaching.   3. Temple of God.   I. Title.
BS1192.5.L47   221.6   87–45186
ISBN 978–0–06–254828–3

13 14 15 RRD(H) 29 28

TO THE MEMORY OF MY FATHER
Donald W. Levenson, זצ"ל
Montani semper liberi.

CONTENTS

Preface   viii
Table of Abbreviations   ix
Introduction   1

PART 1: SINAI,
THE MOUNTAIN OF THE COVENANT

1. The Sinaitic Experience or the Traditions about It?   15
2. YHWH's Home in No Man's Land   19
3. Sinai and the Covenant Formulary   23
4. The Theology of the Historical Prologue   36
5. *Mitsvot* as the End of History   42
6. Are Laws the Same as Commandments?   45
7. Ethics and Ritual in the Light of Covenant Theology   50
8. One God or One Lord?   56
9. The Kingship of God and the Kingship of Man   70
10. The Wedding of God and Israel   75
11. The Ever-Renewed Covenant   80

PART 2: ZION,
THE MOUNTAIN OF THE TEMPLE

1. The Early History of Zion in Prose Traditions   89
2. The House of YHWH and the House of David   97
3. The Vitality of Myth in Biblical Israel   102
4. Zion as the Cosmic Mountain   111
5. The Temple as Sacred Space   137
6. Sacred Space and Sacred Time   142
7. The Meaning of the Cosmic Mountain in Israel   145
8. Yearning for the Temple   176
9. The Survival of the Temple in Judaism   178

PART 3: THE MANIFOLD RELATIONSHIPS
BETWEEN SINAI AND ZION

1. Zion as the Heir to Sinai   187
2. Sinai and Zion, North and South   188
3. Covenant Renewal on the Cosmic Mountain   206
4. Moses and David   209

Index of Citations   219
Index of Authors   225

PREFACE

Begun in the summer of 1979, this study was completed in a first draft during a leave-year in Jerusalem, in 1980–81. Thanks are due to those who helped make that year so pleasant for my family and me, especially three eminent scholars at the Hebrew University, Moshe Weinfeld, Jonas Greenfield, and Moshe Greenberg. I owe a debt of gratitude to a number of individuals who were kind enough to read all or part of the manuscript and to offer me their expert advice: Gösta Ahlström, Michael Brown, Richard Clifford, Baruch Halpern, Peter Machinist, Melinda Reagor, and my indefatigable and ever supportive editor, John Collins. Although I have profited from their wisdom, the errors that remain are strictly my own responsibility. Two typists, one on each side of the Atlantic, who proved their expertise in decipherment, also deserve special mention: Hannah Groumi and Michelle Harewood.

I have tried to keep the quotations from the Bible to a minimum. Those that do appear are my own translations, which often show the influence of the New English Bible and the new translations from the Jewish Publication Society. As in the latter version, verse numbers in this study refer to the Hebrew, rather than the English, where there is a divergence.

Jewish tradition forbids the vocalization of the four-letter name of God, which is conventionally but inadequately translated as "Lord." Jews pronounce it as "Adonai" or "Ha-Shem." In this book it appears as "YHWH" without vowels, even in references to literature in which it was originally vocalized.

Skokie, Illinois
October 2, 1984

This paperback differs from the hardbound edition only in certain minor corrections, almost all of them typographical. I thank Professor Robert L. Cohn for giving me the list of misprints that he had noted in preparing his review of the volume for the *Journal of Religion*.

In the rush to get out the first edition of *Sinai and Zion,* I neglected to thank Randall Zachman for his last-minute contribution in helping me with the proofreading and in preparing the indices.

August 24, 1986

TABLE OF ABBREVIATIONS

AOAT	Alter Orient und Altes Testament
AB	Anchor Bible
AnBib	Analecta Biblica
AJSR	*Association for Jewish Studies Review*
ANET	*Ancient Near Eastern Texts Relating to the Old Testament*, 3rd ed; ed. J. B. Pritchard (Princeton: Princeton University Press, 1969)
ASOR	American Schools of Oriental Research
BA	*Biblical Archaeologist*
BAR	*Biblical Archaeologist Reader*
BASOR	*Bulletin of the American Schools of Oriental Research*
Bib	*Biblica*
BK	*Bibel und Kirche*
BKAT	Biblischer Kommentar: Altes Testament
BZAW	Beihefte zur *Zeitschrift für die Alttestamentliche Wissenschaft*
CBQ	*Catholic Biblical Quarterly*
CJ	*Conservative Judaism*
ConBOT	Coniectanea biblica, Old Testament
Diss	Dissertion
EJ	*Encyclopaedia Judaica*
EvT	*Evangelische Theologie*
FRLANT	Forschungen zur Religion und Literatur des Alten und Neuen Testaments
HAR	*Hebrew Annual Review*
HR	*History of Religions*
HSM	Harvard Semitic Monographs
HSS	Harvard Semitic Series
HTR	*Harvard Theological Review*
HUCA	*Hebrew Union College Annual*
IDBSup	*Interpreter's Dictionary of the Bible, Supplement*
JAOS	*Journal of the American Oriental Society*
JBL	*Journal of Biblical Literature*
JES	*Journal of Ecumenical Studies*
JNES	*Journal of Near Eastern Studies*
JR	*Journal of Religion*
JTS	*Journal of Theological Studies*

ix

LXX	The Septuagint	
MT	Masoretic Text	
OTL	Old Testament Library	
SBT	Studies in Biblical Theology	
TLZ	*Theologische Literaturzeitung*	
TWAT	*Theologisches Wörterbuch zum Alten Testament*	
VT	*Vetus Testamentum*	
VTSup	Vetus Testamentum, Supplements	
WMANT	Wissenschaftliche Monographien zum Alten und Neuen Testament	

BOOKS IN THE HEBREW BIBLE,
THE APOCRYPHA, AND THE NEW TESTAMENT

Gen	Ps (pl.: Pss)	Sus
Exod	Job	Tob
Lev	Prov	Wis
Num	Ruth	Matt
Deut	Cant	Mark
Josh	Eccl (Qoh)	Luke
Judg	Lam	John
1–2 Sam	Esth	Acts
1–2 Kgs	Dan	Rom
Isa	Ezra	1–2 Cor
Jer	Neh	Gal
Ezek	1–2 Chr	Eph
Hos	1–2–3–4 Kgdms	Phil
Joel	Add Esth	Col
Amos	Bar	1–2 Thess
Obad	Bel	1–2 Tim
Jonah	1–2 Esdr	Titus
Mic	4 Ezra	Phlm
Nah	Jdt	Heb
Hab	Ep Jer	Jas
Zeph	1–2–3–4 Macc	1–2 Pet
Hag	Pr Azar	1–2–3 John
Zech	Pr Man	Jude
Mal	Sir	Rev

ORDERS AND TRACTATES
IN MISHNAIC AND RELATED LITERATURE

m. indictes Mishnah   *b.* indicates Babylonian Talmūd

'Abot	*'Abot*	*Nazir*	*Nazir*
'Arak.	*'Arakin*	*Ned.*	*Nedarim*
'Abod. Zar.	*'Aboda Zara*	*Neg.*	*Nega'im*
B. Bat.	*Baba Batra*	*Nez.*	*Neziqin*
Bek.	*Bekorot*	*Nid.*	*Niddah*
Ber.	*Berakot*	*Ohol.*	*Oholot*
Beṣa	*Beṣa (=Yom Tob)*	*'Or.*	*'Orla*
Bik.	*Bikkurim*	*Para*	*Para*
B. Meṣ.	*Baba Meṣi'a*	*Pe'a*	*Pe'a*
B. Qam.	*Baba Qamma*	*Pesaḥ.*	*Pesaḥim*
Dem.	*Demai*	*Qinnim*	*Qinnim*
'Erub.	*'Erubin*	*Qidd.*	*Qiddušin*
'Ed.	*'Eduyyot*	*Qod.*	*Qodašin*
Giṭ.	*Giṭṭin*	*Roš Haš.*	*Roš Haššana*
Ḥag.	*Ḥagiga*	*Sanh.*	*Sanhedrin*
Ḥal.	*Ḥalla*	*Šabb.*	*Šabbat*
Hor.	*Horayot*	*Šeb.*	*Šebi'it*
Ḥul.	*Ḥullin*	*Šebu.*	*Šebu'ot*
Kelim	*Kelim*	*Šeqal.*	*Šeqalim*
Ker.	*Keritot*	*Soṭa*	*Soṭa*
Ketub.	*Ketubot*	*Sukk.*	*Sukka*
Kil.	*Kil'ayim*	*Ta'an.*	*Ta'anit*
Ma'aś.	*Ma'aśerot*	*Tamid*	*Tamid*
Mak.	*Makkot*	*Tem.*	*Temura*
Makš.	*Makširin (=Mašqin)*	*Ter.*	*Terumot*
Meg.	*Megilla*	*Ṭohar.*	*Ṭohorot*
Me'il.	*Me'ila*	*Ṭ. Yom*	*Ṭebul Yom*
Menaḥ	*Menaḥot*	*'Uq.*	*'Uqṣin*
Mid.	*Middot*	*Yad.*	*Yadayim*
Miqw.	*Miqwa'ot*	*Yebam.*	*Yebamot*
Mo'ed	*Mo'ed*	*Yoma*	*Yoma (=Kippurim)*
Mo'ed Qat.	*Mo'ed Qatan*	*Zabim*	*Zabim*
Ma'as. Š.	*Ma'aser Šeni*	*Zebaḥ*	*Zebaḥim*
Našim	*Našim*	*Zer.*	*Zera'im*

INTRODUCTION

One of the distinctive aspects of the modern study of the Bible, as it has developed in the past century and a half, has been the effort to delineate a theology of the Old Testament alone, with minimal or negligible reference to the New Testament, which, in turn, has received its own separate treatment. What makes this innovation possible is the awareness that the canon of the Christian Bible, like any canon, flattens historical differences. A canon is a synchronic statement; every book in it, every chapter, every verse is contemporaneous with every other one. But history is diachronic, a film-strip rather than a snapshot. The awareness of this element of change and development, which is obscured by the canonical statement, makes it possible to speak of earlier stages on their own, and not simply in reference to the totality of the book as understood by one confessional community, in this case, the church.

One would think that the new approach to the Bible, the historical-critical approach, would have attracted a goodly number of Jews, since it offers the prospect of dealing with their Bible, the Hebrew Bible, on its own and not simply as a preparation or foil for the literature of some other community. Conversely, one would predict a new openness to Judaism as one source of insight into the Hebrew Bible, an openness that is impossible so long as that book is subordinated to the New Testament. One would have expected biblical theologians of Christian persuasion to have asked whether Jewish tradition sheds any light upon the religion of most ancient Israel which their own religious orientation has prevented them from glimpsing for nearly two thousand years. The sad fact, however, is that the endeavor known as "Old Testament theology" has been, as its name suggests, an almost exclusively Gentile affair. Indeed, its evaluation of the central institutions of ancient Israel does not depart in substance from those provided by the premodern Christian tradition. It is as though the historical-critical methods have yet to take deep root. Pockets of old bias remain untouched.

The two major institutions of the religion of ancient Israel in which Christian, especially Protestant, stereotypes continue to dominate are also, it can be argued, the two major foci of ancient Israelite religion itself: law (Torah) and Temple. Critical scholarship has not been very successful at shaking the view of the Torah of the Christian apostle Paul, the view that it is something deadening, a bearer of curse, and a temporary measure (Galatians 3). Julius Wellhausen, the greatest Old Testament scholar of the nineteenth century, saw law as a symptom of spiritual desiccation. "After the spirit of the oldest men of God, Moses at the head of them, had been in a fashion laid to sleep in institutions," he wrote, "it sought and found in the prophets a new opening," and the prophets do not stand in debt to those institutions, but precede them and are free of them.[1] Wellhausen was not an orthodox Christian. His critical methods shook the church and endangered his career. But in his negative view of Torah and of Judaism, the religion of Torah, he was both a staunch traditionalist and an adumbration of future trends in "Old Testament theology." For example, half a century later, Walther Eichrodt, whose *Theology of the Old Testament* rejects most of Wellhausen's attutudes, still wrote of Judaism as the degradation of the law.[2] Eichrodt's evaluation of law in the Old Testament itself is higher than Wellhausen's. But he is no more willing than his predecessor to consider the possibility that Judaism, which regards the Mosaic law as still valid, might have something to teach Christians, who see it as something superseded. The more things change, the more they stay the same.

1 J. Wellhausen, *Prolegomena to the History of Ancient Israel* (Gloucester, MA: Peter Smith, 1973) 398–99. (This is a translation of the German work which appeared originally in 1878.)

2 W. Eichrodt, *Theology of the Old Testament* (Philadelphia: Westminster, 1961) 1:168–69. The *Theology* was first published in 1933. A fuller discussion can be found in J. D. Levenson, "The Theologies of Commandment in Biblical Israel," *HTR* 73 (1980) 17–21.

The Temple has fared no better. Sometimes one is inclined to think that Old Testament theologians are simply looking for new words in which to re-enact Jesus' curse upon the Temple (Matt 24:1-2). In Wellhausen's mind, the priestly school which established and regulated an elaborate cultus was a manifestation of spiritual decadence and aridity, the true father of Judaism.[3] Three quarters of a century later, in America, the most widely used textbook of Old Testament studies describes Solomon's Temple as an "invasion of Canaanite culture right into the center of Israel's life and worship."[4] In this instance, the affinities of Solomon's edifice with temples throughout the ancient Near East (which any critical historian would have predicted) furnishes a new club with which to beat the old boogeyman. Only the weapon is different.

What these examples suggest is not that biblical studies are stagnant; on the contrary, there have been immense discoveries in archaeology, epigraphy, and history. Whole civilizations have been discovered. Infinitely more is known about the biblical world now than in Wellhausen's time, *a fortiori* the era of the Talmudic rabbis, the apostles, and Church Fathers. What is suggested, however, is that change has been more rapid and more general in these "ancillary" disciplines than in the theological study of the Hebrew Bible, where old habits of mind remain intact, either ignoring the new data or awkwardly fitting them into the inherited structures. The image of scholars who deprecate some of the major features of a religion which they aim to present sympathetically has always been odd. The new discoveries and new perspectives which they seem to open make it all the odder.

The goal of the present volume is to present these two foci of the religion of ancient Israel, Torah and Temple, from a perspective which is different from that of the consensus. Use will be made of the new discoveries, and the post-biblical Jewish tradi-

3 Wellhausen, *Prolegomena,* esp. Part III.
4 B. W. Anderson, *Understanding the Old Testament* (Englewood-Cliffs: Prentice-Hall, 1957) 146.

tion will often be brought in where it is relevant. I make no claim
that Rabbinic Judaism offers the correct understanding of the
Hebrew Bible. One need not subscribe to the regnant prejudice to
see that Talmudic religion is different from its biblical ancestor,
one of the major differences being the presence in it of a Bible. But
the change seems more evolutionary than revolutionary; it lacks
the "quantum leap" apparent in the Christian claim of a new
Israel and, ultimately, a New Testament. It is this willingness to
consider rabbinic tradition on occasion and to highlight its relevance to the Hebrew Bible and *vice versa* which makes this
volume "An Entry into the *Jewish* Bible." The ultimate measure
of success or failure adopted here, however, is not conformity to
the Jewish tradition, but whether or not the reading proposed is
true to the biblical texts themselves. My claim is that because
Judaism lacks an overwhelming motivation to deny the pluriform
character of the Hebrew Bible in behalf of a uniform reading—
such as the christological reading—Jewish exegesis evidences a
certain breadth and a certain relaxed posture, both of which are
necessary if the Hebrew Bible is to receive a fair hearing. The
fruits of these should not be excluded in advance.

An approach which is open to the texts as they stand (and not
only as later tradition conceives them), to Near Eastern research,
and to Jewish tradition as a resource is still a relative rarity, for
the modern Jew is heir to a legacy of biblical study which he is
often loath to claim. The medieval era was one of exciting advance
in the exegesis of the Hebrew Bible. Between 900 and 1500 C.E.,
commentaries and studies of great and enduring value were
produced in large numbers in the Near East and in Europe, and
these drew special strength from the fact that they were often
fertilized by deep involvement on the part of their authors in the
larger cultures in which Jewry found itself. In contrast, in the
modern period, the Jew's approach to his Bible has just as often
been marked by a defensiveness whose counterpart in the world of
scholarship is timidity or minimalism, a reluctance to address
religious issues and a preference for other aspects of modern

biblical study. This defensiveness is a reflection of the fact that Jewry has not, on the whole, responded well to the challenges of modernity, or at least to its theological dimension. There is, in fact, a quantum leap between the traditional rabbinic approach to the Hebrew Bible and modern critical study. The latter is often said to have begun with the isolation, some two centuries ago, of four sources identified by the letters, J, E, D, and P.[5] What was most threatening about the emergence of source criticism was that it undermined belief in the historical unity of the Torah and in the belief that it was revealed, as tradition held, to Moses upon Mount Sinai. On the contrary, the modern critic sees all four sources as post-Mosaic (if Moses may be considered historical) and as reflections of the eras in which they were composed. The recovery of these differences in eras allows the modern scholar to reconstruct the history of biblical Israel, for it frees him from the need to see the religion as revealed in its entirety at one moment, in other words, as lacking a history altogether. Thus, the historical study and the contemporary practice of the tradition came to be seen as opposed to one another. In the minds of probably most Jews, one had to choose between historical consciousness or an allegiance to traditional religion (Torah); one could not have both. "Judaism," wrote Joseph H. Hertz, Chief Rabbi of Great Britain earlier in this century, "stands and falls with its belief in the historic actuality of the Revelation at Sinai."[6] Rabbi Hertz' implication was that the only way one can be a biblical historian and a faithful Jew is by developing empirical corroboration for what he already knows by faith, namely, the contents of the Torah as rabbinic tradition understands them. In other words, biblical history is not really to be empirical at all.

5 See E. A. Speiser, *Genesis*, AB 1 (Garden City: Doubleday, 1964) xx-xxxvii; and M. Weinfeld, "Pentateuch," *EJ* 13:231-61.

6 J. H. Hertz, *The Pentateuch and Haftorahs* (London: Oxford University, 5695/1935) 2: (Exodus) 234. See the discussion of the issue in E. L. Fackenheim, *Quest for Past and Future* (Bloomington and London: Indiana University, 1968) 66-82.

The ultimate criterion for acceptance of an idea is not the intrinsic cogency of the argument and of the evidence upon which it stands, but whether it conforms to inherited dogma. Biblical history is to be merely confirmatory. Anything new that it finds must not be discordant with what is known, or assumed on faith. Real discovery becomes impossible.

The argument might be offered that the orthodoxy of which Rabbi Hertz' statement is characteristic imagines that the tradition was monolithic on the issues of the conflict of empirical evidence and faith, when it really was not. In the great work of post-biblical Judaism, the Talmud, for example, one rabbi doubts that Moses wrote the last eight verses of the Torah (Deut 34:5–12) on the grounds that he could not have written about his own death and burial. The retort is immediately offered that it was not Moses, but God, who composed these verses; Moses wrote them down in tears.[7] The revealing point is that the first position assumes that a commitment to tradition does not require the Jew to ignore empirical evidence in the name of an increasingly blind faith. One wonders where the Talmudic sage who voiced the doubt would have stood in the modern dispute, when so much more evidence against Mosaic authorship has been developed. In any event, doubts or ambivalence about Mosaic authorship of the Torah and a host of other traditional beliefs appear on occasion in medieval commentaries which the tradition accepts.[8] Even the possibility of scribal error in the text of the Torah as it reaches us seems to have occurred to some of the great rabbinic exegetes.[9] It is surely the case that a few of them were willing to entertain the

---

7   *b. B. Bat.* 15a.
8   E.g., Ibn Ezra to Gen 12:6.
9   This was demonstrated by N. M. Sarna in his paper, "Medieval Biblical Commentary and the Modern Jewish Bible Scholar," delivered at the annual national conference of the Association for Jewish Studies, Dec. 19, 1975. The paper presented examples which are much more daring and far-reaching than those that had appeared in his study of "Hebrew and Bible Studies in Medieval Spain," in *The Sephardi Heritage,* ed. R. D. Barnett (London: Valentine, Mitchell, 1971) 1:344–51.

notion that the plain sense of a verse can contradict the normative law (*halakhah*) which the Talmudic rabbis derived from it.[10] In instances of this sort, what is interesting and possibly enlightening for the modern situation is that awareness of the contradiction does not seem to have dampened the exegetes' commitment either to observance of *halakhah* or to the exposition of the plain sense of scripture. This would imply that Jewish tradition includes a form of biblical scholarship which is more than the mere repetition, rearrangement, or extension of data known through the tradition itself. Tradition, so understood, will include novelty, even contradiction. It will not be fossilized, but vital, growing, and, to a certain extent, changing.

Whatever dim adumbrations of modern methods antiquity and the Middle Ages may have bequeathed us, it is certainly the case that biblical criticism poses a massive challenge to premodern tradition, for historical consciousness in the modern mode was not part of the mental apparatus of those who formulated the classic tradition.[11] The great question for those of a modern cast of mind who also desire to affirm the rabbinic tradition is: How can we fit history as it is perceived and reconstructed by modern individuals into a theological (rather than humanistic) framework? We have seen that Rabbi Hertz' answer was that we cannot, and this remains the answer of most of those who strive to observe *halakhah*. The presupposition underlying it is that "no interpretation," in Rabbi Hertz' words, ". . . is valid or in consonance with the Jewish Theistic position, which makes human reason or the human personality the *source* of such revelation."[12] The question must be asked, however, whether the choice really lies between "belief in the historic actuality of the Revelation at Sinai" and a

10 E.g., Rashbam to Exod 21:34.

11 On the emergence of an awareness of history in biblical scholarship, see J. H. Hayes, "The History of the Study of Israelite and Judean History," in *Israelite and Judean History*, OTL, ed. Hayes and J. M. Miller (London: SCM, 1977) 1–69.

12 Hertz, *The Pentateuch*, 2:235.

liberal humanism which substitutes man's conscience for God's word. Can it not be the case that the literary form of the Torah conveys a truth which is not historical in nature? Is not fiction a valid mode of knowledge,[13] a mode of which God himself may have made use? Must we assume that the conventions of attribution of authorship among ancient semites were the same as those of later eras, so that all pseudepigraphical literature is only forgery? In short, what needs to be developed—and this is the prime task of Jewish philosophy in our time[14] —is a model of divine revelation which takes account of the involvement of the Hebrew Bible in history and its character as imaginative literature and does not seek to deny this involvement and this character in the name of faith. The new model, when it emerges, will surely diverge significantly from what has been the tradition, but some elements of the tradition, such as the study of the Hebrew Bible, will grow stronger as a result. For the fact is that the belief in the Mosaic authorship of the Pentateuch and kindred items of premodern conviction claim the allegiance today only of those Jews and Christians whose prior commitment of faith forbids them to accept anything else. As a result, among Jews at least, they have become a small minority, and most of "the people of the Book" are alienated from the Book, even at times repelled by it.

Two misconceptions about the isolation of J, E, D, and P (the "documentary hypothesis") are common in the Jewish community. First, there is the notion that modern biblical scholarship (biblical criticism) is a Gentile entity and the product of the traditional Christian impulse to undermine Judaism.[15] The truth is

---

13 See R. Alter, "Joseph and His Brothers," *Commentary* 70:5 (Nov., 1980) 50–60; and *The Art of Biblical Narrative* (New York: Basic, 1981), esp. pp. 157–77.

14 Fackenheim, *Quest*, is largely devoted to this question. For the most part, however, the term "Jewish philosophy" is used in the academic world to mean only the *history* of Jewish philosophy, and the effort to face distinctly modern problems in religious thought is often regarded as inauthentic and treated with disdain.

15 See J. A. Miles, "Radical Editing: *Redaktionsgeschichte* and the

that the new methods undermine premodern Christianity as much as they undermine premodern Judaism, as one sees from the original reception of Wellhausen's work among Christian believers. The flash points are different: the Christian arch-traditionalist may be more upset by evolution, for example, than by the documentary hypothesis. The underlying theology is different: the Christian demands literalism, whereas the Jew demands conformity to post-biblical traditions of exegesis, which are often remote from the literal sense. But in each case, the opposition is not between Judaism and Christianity. This does not shake my point that the evaluation of elements of ancient Israelite religion more central to Jews than to Christians has often tended among Christian biblicists to be negative. The anti-Jewish bias, however, is a carry-over from religious traditionalism and not a contribution of critical methods *per se*.

The second misconception is that the isolation of documentary sources remains the center of attention among biblical critics. The truth is that a whole host of other methods and other interests have come to the fore over the past three-quarters of a century, although seldom do these newer approaches impugn the need to identify and to date literary sources behind the present form of the text. In America, the dominant approach has been the application of insights into the world of biblical Israel, the ancient Near East, to the Hebrew Bible itself. Over the course of the last century, there has been a geometric expansion of our knowledge of the biblical world. The Hebrew Bible, essentially the only source of such knowledge available to the medieval commentators, now provides only a small proportion of our knowledge, one that becomes smaller with each new discovery. To a limited degree, the recovery of the cultural context of the Hebrew Bible does not threaten, but rather enriches the premodern traditions of exegesis. For example, the classic commentator, confronting an obscure Hebrew word, would turn to related languages, Aramaic and

Aesthetic of Willed Confusion," in *Traditions in Transformation*, ed. B. Halpern and J. D. Levenson (Winona Lake: Eisenbrauns, 1981) 19–20.

Arabic, or even to an unrelated language, like Greek,[16] for an etymology. Presumably, if he could have benefited from the discovery of other ancient languages from the region—Akkadian, Egyptian, Ugaritic, Phoenician—he would have made ample use of them as well. The problem comes from the fact that the archaeological discoveries have provided more than information on individual words. They have also provided data about the history of Israel and of the culture of the surrounding people, and these data often cannot be absorbed into the tradition as it stands. Although in the popular mind, archaeology is often thought to prove the Bible true (i.e., historical), this is seldom the case, and it is occasionally the opposite of the truth.[17]

To give only one example, a recent survey of the traditions about the Patriarchs (Abraham, Isaac, and Jacob) in the light of Near Eastern sources, including excavations, concludes that these traditions cannot be accurate historically.[18] No less revolutionary is the discovery that the claim Israel makes to being "a unique people in the world" (1 Chr 17:21) is also open to grave doubt. The Near Eastern approach has developed parallels to almost every aspect of Israel's culture.[19] Her laws resemble Mesopotamian law; her Temple is typically Canaanite; even her monotheism, as we shall see in Part 1, is composed of elements attested outside herself, all of them older than she. It could, of course, be argued that the overall configuration of these elements is unique to Israel, that the bricks may be found elsewhere, but the building is distinctive. This is true. It is, however, also true of the other cultures. There never was another Egypt, another Sumer, another Babylonia, another Canaan, another Greece, another Rome. Every complex culture is, in its totality, unique.

16   E.g., Rashi to Gen 49:5.
17   See the trenchant analysis by J. J. Finkelstein, "The Bible, Archeology, and History," *Commentary* 27:4 (April 1959) 341–49.
18   T. L. Thompson, *The Historicity of the Patriarchal Narratives,* BZAW 133 (Berlin and New York: de Gruyter, 1974).
19   See H. W. F. Saggs, *The Encounter with the Divine in Mesopotamia and Israel,* Jordan Lectures (London: University of London/Athlone, 1976).

My experience has been that the desire to uphold a belief in the uniqueness of Israel is strongest among Jews.[20] It is a species of argumentation in support of supernatural beliefs by means of rationalistic arguments. In other words, if Israel can be shown to be radically discontinuous with her environment, then the likelihood is increased that her identity is the result of supernatural intervention, just as the bible says (e.g., Gen 12:1-3). Or, if one prefers secular nationalism to traditional theology, then the discontinuity would seem to validate a heroic interpretation of Jewish survival: the Jewish spirit overcomes history. In either case, the argument is weak. There is no logical necessity that something be unprecedented or unparalleled when it is revealed; God can work through history as well as in spite of it. Nor can one assume that a feature is essential to the Hebrew Bible simply because it is, so far as we now know, unparalleled. On the contrary, what is essential may also be a Near Eastern commonplace. For example, few would see philanthropy towards the poor, the widow, and the orphan[21] as peripheral to the biblical vision of justice. The fact that it is well attested throughout the ancient Near East[22] does not present any logical challenge to its centrality in Israel. The nationalistic approach is no better; the Jews are in history, both benefitting and suffering from it, and not divorced from it by some factor of mysterious but natural origin.

II

In spite of the changes which the tradition underwent throughout biblical times, there are certain generalities which an awareness of history does not substantially undermine. The purpose of

20   It is reflected in the powerful influence of the late Yehezkel Kaufmann upon Jewish biblical scholars. See the discussion of his views of myth (pp. 107-9).

21   E.g., as mandated in Exod 22:21; 23:6; Lev 19:10; and Deut 27:19.

22   See F. C. Fensham, "Widow, Orphan, and the Poor in Ancient Near Eastern Legal and Wisdom Literature," *JNES* 21 (1962) 129-39.

this volume is not to trace the history of the ideas and institutions in question, but, rather, to utilize the historical background in order to elucidate the texts which are their classic statement. Some concern with historical change, with the diachronic dimension, is inevitable if we are not to slip into a comfortable but discredited form of traditionalism. But the essential approach of this book is synchronic and literary, with the focus not on the minor permutations in time, but on the enduring continuities understood in the broad historical context. Most of the literature which is its subject is from the period of the Israelite monarchies, the last of which came to its end in 587 B.C.E., and from the immediate aftermath of that calamity. The question of how Israel faced the loss of land, Temple, and throne, the great theological crisis of the Exile, does not fall within our purview. Nonetheless, a discussion of the two great mountain traditions, that of Sinai and that of Zion, can clarify the ideas which gave Israelite religion and all later forms of Judaism, including the Judaism of our day, their characteristic shape and their phenomenal durability. To what extent such a clarification can enrich a Christian's reading of his "Old Testament" is ultimately not for me to judge. But if a Jew can recapture something of the original context of his Bible without thereby undermining rabbinic tradition, it would seem possible for a believing Christian as well to read this Old Testament in such a way as to hear anew tones that his tradition has muted or hushed. If both communities can grow through a common reappropriation of a book for which they do not share even a name, then the possibilities for fraternal respect may grow as well.

1

Sinai,
the Mountain
of the Covenant

1. THE SINAITIC EXPERIENCE
OR THE TRADITIONS ABOUT IT?

Whatever the experience of the people Israel on Mount Sinai was, it was so overwhelming that the texts about it seem to be groping for an adequate metaphor through which to convey the awesomeness of the event. For example, in the description in Exod 19:16–22, the first verse seems to describe a hurricane—thunder, lightning, a mysterious cloud. But v 18 presents an image more like that of a volcano—smoke and fire on the mountain, like the fire of a furnace. Both verses mention quaking, the quaking of the people before this momentous sight (v 16) and the quaking of the mountain itself (v 18), which is no more secure than the people against the descent of YHWH, the God of Israel. Fear pervades the spectacle, a fear that infects nature as much as humanity. At the same time, the sight exerts an eerie appeal, which tempts the people to "break through" to catch a glimpse (v 21), but to yield to this temptation is to risk YHWH's displeasure. If they "break through" to him, he will "break out" against them (v 22). Even the priests, who have been singled out—or will be, as the received text has it, a few chapters later—to minister in the presence of God, must submit to special rites of sanctification if they are to survive the Sinaitic experience. In other words, we see here two contrasting movements. The first speaks of an intersection between the lives of God and of Israel. The two meet at Mount Sinai. Moses, the representative of Israel, ascends the mountain onto which YHWH has descended. The second movement, however, speaks of a barrier between God and Israel, which if transgressed, will turn the moment of destiny into one of disaster. Only Moses may ascend. Even the priests are in jeopardy until they have renewed their sanctity. It is as though God beckons with one hand and repels with the other. The twofold quality of the experience narrated in these verses has been explored by the theologian and historian of religion, Rudolf Otto. As is well known, Otto defined "the holy" by the words *mysterium tremendum et fascinans*, a Latin expression that admits of no good English equivalent, but which we can render as "a fearsome and fascinating mystery."[1] It is just such an ambivalent sense of mystery that pervades the account of the theophany, the apparition of God, that was believed to have occurred on Mount Sinai. The Sinaitic experience is here presented as simultaneously supremely relevant to human experience and distant from it and foreign to it. In its quality of indivisible charm and threat, it is eminently exotic, lying outside the boundaries of what is familiar.

What really happened on Mount Sinai? The honest historian must answer that we can say almost nothing in reply to this question. We do not know even the location of the mountain. Its identification with Jebel Musa, on which a Christian monastery stands today, is relatively recent and open to doubt.[2] In fact, some streams of biblical tradition know the mountain by a different name, Horeb, and we cannot affirm with any confidence that the two sets of tradition, that of Sinai and that of Horeb, derive from the same event and were not welded together in the centuries of retelling the stories. In fact, the expression *Mount* Horeb occurs only once (Exod 33:6), although two passages speak of "Horeb, the mountain of God."[3] The other fourteen occurrences of "Horeb" mention no mountain at all. Instead, things tend to happen "at Horeb." For example, the incident in which Moses struck the rock to produce water took place "at Horeb" (17:6), some time before Israel arrived at the Sinai Desert (19:1), where the awesome revelation was to take place. In short, although some passages speak of Horeb as the site at which YHWH spoke to Israel in the midst of fire (Deut 4:15) and proclaimed the terms of

1   R. Otto, *The Idea of the Holy* (New York: Oxford University, 1923).

2   See J. Bright, *A History of Israel*, 3rd ed. (Philadelphia: Westminster, 1981) 124–25.

3   Exod 3:1 and 1 Kgs 19:8.

the covenant to them (e.g., v 10), we cannot assume that Horeb was always simply synonymous with Sinai.[4] And even if we could make such an assumption, the presence of two names would suggest that we do not have a straightforward and continuous tradition linking us with the putative event, but, instead, a document whose complex literary history makes the recovery of the event well-nigh impossible. We know nothing about Sinai, but an immense amount about the traditions concerning Sinai. It is the consensus of those who approach these traditions empirically rather than dogmatically that their written form—which is the only way in which we can encounter them today—derives for the most part from periods hundreds of years after the event they purport to record.[5] In Part 2, for example, we shall see that the Sinaitic experience was re-enacted in the Temple at Jerusalem, which was not built until hundreds of years later. Or is it the case that the Sinaitic experience, as portrayed in Exodus, is retrojected from, or at least colored by, the experience of YHWH's theophany in the Temple? About such issues we can only speculate.

It is my contention, however, that the historical question about Sinai, as important as it is in some contexts, misses the point about the significance of this material in the religion of Israel. The Sinaitic experience is not narrated as if it occurred on the level of mere fact. In truth, unbiased historiography of the sort to which modern historians aspire did not exist in biblical times. Instead, biblical historians always enlisted history in the service of a transcendent and therefore metahistorical truth. It is that truth, conveyed to us through historical narrative, whether accurate historically or not, that interests the narrator, not the details, without which modern historians cannot work at all. What modern historian would tell the story of World War II without ever giving the name of the German *Führer?* Yet, the Torah, the first

4 See R. J. Clifford, *The Cosmic Mountain in Canaan and the Old Testament,* HSM 4 (Cambridge: Harvard University, 1972) 121–22.

5 On the dating and nature of the Pentateuchal sources, see M. Weinfeld, "Pentateuch" in *EJ* 13:231–61.

five books of the Hebrew Bible, never tells us the name of the king of Egypt—to the endless vexation of ancient historians—but refers to him by his royal title only, Pharaoh. Similarly, history in the modern sense is not the goal of the Sinai narratives: they present the Sinaitic experience as disclosing the essential, normative relationship of YHWH to his people Israel. Sinai was a kind of archetype, a mold into which new experiences could be fit, hundreds of years after the original event, if such there was. That mold served as a source of continuity which enabled new norms to be promulgated with the authority of the old and enabled social change to take place without rupturing the sense of tradition and the continuity of historic identity. For example, anyone who reads the whole Torah cannot avoid noticing that one sees law-codes separated by blocks of narrative. Soon after the giving of the Ten Commandments, we meet the "Book of the Covenant" (Exod 20:22–23:33); later we see another law-code in Leviticus 17–26, which concludes thus:

These are the laws, rules and instructions, which YHWH established between himself and the Israelites on Mount Sinai by the hand of Moses. (Lev 26:46)

One would think from this conclusion that the revelation of law was at last over. And yet individual blocks of law come in the very next chapter, in the book of Numbers, and another whole code, the longest in the Bible, will appear in Deuteronomy 12–26. This Deuteronomic code is most interesting in that it is proclaimed not at Sinai/Horeb, but on the plains of Moab, just before Israel is to dispossess the Canaanites; yet it, too, is presented in the mouth of Moses and as an outgrowth of the revelation of the Ten Commandments (chs. 4; 9–10). Modern scholars date these various codes to different periods in Israel's history, all of them post-Mosaic. What their common ascription to Moses on Sinai suggests is that the Sinaitic "event" functioned as the prime pattern through which Israel could re-establish in every generation who she was, who she was meant to be. The experience of Sinai, whatever its historical basis, was perceived as so overwhelming, so charged with meaning, that Israel could not imagine that any truth or commandment from God could have been absent from Sinai.

2. YHWH'S HOME
IN NO MAN'S LAND

Those who wish to speculate about the meaning of Sinai in the period of Israel's first association with it will take special interest in those passages which mention the mountain and can be dated on independent, formal grounds to a very early period. Psalm 68 is a choice example, as linguistic, orthographic, and other criteria suggest to some scholars that it is one of the oldest pieces of Israelite poetry.[6] Vv 8–9 and 16–19 are quite relevant to any discussion of the conception of Sinai that diverges from, and thus most likely predates, the conception in our Pentateuchal narrative sources. These verses, obscure as they are, clearly record a march of YHWH from Sinai, a military campaign in which the God of Israel and his retinue, divine, human, or something of each, set out across the desert. The point not to be overlooked is that YHWH's home, the locus of this presence, is not a site inside the land of Israel, but rather Mount Sinai, which is separated from Israel's home by forbidding wasteland. The mention of Sinai (vv 9, 18) clearly implies a connection between YHWH and that mountain much closer than what we would expect from the Pentateuchal narratives in which Mount Sinai seems to be no more than the place in which the revelation of law took place. Instead, in Psalm 68, YHWH is "the One of Sinai" (v 9), an

6 See W. F. Albright, "A Catalogue of Early Hebrew Lyric Poems (Psalm LXVIII)," *HUCA* 23 (1950) 1–39. Albright dates the compilation of Psalm 68 to the period from the thirteenth to the tenth centuries B.C.E. (p. 10) and vv 8–9 to the twelfth and eleventh centuries (p. 20), well before the writing of the present Pentateuchal narrative sources. The general method employed can be seen lucidly in F. M. Cross and D. N. Freedman, *Studies in Early Yahwistic Poetry* (Missoula: Scholars, 1975).

epithet that provokes jealousy on the part of Mount Bashan, in the lands of the Trans-Jordanian branch of the tribe Manasseh. In spite of his ritual march to the land of Israel, YHWH's favored abode is still Mount Sinai. "The One of Sinai" is the numen, the deity, of that mountain, the God of whom Sinai is characteristic. The same expression occurs in an identical context in the famous Song of Deborah (Judg 5:4–5). It is possible that "Sinai" in Ps 68:9, 18 and Judg 5:5 is a gentilic adjective related to the "Wilderness of Sin," a desert probably in the Sinai peninsula (e.g., Exod 16:1). If so, the expression refers to a broader area than the mountain itself in its designation of the divine abode. On the other hand, there is an unmistakable play on Sinai in the account in Exod 3:1–6 of the burning bush (sĕnê), which Moses encountered at Horeb. The marvel that attracts Moses' attention here is a bush that burns and burns, but is never burnt up—the prototypical renewable source of energy. The document from which this narrative is drawn refers to the mountain of God not as Sinai, but as Horeb (v 1). Still, the closeness in sound of sĕnê ("bush") and Sînay ("Sinai") cannot be coincidental. Perhaps the play on words here derives from the notion that the emblem of the Sinai deity was a tree of some sort; hence the popular association of Sînay and sĕnê. In fact, a blessing on the tribe of Joseph identifies YHWH with "the one who dwells in the bush" (Deut 33:16). If "bush" is not a scribal error for "Sinai," the tree here is not merely a device to attract attention, as one might think from Exodus 3, but is, rather, an outward manifestation of divine presence. YHWH is the numen of the bush. The conjunction in Exodus 3 of bush or tree (we do not know the precise meaning of sĕnê) and fire is not surprising in light of later YHWHistic tradition. "YHWH your God," thunders a Deuteronomistic homilist, "is a devouring fire, a jealous God" (Deut 4:24). In the encounter of Moses and the burning bush, two of YHWH's emblems—tree and fire—clash, and neither overpowers the other. The two will appear again in tandem in the mĕnōrâ, the Tabernacle candelabrum which is actually a stylized tree, complete with "branches," "almond-shaped cups," "calyces," and "petals" (Exod 25:31-39).[7] This arborescent lampstand appears not only in the Tabernacle which served as Israel's central sanctuary in the period of wandering in the wilderness, but also in the Temple that was to be built by Solomon in the early monarchical era (1 Kgs 7:49). The Temple at Jerusalem was lit by the fires of the burning tree.

What accounts for our inability to locate the site of the great mountain of Mosaic revelation with any certainty? The failure is not simply one of the modern science of topography. Rather, there is a mysterious extraterrestrial quality to the mountain in the most developed and least allusive biblical references to it. Sinai/ Horeb seem(s) to exist in no man's land. Moses' first trip "to the mountain of God" occurs after he has fled Egypt. The mountain of God is not under Pharaoh's control. It seems to be closer to Midian, a confederation of tribes living near what is today known as the Gulf of Eilat (or Gulf of Aqaba), the body of water that separates the Sinai from Arabia. Still, according to Exod 3:1, Horeb does not seem to lie within Midianite territory, since Moses must drive his Midianite father-in-law's flocks into the wilderness to arrive at the sacred spot. Further proof of this follows from Num 10: 29-33, in which Jethro (also known as Hobab and Reuel) announces that he will return to his native land and not accompany Israel in her march from the Sinai into Canaan, the promised land. Mount Sinai may be near, but it is not within Jethro's territory. Instead, "the mountain of God," under whatever name and with whatever difference the names may indicate, is out of the domain of Egypt and out of the domain of the Midianites, an area associated, by contrast, with the impenetrable regions of the arid wilderness, where the authority of the state cannot reach. YHWH's self-disclosure takes place in remote parts rather than within the established and settled cult of the city. Even his mode of manifestation reflects the uncontrollable

7 On the symbolism of the tree in biblical Israel, see C. L. Meyers, *The Tabernacle Menorah,* ASOR Diss Series 2 (Missoula: Scholars, 1976), esp. pp. 143-56.

and unpredictable character of the wilderness rather than the decorum one associates with a long-established, urban religion, rooted in familiar traditions. As Moses and Aaron put it to Pharaoh:

> The God of the Hebrews has chanced upon us. Please let us go a journey of three days into the wilderness to offer sacrifices to YHWH our God, lest he strike us with plague or sword.
> (Exod 5:3)

In other words, the deity is like his worshippers: mobile, rootless and unpredictable. "I shall be where I shall be" (3:14)—nothing more definite can be said. This is a God who is free, unconfined by the boundaries that man erects. To man, especially to a political man in a civilization as urban and complex as that of Egypt, this request of the Hebrews must have seemed unspeakably primitive. And so Pharaoh, ruler of a great power, responds contemptuously to Moses and Aaron's plea that the people be allowed to journey into the desert to appease their God, lest he afflict them:

> Who is this "YHWH" that I should obey him and let Israel go? I do not recognize YHWH and I will not let Israel go! (Exod 5:2)

Artlessly, an opposition has been set up between service to YHWH and service to Pharaoh. Two masters, two lords, are in contention for the service of Israel in these first chapters of Exodus. As the narrative develops, it becomes clear that one master represents human pride, the security of an ancient and settled regime which has lasted for millennia and will, so its ruler believes, outlast the demand of these Asiatic barbarians for the liberty to serve their God in his desolate home. The other master is that unpredictable deity himself, unknown in the urban world of Egypt, a deity whose home and whose power lie outside Egyptian sovereignty, increasingly threatening it and continually reminding Pharaoh of the limits of his power, which he and his subjects regard as infinite and, in fact, divine. The contrast is also between the desert and the urban state. As Zev Weisman puts it, "the desert serves as a cradle for this primitive universalism of social elements which are outside the control of government, in that it is a space free of any political authority whatsoever and of any organized governmental-cultic establishment."[8] Note that I am not saying that the desert was the goal or ideal of life in ancient Israel. It was not. The desert was mostly conceived as a forbidding, even demonic area.[9] Nor am I saying that YHWH's essential nature was perceived throughout biblical history as that of a desert deity. It was not. What I do claim is that the desert, which some poetry (which is probably early) regards as the locale of YHWH's mountain home, functions in early prose as a symbol of freedom, which stands in opposition to the massive and burdensome regime of Egypt, where state and cult are presented as colluding in the perpetuation of slavery and degradation. The mountain of God is a beacon to the slaves of Egypt, a symbol of a new kind of master and a radically different relationship of people to state. Sinai is not the final goal of the Exodus, but lying between Egypt and Canaan, it does represent YHWH's unchallengeable mastery over both.

3. SINAI AND THE COVENANT FORMULARY

The traditions we have been discussing are of the infancy of Mount Sinai as a symbol in Jewish tradition. They present an image of a religion close to animism. YHWH is, in part, the genie of a scrubby tree, a desert deity who, in a quite literal way, dwells on a mountain, from which he ventures to wage war. It may be dangerous to dismiss these primitive hierophanies too quickly, for there lies within them the germ of ideas which will prove of

8 Z. Weisman, *"Hr H'lhym,"* *Tarbiẓ* 47 (1978) 119. The English translation is my responsibility.

9 See S. Talmon, "The 'Desert Motif' in the Bible and in Qumran Literature," in *Biblical Motifs,* Studies and Texts 3, ed. A. Altmann (Cambridge: Harvard University, 1966) 31–63.

world-historical, in fact revolutionary import. It may be the case primitive men are in deeper contact with some truths than are their more advanced brethren.

It is essential, nonetheless, not to fall into the blunder known as the "genetic fallacy," the idea that origins explain developments. Just as one would hardly grasp the greatness of Abraham Lincoln by discussing what he was at the age of six months, so would it be a mistake to take these earliest traditions of Sinai as definitive for what the mountain signified throughout biblical tradition. For most of that tradition, Mount Sinai is remembered for something other than the manifestation of an arborescent wilderness deity. Rather, Sinai commemorates something that is alleged to have occurred on the plain of human history, but of an awesome and transcendant nature. In short, it is not Sinai in its prehistorical or protohistorical somnolence which should claim the better part of our attention, but the Sinaitic event, what the traditions allege, in their varying ways, to have happened there. The following text expresses that event in a particularly concise form:

> ³YHWH called to him from the mountain, saying,
>   Thus shall you say to the House of Jacob,
>   And declare to the Israelites:
> ⁴"You have seen for yourselves what I did to Egypt, how I bore you on eagles' wings and brought you to me. ⁵Now, then, if you will obey me faithfully and keep my covenant, you shall be my treasured possession among all peoples—for all the world is mine. ⁶You shall be to me a kingdom of priests and a holy nation. These are the words which you shall speak to the Israelites." ⁷Moses came and summoned the elders of the people and put before them all the words which YHWH had commanded him. ⁸And all the people answered as one and said, "All that YHWH has spoken we will do!" Moses took the words of the people back to YHWH. (Exod 19:3b–8)

These verses serve as a kind of introduction to the entire revelation on Sinai. In them, YHWH and Israel conclude a bilateral relationship: he will grant them a special status, one shared by none of his other people, if only they will obey him. This they agree to do, sending their assent up the mountain to God by way of the mediator of this new relationship, Moses. The text above is significant for two reasons. First, recent scholarship tends increasingly to recognize in this passage old traditions, in spite of telltale signs of literary reworking. Which of the old epic sources, J or E, is responsible for the larger part of these verses is not relevant here, but it is essential to note that some scholarship that has come out in the last several years is quite skeptical about the possibility that Exod 19:3b–8 is the product of a Deuteronomic source. Instead, the passage more likely reflects a relatively early phase in the religion of Israel.[10] My second reason for beginning

10 On the dating of Exod 19:3b–8, see K. Baltzer, *The Covenant Formulary* (Oxford: Blackwell, 1971) 28–29, esp. p. 28 n. 45; and W. Beyerlin, *Origins and History of the Oldest Sinaitic Traditions* (Oxford: Blackwell, 1965) 6–11, 67–77. Beyerlin (*Origins*, p. 11) concludes that it "could most easily belong to the E source." See also D. J. McCarthy, *Treaty and Covenant,* 2nd ed. AnBib 21A (Rome: Pontifical Biblical Institute, 1978) 270–73, in which McCarthy notes that "the details of the language in the pericope, therefore, have little which is strictly in common with Dtr." Note also B. Childs' discussion in *The Book of Exodus,* OTL (Philadelphia: Westminster, 1974) 344–47; 360–61. It will become evident that I cannot agree with the thesis of L. Perlitt (*Bundestheologie im Alten Testament,* WMANT 36 [Neukirchen-Vluyn, 1969]) that the covenant theology in Israel originates with Deuteronomy. See the discussion on Perlitt in McCarthy, *Treaty,* 22–23. A fine comment on the strengths and the weaknesses of Perlitt's book is made by J. Barr, "Some Semantic Notes on the Covenant," in *Beiträge zur Alttestamentlichen Theologie: Festschrift für Walther Zimmerli,* ed. H. Donner et al. (Göttingen: Vandenhoeck and Ruprecht, 1977) 37: "Yet with all the will in the world it is a little hard to believe that the covenant of YHWH with Israel became significant only so late."

I disagree very sharply also with the thesis of E. Kutsch (*Verheissung und Gesetz,* BZAW 131 [Berlin and New York: de Gruyter, 1972]) that *běrît* does not mean "covenant" (*Bund*), but "obligation" (*Verpflichtung*). See the review of M. Newman in *JBL* 94 (1975) 117–120. Newman concludes that "Relationship is also an essential feature. *Běrît* always involves two parties and a specific *relation* between them." (p. 120). See also McCarthy's demurrer in *Treaty,* 16–22. Once again, it is Barr ("Some Semantic," 37) who identifies the underlying misconception of Kutsch: ". . . the whole discussion seems dominated by a strong sense of the opposition between grace and law, promise and law, which makes the reader uncomfortable." Kutsch does not

here is that this text actually names the sort of relationship inaugurated on Mount Sinai. It is a *covenant*. If we can shed light on this term, we may be able to understand the basis of this special status conferred upon Israel and of the obligations that are inextricable from her identity.

About three decades ago scholars, especially George Mendenhall in the United States and Klaus Baltzer in Germany, began to compare biblical literature with certain treaties whose structure had been known for about two decades.[11] These treaties derived from the Hittite Empire, which occupied essentially what is now the eastern part of Turkey and whose language was of the Indo-European family, like Greek and unlike Hebrew, which is from the Semitic family. In the Late Bronze Age (ca. 1500–1200 B.C.E.), the Hittite emperors were attempting to control the critical landmass to their south, Syria, by entering into treaties with the kings of the lesser states of that region. The purpose of these treaties was to secure the allegiance of the smaller states to make sure that they stood faithful in alliance with the Hittites and did not pursue an independent foreign policy. Treaties, in the ancient world, were of principally two types, *parity* and *suzerainty*. Parity treaties were between equals; suzerainty treaties were between unequals, the great king whom we shall call the *suzerain* and the petty monarch, whom we term the *vassal*. From now on, we shall be concerned with suzerainty treaties only.

The sequence of steps characteristic of these treaties has come to be known as the *covenant formulary*. To be sure, the extant

see that responsibility arises from the ability to respond.

On the significance of Exod 19:3b–8 for the continuing Sinai traditions, see J. Muilenburg, "The Form and Structure of the Covenantal Formulations," *VT* 9 (1959) 347–65.

11   G. E. Mendenhall, "Ancient Oriental and Biblical Law," *BA* 17 (1954) 26–46; and "Covenant Forms in Israelite Tradition," *BA* 17 (1954) 50–76. Both essays are reprinted in *BAR* 3, ed. E. F. Campbell and D. N. Freedman (Garden City: Doubleday, 1970) 3–53; Baltzer, *Covenant Formulary*. The first scholar to point out the resemblance, however, seems to have been Elias Bickerman, in 1951. See McCarthy, *Treaty*, 5, esp. n. 1.

documents, even those from the Hittites of the Late Bronze Age which have proved so important to biblical studies, show a wide variety of forms. All that seems to have been essential to a treaty in the ancient Near East was a set of stipulations binding the vassal, and an oath sworn by at least the vassal and guaranteed and sanctioned by the gods. Nevertheless, despite this fluidity of forms, many of the treaties show a sequence of six steps, although not always in the same order.

In the first step, the *preamble* or *titulary,* the suzerain identifies himself.[12] The second step is the *historical prologue* or *antecedent history.* Whatever one calls it, it is a statement of the past relationship of the parties. Sometimes the suzerain stresses his benefactions towards the vassal. In one such treaty, the Hittite emperor Mursilis points out that he put his vassal, Duppi-Tessub on his throne, in spite of the latter's illness, and forced an oath of loyalty upon his brothers (any new king fears his brothers) and upon his subjects, the land of Amurru.[13] The covenant obligates the people of Amurru to recognize the kingship of Duppi-Tessub. In other words, the suzerain ensures the vassal's royal status. The implication is that, left to his own devices, Duppi-Tessub would not have retained the throne. In fact, this seems to have been one of the central purposes of the historical prologue—to encourage a feeling of gratitude in the vassal so as to establish firmly the claim of the suzerain upon him. He owes something to his suzerain, and it is only right that he should respond to him out of a sense of obligation.

The historical prologue thus leads smoothly to the third step, the *stipulations,* the terms of the treaty. The purpose of the stipulations is to secure the fidelity of the vassal, to insure that the

12 A good example is the "Treaty Between Mursilis and Duppi-Tessub of Amurru," translated by A. Goetze in *Ancient Near Eastern Texts,* 3rd ed., ed. J. B. Pritchard (Princeton: Princeton University, 1969) 203-5. Hereafter, this volume will be identified as *ANET.* See also D. R. Hillers, *Covenant* (Baltimore: Johns Hopkins, 1969).

13 *ANET,* 203-4.

centerpiece of his foreign policy is faithfulness to his liege lord. The stipulations are in the nature of direct address; they are in the second person. It is important to understand the difference between this kind of phrasing and that typical of a modern treaty or contract. The ancient Near Eastern covenant was not an impersonal code, but an instrument of diplomacy founded upon the personal relationship of the heads of state. The essence of the covenant lies in the fact that the latter pledge to be faithful to one another. It is important to remember that even within one state, government was conceived as personal, as it emphatically is not in modern states. Modern man wants a government of laws, not of men, one in which all legal relationships are described in abstract terms without reference to personalities—thus phrased in the third person only. By contrast, in the ancient Near East, the king was thought to look after his subjects solicitously. In a ubiquitous metaphor, he was their shepherd and they were his flock. They loved him and feared him. In parity treaties, the two kings are "brothers"; in some suzerainty treaties, the greater king is the "father" of the lesser king, not in a biological sense, of course, but in a powerful metaphorical way. Thus, we find that the vassals are sometimes commanded even to love their suzerain. In one Assyrian (i.e., Northeast Mesopotamian) treaty drawn up by King Esarhaddon (680–669 B.C.E.) to insure that his vassals will be loyal to his son Assurbanipal, we read: "You will love as yourselves Assurbanipal." And in another document, the vassals declare under oath: "... the king of Assyria, our Lord, we will love."[14]

The purpose of the covenant would be defeated if the vassal were allowed to enter into such a relationship with another suzerain as well, for that would undermine the great king's control over the area ruled by his partner. Therefore, although a suzerain may have many vassals, a given vassal must recognize only one suzerain. "Do not turn your eyes to anyone else," warns

14 Quoted in W. L. Moran, "The Ancient Near Eastern Background of the Love of God in Deuteronomy," *CBQ* 25 (1963) 80.

Mursilis.[15] "Henceforth however," another suzerain admonishes, "recognize no other lord."[16] This demand for exclusive loyalty is central to the stipulations. From it the others follow naturally. Without it, they make no sense.

The fourth step in the covenant formulary is the *deposition* of the text. Any legal document should be deposited in some place agreed upon at the signing. In a society in which gods served as guarantors of the treaty, it was often deemed appropriate to put a public document in their temples, where they would be continually reminded of its provisions, lest a perfidious ally go unpunished. The formality of deposition need not occupy our attention. Furthermore, some treaties required that the text be periodically read to the vassal in a kind of liturgical reaffirmation of the pact:

> Furthermore, this tablet which I have set [forth] for you Ala[kšanduš], shall be re[cit]ed to you three times each year, and you Alakšanduš shall know it.[17]

Here, recitation has as its goal knowledge of the terms of the covenant. One must know the treaty in order to fulfill it.

The fifth item is the *list of witnesses*. These are the gods before whom the sacred oath is sworn. To violate the treaty, solemnly entered into, is to risk the wrath of these deities. The list is often quite lengthy, since the treaties tend to invoke the pantheon of each of the two parties. In addition, certain natural phenomena, such as mountains, rivers, heaven and earth, stand in witness. In a culture in which words were believed to have effects and in which one therefore did not utter the names of the deities lightly, the list of divine or cosmic witnesses served as a potent inducement to observance of the stipulations.

The sixth and last element in the covenant formulary is called *curses and blessings*. Violation of the stipulations, perfidy and betrayal, will surely result in a cursed life. Conversely, com-

15 *ANET*, 204. Cf. Num 15:39.
16 Quote in Baltzer, *Covenant Formulary*, 21 n. 10.
17 Baltzer, *Covenant Formulary*, 84 n. 2.

pliance with the stipulations, loyalty and faithfulness to the suzerain, result in a state of beatitude. The curses include such things as annihilation, epidemic, sterility, drought, famine, dethronement, and exile. It is clear that the covenant contains within it a moral mechanism based on the principle of retribution, reward for the faithful, punishment for the faithless. The moral principle was thought to be implemented not so much by the workings of the human political order, as by a transcendent element, the trustworthiness of the gods to respond to an oath sworn in their holy names.[18]

If we turn back to the passage in Exodus 19 that we have taken as indicative of the broad outlines of the Sinaitic traditions, we hear echoes of this covenant formulary. To be sure, Exod 19:3b–8 is not *per se* the text of a covenant. It is a proclamation to the people announced through a prophet, Moses, the prophet functioning as a mediator in the establishment of a covenant relationship. Such a mediating role does not appear in the classic Hittite covenants. Once one makes allowances for the context in which this vignette functions, however, it is difficult to deny the reflexes of the covenant formulary to be heard therein. V 4, for example, is a miniature historical prologue. V 5 voices the stipulation in the form of a conditional blessing. We should not be surprised or led to doubt the covenantal nature of the passage simply because the stipulative aspect of this latter sentence is cast in the most general terms, obedience to YHWH and observance of the covenant, for, in fact, the whole passage is embedded in a context which serves as an introduction to the actual stipulations of the Sinaitic covenant.[19] It would have made no sense to present them in detail here. There is a covenantal aspect to the next verse, which,

18 See, for example, the treaty between Suppiluliumas and Kurtizawa, translated by Goetze, *ANET*, 206.
19   In fact, v 8 makes it clear that the stipulations have already been proclaimed, in spite of the fact that they do not begin until the next chapter. Obviously, Exod 19:3b–8 is not now found in its original location, a point noticed also in premodern times (e.g., Rashi to v 11). See Childs, *Exodus*, 364.

although very important, has escaped the notice of other commentators:

> You shall be to me a kingdom of priests and a holy nation. (v 6)

Here, as a reward for loyalty in covenant, YHWH confers upon Israel the status of royalty.[20] Their special position in a world entirely God's is the position of priestly kings. The analogy with the treaty of Mursilis and Duppi-Tessub is quite close. Just as the Hittite emperor insured the kingship of his vassal by taking "your brothers (and) sisters and the Amurru land in oath for you," so does YHWH guarantee that his loyal vassal Israel will be the "kingdom of priests" among all the nations of the world, a special people consecrated in covenant to him. "The whole world" is to Israel as the Amurru land (including the royal siblings) is to Duppi-Tessub. In each case, the suzerain establishes the vassal as the royal figure in a larger community which is itself under the great king's suzerainty. The commandments, which are the stipulations of covenant, delineate a service which is also a form of lordship, an aristocracy of humility. Finally, in v 8, the people solemnly undertake to fulfill the terms of the covenant:

> And all the people answered as one and said,
> "All that YHWH has spoken we will do!"

The covenant is now in force.

In sum, we detect in Exod 19:3b–8 reflexes of the formulary first worked out for the Hittite suzerainty treaty of the Late Bronze Age. Behind v 4 lies the historical prologue. V 5b reflects the stipulations, which are syntactically linked to the blessings (vv 5b–6a). Not every one of the six steps appears here; only three are

20 See W. L. Moran, "A Kingdom of Priests," in *The Bible in Current Catholic Thought*, St. Mary's Theological Studies 1, ed. J. L. McKenzie (New York: Herder and Herder, 1962) 11–12, for evidence that *mamlākâ* can denote the king. But whereas Moran translates "a royalty of priests," parallelism would suggest that it is the entire people who bear the royal/priestly identity.

clear. But even in the Hittite texts, we cannot expect to find each item attested. Hence, Dennis McCarthy's warning about our passage is sound: "The covenant formulary is not a frozen form. ... To control a literary form is precisely to use it effectively and freely like this."[21] Exod 19:3b–8 is powerful evidence for the relatively early conception of the Sinaitic experience as the institution of a covenant between two kings, YHWH and the people Israel.

If in Exod 19:3b–8 there lurks a covenant ceremony beneath a text that is now a prophetic proclamation, in the last chapter of the book of Joshua (Josh 24:1–28) the covenant ceremony comes to the fore, and it seems that we can detect each of the six steps of the formulary, to one degree or another. This passage is not the text of a covenant, but it is the description of the negotiations which lead up to one and of the ceremony in which the covenant is concluded. What about the formulary? The first step, the preamble or titulary, is perhaps reflected in v 2: "Thus said YHWH the God of Israel." I say "perhaps" because Joshua here, like Moses in Exodus 19, functions as a prophet, and "Thus said YHWH" (the *messenger formula*) is the most common way for a prophet to introduce his oracle. The most famous echo of the preamble, however, is the verse that Jews count as the first of the Ten Commandments, although it is technically no commandment at all:

I am YHWH your God who brought you out of the land of Egypt, out of the house of slavery. (Exod 20:2)

The First Commandment is emphatically not a messenger formula, but the self-presentation of the suzerain followed by his recitation of his essential benefaction to the vassal. In Joshua 24, the historical prologue occupies the greater part of the divine address. It begins with the generation before Abraham and summarizes the three immediately succeeding eras in Israel's sacred

21 McCarthy, *Treaty,* 273.

history—the patriarchal period, the Exodus from Egypt, and the conquest of the land (vv 2-13). The dominant theme of this recitation of history is the unceasing grace of YHWH toward Israel. He has given them more than they deserve. Time and again he has rescued them; time and again he has frustrated their enemies. Thus, at this moment at the end of the book of Joshua, as the great epic of deliverance and conquest draws to a close, Israel profits from victories that her own sword and her own bow have not won, lives in cities she did not build, and eats of vineyards and orchards she never planted. The message is clear; God has benefitted Israel beyond her deserts. Like the ailing Duppi-Tessub, whom Mursilis nevertheless put on the throne, Israel benefits from goodwill she has not earned. In this covenant, the suzerain, at least, has demonstrated that he is possessed of the fidelity and reliability such a pact required of its partners.

Awareness of divine grace sets the stage for the stipulations. These are expressed in the form of three imperatives: "hold YHWH in awe," "serve him with undivided loyalty and in truthfulness," and "banish the [alien] gods" (v 14). This expression of the stipulations is quite minimal, as covenants go; Joshua 24 required merely that Israel acclaim YHWH as her suzerain. But these minimal stipulations are all that is required, as the text must presuppose some corpus of Sinaitic law already revealed in the lifetime of Moses. It should be noted that the people swear they will not *abandon* YHWH (v 16); this is a persuasive indication that they have aleray entered into a relationship of fealty with him.[22] These are not newcomers to YHWHism, at least in the text as we presently have it. Instead of mediating a new covenant, Joshua is reinstituting the old one, reclaiming a wayward people for the essential relationship to God. Hence, his main concern is to insure that YHWH is her suzerain, YHWH alone. "Banish the gods" is the equivalent of Mursilis' demand, "Do not turn your eyes to anyone else! . . ." But whereas Mursilis goes on to lay

22 M. Buber, *The Kingship of God,* 3rd ed. (New York: Harper and Row, 1967) 203 n. 23.

down detailed terms in which this exclusive fidelity must find expression, Joshua relies upon the stipulations of his predecessor's time. By banishing YHWH's rivals, Israel rededicates herself to him.

The deposition of the covenant text takes place in v 26, when Joshua records the terms of the covenant in a scroll which he appears to deposit by a boulder at the foot of the sacred tree growing in the (now YHWHistic) Temple at Shechem. Both the tree and the rock will serve as landmarks for the location of the treaty-text inside the Temple. There is no provision here for the periodic reading of the text, but we do find exactly such a requirement in connection with the covenant Moses drew up on the plains of Moab, for there Moses charges Israel to hear a Torah read every seventh year during the festival of Booths (Deut 31:10-13).

The fifth step of the covenant formulary, the witnesses, presents a problem. In the extra-biblical treaties, the witnesses were mostly the gods of the two contracting states. But the suzerain in Israel being divine himself, to have him and them swear by another god would defeat the purpose of the covenant, for Israel would thus recognize another potential suzerain of the same status as YHWH. Instead of divine witnesses, therefore, Joshua first utilizes Israel as a witness against herself (v 22)—perhaps not very convincing legal procedure, but there is no good alternative. As if sensing that Israel would not prove most trustworthy in the role of witness against herself, the account then offers another adaptation of the old treaty formulary. In v 27, the large rock assumes the role of the gods as witness to the covenant, "for it has heard all the words YHWH has spoken to us."

The only hint in Joshua 24 of curses and blessings, the last item in the covenant formulary, occurs in v 20. YHWH has brought Israel success up to now, but if she abandons him and serves another suzerain, he will in turn reverse himself and annihilate Israel. The blessings are simply the continuation, after the conclusion of a covenant, of the life of grace stressed in the historical prologue. Two passages in the Pentateuch, Leviticus 26 and Deuteronomy 28, develop this theme of blessing and curse in great and, at times, horrific detail. It is hardly surprising that these curses are read every year in the synagogue in an undertone.

We have seen that in Joshua 24, it can be argued that each of the six steps of the covenant formulary is present to one degree or another. The historical prologue, the stipulations, the deposition of the text, and the witnesses are well represented. The curses and blessings appear in a very skeletal form, and the preamble may or may not be there at all. The correlation between these elements and the covenant formulary evident in the Hittite and other Near Eastern suzerainty treaties cannot be coincidental. Israel has become the vassal of YHWH; YHWH has become the suzerain of Israel. There can be no profound understanding of the traditions of Sinai without recognition of the source or analogue for the kind of relationship which YHWH was thought to have inaugurated there, a relationship of covenant in which he became their sole God, and they, his special possession, the *dominium Dei*. To be sure, it is difficult to be definitive as to the date when this conception took hold. As I noted in the Introduction, without fundamentalist presuppositions we cannot assume that a passage is synchronous with the events it purports to record. The historical Joshua—if such there was—may have had nothing to do with a covenant ceremony of the sort that closes the book that has been given his name. One must, instead, date the passage by its literary features and its religious ideas. It is interesting in this connection that one of the greatest scholars of covenant, Dennis McCarthy, dated this material quite early, earlier, in fact, than much of the Pentateuch.

The book of Joshua is usually regarded as the product of reworking (redaction) at the hands of editors highly influenced by Deuteronomy. The core of Deuteronomy, in turn, is usually dated to the late seventh century B.C.E., since parts of it seem to be closely related to, perhaps identical with, the book of the Torah found in the Temple during the reign of King Josiah (2 Kings 22–

23). If Joshua 24 is the product of a Deuteronomistic school, it is relatively late in the history of the religion of biblical Israel, and the old argument that covenant in Israel is late, an argument recently revived, gains in plausibility.[23] McCarthy, however, notes the presence of some distinctly un-Deuteronomic elements in the chapter. For example, the "choice between gods as equal alternatives ... is *unthinkable*" in Deuteronomic tradition, as is the nonjudgmental attitude toward a sacred tree and a Temple outside of the central shrine (v 26),[24] elements of old tradition against which the reforming book of Deuteronomy polemicized uncompromisingly (e.g., Deut 12:2). All this suggests that the Deuteronomistic historian has redacted, but not authored the account of the covenant ceremony at Shechem. In any event, the likelihood remains that the Sinaitic experience was conceived as covenantal relatively early in Israel and that the format of covenant served as the controlling metaphor for Israel's relationship to God through most of biblical history. This covenantalization of Israelite religion was so thoroughgoing that we are almost reduced to hypothesis in our effort to reconstruct the prior stages. The literary legacy of ancient Israel is incomprehensible apart from covenant theology.

4. THE THEOLOGY OF
THE HISTORICAL PROLOGUE

The elucidation of the covenant metaphor in Israel, which began nearly three decades ago, has given us insights into the nature of much biblical literature that we would not otherwise have garnered. On the basis of the occurrence together of forms in

23 See n. 10. The lateness of the covenant theology was the cornerstone of Julius Wellhausen's reconstruction of the history of Israel's religion. See his *Prolegomena to the History of Ancient Israel* (Gloucester, MA: Peter Smith, 1973) 417. Of course, central to Wellhausen's approach is the paralogism that lateness indicates inauthenticity and lack of value.

24 McCarthy, *Treaty*, 223. See also G. Schmitt, *Der Landtag von Sichem*, Arbeiten zur Theologie 1/15 (Stuttgart: Calwer, 1964) 30–32. Schmitt sees in

certain passages, scholars might have been able to reconstruct a covenant ceremony as their underlying setting or background, but such a reconstruction on formal grounds alone would have remained speculative and unrooted in any secure knowledge of the biblical world. The Near Eastern suzerainty treaties, on the other hand, provide sound data for determining the connections between the elements that we now know to be derived from the formulary. In the previous section, we demonstrated this connection, this organic coherence, for two passages, Exod 19:3b–8 and Joshua 24:1–28. There are, in fact, dozens and dozens of other texts whose structure and setting become lucid in the light of the discoveries about covenant that were made only in this century.[25]

The contribution of the research into covenant to the theology of the Hebrew Bible, however, has been less impressive. From Mendenhall's original essay on, scholars have been trying to ascertain the theological significance of this discovery, but with little consensus. Philological studies thus continue to outnumber and outweigh theological studies. But surely something of such great historical and literary importance must have profound implications for our understanding of the religous life of ancient Israel as well. After all, what we are dealing with is a central image, perhaps *the* central image, for the relationship of Israel to her God.

Let us begin our discussion of the theology implicit in the covenant metaphor with a consideration of the assumptions behind the historical prologue. We have already seen that the function of the prologue is to ground the obligations of Israel to YHWH in the history of his gracious acts on her behalf. The unstated assumption is that meaning can be disclosed in history.

the demand that Israel choose without ambivalence for YHWH or the gods a parallel to Elijah's challenge on Mount Carmel (1 Kings 18) and thus dates Joshua 24 to the ninth century. Since McCarthy quotes him evidently with approval (*Treaty*, 234 n. 38), it seems inconsistent that McCarthy still maintains that "Ur-Dt sometime after 700 . . . first articulated the relationship between Israel and YHWH according to the treaty genre." (p. 15).

25 See Baltzer, *Covenant Formulary*, 19–38.

History is the arena in which Israel has met and come to know the deity who now becomes her suzerain. The past is a preparation for the present moment of destiny; the present is the consummation of the past, the assurance that it can continue. But what is the nature of the historical past? History is not simply one's personal past. It has a collective dimension. It is the past of the whole people Israel which grounds the obligation of the individual Israelite of any generation. In the case of Joshua 24, there is a subtle but revealing fluidity between the Exodus experience of the ancestors and the experience of the present generation whom Joshua challenges to follow YHWH. "You came to the Sea, but the Egyptians chased after your fathers" (v 6). Literally, of course, the "you" was not, as the narrative has it, present at the Sea of Reeds; only their fathers were. The difference, however, between "you" and "your ancestors" is of no literary significance; it surely does not testify to two separate documents that have been awkwardly combined in the present text. On the contrary, a major function of the historical prologue is to narrow the gap between generations, to mold all Israel, of whatever era, into one personality that can give an assent to the divine initiative. "Your own eyes have seen what I did to the Egyptians" (v 7). History is telescoped into collective biography. What your ancestors saw is what *you* saw. God's rescue of them implicates *you*, obliges *you*, for *you*, by hearing this story and responding affirmatively, become Israel, and it was Israel whom he rescued. Telling the story brings it alive. The historical prologue brings the past to bear pointedly on the present. In the words of the rabbinic Passover liturgy (Haggadah), "Each man is obligated to see himself as if he came out of Egypt."

It is significant for our understanding of the nature of the religion of Israel among the religions of the world that meaning for her is derived not from introspection, but from a consideration of the public testimony to God. The present generation makes history their story, but it is first history. They do not determine who they are by looking within, by plumbing the depths of the individual soul, by seeking a mystical light in the innermost reaches of the self. Rather, the direction is the opposite. What is public is made private. History is not only rendered contemporary; it is internalized. One's people's history becomes one's personal history. One looks out from the self to find out who one is meant to be. One does not *discover* one's identity, and one certainly does not forge it oneself. He *appropriates* an identity that is a matter of public knowledge. Israel affirms the given.

The given that is affirmed in the covenant ceremony is not a principle; it is not an idea or an aphorism or an ideal. Instead, it is the consequence of what are presented as the acts of God. Israel accepts her place in the suzerain-vassal relationship. "YHWH our God we will serve; him alone we will obey" (v 24). In other words, those who come to the Hebrew Bible in hopes of finding a philosophical system flowing smoothly from a theorem will be disappointed. The religion of Israel was not a philosophical system; it had no such theorem. To be sure, every religion is the heritage of a particular community with a history of its own, and this element of history introduces a factor that frustrates the philosophical impulse in every religion. But in the religion of the Hebrew Bible, the philosophical impulse, if it exists at all, is stunted. We see no profound observation at the base of it, like the observation in Buddhism that desire is the source of suffering. Even the oneness of God, we shall soon see, is a consequence of other factors and not a proposition from which the essential religion of Israel can be derived.

Israel began to infer and to affirm her identity by telling a story. To be sure, the story has implications that can be stated as propositions. For example, the intended implication of the historical prologue is that YHWH is faithful, that Israel can rely on God as a vassal must rely upon his suzerain. But Israel does not begin with the statement that YHWH is faithful; she infers it from a *story*. And unlike the statement, the story is not universal. It is Israel's story, with all the particularities of time, place, and *dramatis personae* one associates with a story and avoids in a statement that aims at universal applicability. In other words, if there is a universal truth of the sort philosophers and even some religions aim to state, Israel seems to have thought that such truth will come *through* the medium of history, through the structures of public knowledge, through time, and not in spite of these. History, the arena of public events (as opposed to private, mystical revelation and to philosophical speculation), and time are not illusions or distractions from essential reality. They are means to the knowledge of God. The historical prologue is a miniature theology of history.

When did the history summarized in the prologue commence? If one wishes to read the entire Torah as a covenant text, history begins at the beginning, the creation of the world and the story of primordial humanity (Genesis 1–11). But this is not where the historical prologues in the proper sense start their story. In Exodus 19:3b–8, the story begins and ends with the Exodus from Egypt, when YHWH brought Israel, as on eagles' wings, to himself. In Joshua 24, the horizon is larger: history begins with the backdrop to Abraham's migration, the generation of his father, the Mesopotamian Terah. Most of the recapitulations of the sacred history begin, like Joshua 24, some time in the Patriarchal period. "An Aramean about to perish was my father," begins one little summary (Deut 26:5) in an allusion to Jacob/Israel, from whom the nation took its name, and it is the descent into Egypt by the eponymous ancestor which tends to function there as the trigger for the action of the whole history of redemption, what German scholars call *Heilsgeschichte*.[26] Theologically this means that Israel's identity is not rooted in cosmic symbols, such as those that appear in the first account of creation in the

---

26 On these summaries of *Heilsgeschichte,* see the title essay in G. von Rad, *The Problem of the Hexateuch and Other Essays* (New York: McGraw-Hill, 1966) 1–78. I do not endorse von Rad's belief that the *Heilsgeschichte* narratives grew out of short historical credos, but I do believe that he rendered a service in drawing attention to them. They are abstracts of the *Heilsgeschichte* stories presented in order to evoke an affirmation of covenant.

Torah (Gen 1:1–2:4a). Her identity is not cosmic and primordial, but historical in a sense not so distant from that in which modern people use the term. Israel was not created on day one or at any other moment in the seven days of creation. Instead, she was called into existence at a moment in ordinary time and at a specifiable place, Haran (11:31). Israel is to carry a metahistorical identity through her journeys in history. This preference for historical terms over cosmic-primordial symbols sets the Sinai traditions off markedly from those of Zion, which will occupy our attention in Part 2.

In one of his earliest essays, Mendenhall wrote that

> the covenant form itself furnished at least the nucleus about which the historical traditions crystallized in early Israel. It was the source of the "feeling for history" which is such an enigma in Israelite literature.[27]

He was surely right that the historical prologue has come to serve as the organizing principle for the presentation of history in biblical Israel. Covenant discloses the meaning of history. YHWH performed those wonders in Egypt in order to bring Israel to himself, to Sinai, where the relationship would be institutionalized, and thus perpetuated, through covenant (Exod 19:4). But Mendenhall erred on one point. The covenant form cannot be the source for Israel's enigmatic "feeling for history," for without a prior historical orientation, Israel could not have formulated her relationship to her God in the terms of covenant. Mendenhall wrote as if covenant were a given and thus Israel concerned herself with history because that is what covenant calls for. The reverse is true. It is an orientation toward history, a "feeling" that history points to something transcendent, which prepares the ground for an image of relationship that is drawn from the historical sphere. Where the ground has not been prepared, where there is no historical identity and consciousness, the seed of covenant will die, and the covenantalization of religion

27 Mendenhall, "Covenant Forms," 70.

cannot take place. Unless historical experience seems purposive and significant, one does not formulate or accept an interpretation of history which sees the hand of God lying behind events. Covenant does not explain the "feeling for history." The "feeling for history" is consummated in covenant, but its origins remain an enigma.

The leading theological implication of the historical prologue, then, is that it provides a grounding for the obligations Israel felt to God, a grounding that comes not from introspection or philosophical speculation, but from the recitation of a story. Telling the story brings it alive, actualizes it, turns it from past into present and bridges the gap between individual and collective experience, by enabling Israelites of the present generation to become the Israel of the covenant, the Israel of the classic, normative relationship with God. In sum, the historical prologue provides the data from which the nature of YHWH the reliable suzerain can be known.

5. MITSVOT AS
THE END OF HISTORY

No scholar has ever stressed the importance of history as the arena in which the God of the Hebrew Bible discloses himself more often and more powerfully than the late G. Ernest Wright.[28] In his thinking, the religion of Israel was a religion of recital, in which the highest spiritual level consisted of narrating the mighty acts of God. The key term is *event*:

> Israel's creative events were events in time and place, which were celebrated in worship in a great variety of ways. History was not done away with but taken up into worship because God's revelation is in historical action, in events selected as especially "newsworthy" for what they

28 See G. E. Wright, *The Old Testament Against Its Environment*, SBT 2 (London: SCM, 1950); *God Who Acts* (London: SCM, 1952); and *The Old Testament and Theology* (New York: Harper and Row, 1969). Wright's influence on the last section should be obvious.

reveal. Around them the sacred literature took form. Teaching, rituals, and oracles are present in abundance, but they receive their context in and are secondary to the special events, the historical tradition.[29]

In other words, for Wright, God is known only through the event. All else—"teaching, rituals, and oracles"—are consequences of the knowledge of God obtained through empirical observation of his acts in the historical order. These things may serve to orient the community towards that order, but they do not compromise the priority of the event. They remain "secondary."

Consideration of the covenant formulary, however, suggests that Wright's formulation is backwards. The revelation of God in history is not, according to covenant theology, a goal in and of itself, but rather, the prologue to a new kind of relationship, one in which the vassal will show fidelity in the future by acknowl-edgement of the suzerain's grace towards him in the past, in history. The historical prologue is only the prologue. It ceases to be at point when the covenant takes effect. From that moment on, what is critical is not the past, but the observance of the stipu-lations in the present and the sort of life that such observance brings about. To be sure, the recital of the acts of God which Wright emphasizes is indeed central to Israel's religious life. But the purpose of recital was to evoke anew an affirmation, namely the affirmation of the suzerainty of YHWH. And this affirmation was not expressed through the endless recitation of the *magnalia Dei* as a goal in itself. Instead, the affirmation was rendered in the form of observance of the commandments (*mitsvot*), which were to Israel the stipulations of covenant. The knowledge of God is the "recognition" of God in a diplomatic sense. "And you, Huqqanas," reads one extra-biblical treaty, "Know only the sun regarding lordship." Here, in the context of covenant, knowledge refers "to mutual legal recognition on the part of suzerain and vassal," a use of the term which is, as we shall see, dominant in the

29 Wright, *Old Testament and Theology*, 44.

biblical covenant theology as well.[30] In other words, all that history reveals about YHWH is that he has been faithful and gracious to Israel. The community comes into the fuller knowledge of God through a life of observance of the *mitsvot*. History is the foreground of observance, but observance is the teleological end of history.

The idea that the recitation of sacred history is the essence of Israelite religion and that the *mitsvot* are subordinate to history is but a secularization of the Christian concept of an "economy of salvation" which enables one to inherit the status of Israel without the obligation to fulfill the Mosaic law.[31] In other words, the vocabulary is modern, but the underlying structure is the Pauline theology of Galatians 3 and Romans 4. The law, understood as a stern taskmaster, impersonal and death-dealing, is valid only at one stage in the providential plan. Once the total plan has been made known, the law, good in its own time, becomes obsolete and even a hindrance to appreciation of the new revelatory event. Thus, it is hardly surprising that Wright's "theology of recital" and kindred notions should have wielded influence over Christian studies of biblical theology, for, by subordinating law to soteriology, they have seemed to legitimate the traditional christological reading of the Pentateuch: Christ as "the end of the law" (Rom 10:4).

But does the Hebrew Bible really suggest this interpretation? The historical prologue does indeed speak of deliverance, but this is not the same as Christian "salvation." For deliverance in the Hebrew Bible is in the main collective and historical, and not individual, and that from which Israel has been saved is not sin in any sense, certainly not sin understood as a cosmic power or an

30 H. B. Huffmon, "The Treaty Background of Hebrew Yada'," *BASOR* 181 (1966) 31. See also Huffmon and S. B. Parker, "A Further Note on the Treaty Background of Hebrew Yada'," *BASOR* 184 (1966) 36–38.

31 The classic statement of that theology is von Rad, *Old Testament Theology*, 2 vols. (New York and Evanston: Harper and Row, 1962). See also the title essay in his *The Problem*.

ontological reality, nor is she saved for eternal life and from damnation.[32] To say otherwise is to read apocalyptic notions very evident in primitive Christianity (much less so in Rabbinic Judaism) back into the Hebrew Bible. Terms like "salvation history" (*Heilsgeschichte*) thus conveniently obscure essential differences. Moreover, when one understands covenant in its Near Eastern context, it becomes clear that it is not law, but the recitation of history, which is subordinate. History is recited so as to elicit a consciousness of obligation, a response to unmerited benevolence, and an awareness of the reliability of the would-be suzerain. History is prologue. What endures is the mutual relationship between unequals which is the substance of covenant. That relationship does not lack concreteness; on the contrary, it is healthy only to the extent that the will to fulfill specific *mitsvot* is present. The covenant without stipulations, the Abrahamic covenant of Genesis 15 and 17, is only a preparation for the Sinaitic covenant, into which it is absorbed. Thus, observance of the Mosaic Torah is the opposite of an obstacle to a loving and intimate relationship with God. It is the vehicle and the sign of just that relationship.

6. ARE LAWS THE SAME AS COMMANDMENTS?

What, precisely, were the commandments which stood in the role of covenant stipulations in Israel? In other words, what did the Sinaitic covenant require of the vassal? Half a century ago, Albrecht Alt, contemplating the vast corpus of law in the Torah came to the conclusion that any given statute falls into one of only two categories.[33] The categories are differentiated essentially by

32 See H. W. F. Saggs, *The Encounter with the Divine in Mesopotamia and Israel,* Jordan Lectures (London: University London/Athlone, 1976) 64–67.

33 A. Alt, "The Origins of Israelite Law," in *Essays on Old Testament Religion* (Garden City, NY: Doubleday, 1968) 101–71. The essay was

syntax. The first type of law, which Alt termed *casuistic*, is couched in a conditional mode, *if ... then* or *when ... then*. It specifies a situation (or case, hence "casuistic") and the penalty that fits it, for example:

> [18]When men quarrel and one strikes the other with a rock or with his fist, and he does not die but takes to his bed, [19]if he then gets up and walks around outside upon his staff, the one who hit him shall go unpunished, except that he must compensate him for his idleness and see that he is cured. (Exod 21:18-19)

The other type of law Alt termed *apodictic*. Apodictic laws tend to be expressed in the second person, *you shall* or *you shall not*.[34] They usually do not make the situation very specific, nor do they specify a punishment. This kind of law, well known from the Decalogue, is, in fact, found throughout the Torah:

> [20]You shall not wrong a resident alien or oppress him, for you were aliens yourselves in the land of Egypt. (Exod 22:20)

> [17]You shall not hate your kinsman in your heart. Reprove your neighbor, but do not incur any guilt on account of him. [18]You shall not take vengeance or bear a grudge against your kinsfolk. You shall love your neighbor as yourself. I am YHWH. (Lev 19:17-18)

What interested Alt were two points. First, the casuistic form is very familiar to any student of ancient Near Eastern law. It was a standard way to frame a norm. Apodictic law, however, seemed to Alt an Israelite innovation. It is not the normal language of extra-

originally published in 1934.

34 Here, I have narrowed Alt's definition somewhat. As the term "apodictic" would suggest, he saw the distinguishing characteristic of this type of law in its absolute, declarative tone. Hence, he classified as apodictic laws ones like that in Exod 21:12 ("He who strikes a man and he dies shall surely be put to death"). This kind of phrasing, however, still lies within the casuistic category. It is indistinguishable from this hypothetical phrasing: "If one strikes a man and he dies, then he shall surely be put to death." See M. Weinfeld, "Lmqwrw šl H'pwdyqṭy Bḥwq Hmqr'" *Tarbiẓ* 41 (5732/1972) 349; The whole article appears in English as "The Origin of the Apodictic Law," *VT* 23 (1973) 63-75.

biblical law-codes. Alt's second point follows closely upon the first: the difference between casuistic and apodictic norms is not simply formal, but also substantive. The first defines matters of "secular jurisdiction" only:

> Purely sacral law, which has as its particular object the regulation of dealings with God in the cult, is completely ignored in the casuistic ordinances; the only matters they legislate for are those which we can see at once were within the competence of the local secular jurisdiction. ...[35]

Quite the reverse is true of norms that assume an apodictic form:

> They deal in part with the sacral realm of man's relations with the divine—although the particular form of the laws, a list of crimes and their punishment, restricts this to the exclusion of all actions which treat other gods and spirits on the same level as YHWH, or imply a misuse of anything that belongs to him, and is thereby holy, such as his name, or the sabbath. ...

> Religion, morality and law are all included without any distinction; for everything is referred to the unconditional will of God.[36]

In short, casuistic law is general and secular in character; apodictic law is Israelite and sacral.

Although Alt's dichotomy of casuistic and apodictic has become a staple of biblical study, some important qualifications have been registered. The *I-You* form of the apodictic law has been found outside Israel in curses, in aphoristic teachings, and, especially, in the stipulations of covenant.[37] As we saw in the treaty of Mursilis and Duppi-Tessub, the suzerain *addresses* the vassal: "With my friend you shall be friend, and with my enemy you shall be enemy." The stipulations are in the second person. This suggests, then, that the apodictic law, no less than the casuistic, possesses analogues in the realm of Near Eastern jurisprudence; the latter

---

35 Alt, "Origins," 117.
36 Alt, "Origins," 146.
37 S. M. Paul, "Dgmy Nyswḥ šl Hḥwq Byśr'l Wbmswpwtmyh," *Lešonenu* 34 (5730/1969) 257–66.

is typical of law-codes, the former, of international treaties. Neither form was unique to Israel. In fact, even the mixture of secular and religious ordinances found in all biblical codes is attested, not in the Mesopotamian codes that Alt knew, but in the *laws* of the Hittites themselves.[38] It, too, is not unique to Israel.

In one of Mendenhall's essays, the connection of the two types of law is made explicit. Casuistic law is to apodictic law as "technique" is to "policy," or as the Book of the Covenant (Exod 20:22–23:33) is to the Decalogue:

> The Decalogue describes the interests of the deity which are protected by the deity, but law protects the interests of the community by averting from itself the punitive action of God. Finally, the Decalogue becomes community policy—the definition of right and wrong to which the community is bound, and law consists of those techniques of community action whereby those policies are served and protected.[39]

Hence, in the covenant code, "nearly all the stipulations of the Decalogue are . . . protected."[40]

There are several serious problems with Mendenhall's formulation. First of all, the word "nearly" in the quote immediately above is a rather major concession. It is not as if there were so many commandments in the Decalogue that a law-code of about one hundred verses could not "protect" them all. The fact is that the Book of the Covenant does not depend exegetically upon the

38 Weinfield, *Lmqwrw*, 349–60, esp. p. 352 n. 22. But Weinfeld's attempt to derive the apodictic form in Israel from the Hittite law-codes rather than from the vassal treaties seems unlikely to me. First of all, as Weinfeld notes (p. 351), these "law-codes" are termed "covenants" in Hittite, and they are accompanied by an oath. In short, we are dealing here with a nuance of covenant that brings us very close to the boundary with the law. Weinfeld's argument (p. 350) that the vassal covenant cannot be the source of apodictic law because the treaty is international in jurisdiction is weak. It is precisely the transposition of the covenant from the political/international realm to that of theology/liturgy which characterizes the Israelite covenant tradition.

39 Mendenhall, "Ancient Oriental and Biblical Law," 28.

40 Mendenhall, "Ancient Oriental and Biblical Law," 38.

Decalogue. It is by no means clear that it even knows of the existence of that list of ten apodictic norms. If the two corpora have some similar interests, in the Sabbath, for example, (Exod 20:8–11; 23:12), this is no indication of relationship. One would expect two bodies of law from the same culture to share the same concerns. One can infer Israelite "policy" quite well from the Book of the Covenant, as from all the biblical codes, without the aid of the Decalogue. On the other hand, there are many norms in the Book of the Covenant for which the Decalogue cannot be said to have provided any policy—the law of the assailant cited above, for example (21:18–19), or the laws of the goring ox (vv 28–32) or the prohibition against eating torn flesh (22:30). In short, Mendenhall's claim that the Book of the Covenant is intended to implement or protect the Decalogue, to which it looks for policy, is not accurate. Alt's conclusion that the two forms of law address different spheres of life, the secular and the sacral, is preferable to Mendenhall's attempt to see the one type of law as a kind of extension of the other, the link between them being "the interests of the community [in] averting from itself the punitive action of God."

The distinction between apodictic and casuistic law is an important insight into literary form, one that bears upon the origin and the function of the laws of ancient Israel. It is a major achievement of the form-critical method which Alt utilized with such brilliance. It tells us much about the history and setting of the material that it analyzes. But I submit that it does not have *theological* significance. It has not been sufficiently noticed that *all* law-codes in the Torah were ascribed to the revelation to Moses on Mount Sinai.[41] That is to say, all law in Israel, whether casuistic or apodictic in form, has been embedded within the

41 The only non-Mosaic code is the program in Ezekiel 40–48, which, interestingly enough, never came into effect. And it, too, would seem to be modelled on the Sinaitic traditions, for all its variance with them. See Levenson, *Theology of the Program of Restoration of Ezekiel 40–48*, HSM 10 (Missoula: Scholars, 1976), esp. pp. 37–53.

context of covenant. In so doing, the tradition has endowed laws with the status of covenant stipulations, whether the individual ordinances show a *formal* connection to stipulations or not. Thus, the artless meshing of apodictic and casuistic norms throughout the Pentateuch, a process which Alt's method seeks to reverse, is a theologically important fact which his form criticism must not be allowed to obscure. In the canonical scripture, Moses mediates both types of law as if they are one. He writes down the Book of the Covenant (24:4), just as he writes down the apodictic norms through which YHWH "made a covenant with you and with all Israel" (34:27). Mosaic authorship of the Pentateuch, therefore, although not literally true, does serve to convey a theological truth. Biblical critics have allowed their well-founded disbelief in the literal assertion of post-biblical tradition to blind them to the religious significance of the Mosaic attribution of the law.[42] There were in ancient Israel more ways of conceiving the laws than simply that of the covenant theology.[43] But by ascribing all normative law to Moses, the canonical Pentateuch has made laws into personal commandments, and it has made the secular into a matter of the greatest sacral concern. The Mosaic Torah is thus anything but a stern and impersonal taskmaster. It is a means of communion with a loving and personal God. The energy and spiritual power of Torah flows in no small measure from its insistence on holding these two dimensions, the outer and the inner, the legal and the affective, in a tight unity, refusing to sacrifice the one on the altar of the other.

7. ETHICS AND RITUAL
IN THE LIGHT OF COVENANT THEOLOGY

Another way of classifying Toraitic law is seen in the rabbinic tradition. The rabbis differentiated commandments that are *be-*

42   See Childs, *Introduction to the Old Testament as Scripture* (Philadelphia: Fortress, 1979) 132–35.
43   On the overextension of the covenant idea at the hands of theologians,

tween man and his neighbor from those *between man and God*. This classification is parallel to the modern distinction between casuistic and apodictic, although it is not identical, for an injunction such as the love of one's neighbor (Lev 19:18) is apodictic in form and yet it obviously affects one's life in society. What is interesting is that the rabbis did not view one class of commandments as more obligatory than the other, nor did they consider a person's obligation to his neighbor autonomous and independent of his duty to God. In other words, unlike some of the proponents of liberal Judaism, the Talmudic rabbis did not distinguish between *ethical* and *ritual* norms with the goal of diminishing the latter. The two sets are equally obligatory. Where there emerges a conflict between a commandment of one set and one of the other, an order of priorities must be articulated. In that sense, one commandment may be more important than another, but not more obligatory. The prioritization is still an item in the law. Ordinarily, one does *all* the commandments. Rabbi Judah the Patriarch, the redactor of the Mishnah (ca. 200 C.E.), put it nicely: "Be as careful about a 'light' commandment as you are about a 'serious' one, for you do not know the reward of the commandments."[44] The commandments, then, are not an autonomous system of ethics which man devises for his own purposes. The "light" ones, at least, cannot be justified before the bar of philosophical ethics. Their importance is known to God—who instituted the whole Jewish legal system (*halakhah*)—but it is concealed from man.

In its broad outlines, this aspect of the rabbinic understanding of law is in continuity with the theology that underlies the final (canonical) shape of the Pentateuch. But, as indicated above, a refinement is necessary. If one wishes to correlate the biblical and the rabbinic approaches, one would do better to speak of three

see Levenson, "The Theologies of Commandment in Biblical Israel," *HTR* 73 (1980).

44 *m. 'Abot* 2:1.

classes of laws. The first describes a case deriving from man's life in society and specifies a punishment that can reasonably be carried out by a human court. This first class is casuistic and between man and his neighbor. The law of the assailant (Exod 21:18–19) is a fine example. The second category is an absolute norm, phrased in the second person, which does not specify a penalty or, if it does, the penalty cannot be imposed by human hands, but the effect of the crime is visibly social in nature. The injunction to love the resident alien (22:20) is of this second kind of commandment. It is apodictic and between man and his neighbor. Finally, there are norms stated as imperatives whose violation would seem to entail no immediate danger to society. The dietary laws of Leviticus 11 and Deuteronomy 14 fall in this category. Whatever an anthroplogist may tell us was their origin or function, Israel took them up into her theology and derived them from the principle of *imitatio Dei,* the imitation of God:

> For I am YHWH, who brought you up out of the land of Egypt to be your God. You shall be holy, for I am holy. (Lev 11:45).

> You shall not eat anything that has died a natural death. Give it to the alien in your towns to eat, or sell it to a foreigner. For you are a people holy to YHWH your God. You shall not seethe a kid in its mother's milk. (Deut 14:21)

This is not to deny that these laws made sense in terms of the society in which they emerged and were alive; they did. They undoubtedly seem more mysterious to us than they did to biblical Israel. For example, a text discovered only in this century has suggested to some scholars the possibility that the prohibition upon seething a kid in its mother's milk was directed against a Canaanite fertility rite,[45] a discovery bolstered by the fact that the preface to the dietary laws in Deuteronomy 14 stresses that "YHWH your God chose you from among all the peoples on the earth to be his treasured people" (v 2). Israel is to be different. But

---

45   See Childs, *Exodus,* 485–86.

what is the nature of her special identity? In these texts, Israel's uniqueness lies not in the area of justice or health or any of the other things which we might consider desirable. It lies in *holiness*. In other words, whatever the more mundane explanation for these norms of the third category, the normative theology of the Pentateuch had no interest in preserving their memory. Instead, it refers the practice to the nature of God alone. Such norms are apodictic and between man and God.

Earlier, we saw that the theology behind the present shape of the Torah endows casuistic law with the status of the apodictic imperatives of covenant. The consequent mesh of the two types, one deriving from law and the other from covenant, stands as a constant warning against interpreting the casuistic laws as instrumental and hence dispensable in nature. Both types of law are owed to God; the one is not presented as a human corollary to the other. Now we must note, in addition, that the presence of apodictic laws between man and God serves as a warning against identifying the Lord of the covenant with any rational principle. Reason is not the suzerain. This category of laws, the least palatable to people of a philosophical cast of mind, stands guard against any effort to depersonalize God. It is because the covenant relationship is founded upon personal fidelity that there can be laws whose only "explanation" is the unfathomable decree of God.

The covenant relationship, then, is not polar but triangular. At the top stands God, and at each of the two angles of the base stand Israelites. Each of them relates to his neighbor through norms decreed by God. Or, to put it differently, individual Israelites relate to each other as vassals of the same suzerain. Whereas Mursilis commands Duppi-Tessub, "With my friend you shall be friend, and with my enemy, you shall be enemy," YHWH commands Israel:

You shall not take vengeance or bear a grudge against your kinsfolk. You shall love your neighbor as yourself: I am YHWH. (Lev 19:18)

The double standard is owing to the fact that one is to relate differently to another son of the covenant from the way he relates to an outsider. The point is not ethnic solidarity, "preferring one's own," but rather the requirement to be a friend to one's suzerain's friends. The covenant binds the vassals to each other, just as it binds each of them to YHWH. In Israel, covenant becomes a basis of social ethics.

In the casuistic law, a human court can inflict the penalties for violations. But what about apodictic law? Here, the curses of covenant come into effect. They are the divine sentence upon a wayward vassal. And since the casuistic law is endowed with the status of stipulations of covenant as well, even here, Israel, if not the individual Israelite, feels the wrath of God when she has transgressed. In fact, one function of the prophet was to put Israel on trial for breach of covenant.[46] The best example of such a trial (Hebrew, *rîb*) is Mic 6:1–8. In this poem, vv 1–2 are a summons. The mountains, hills, and the foundations of the earth are invited to attend the trial of Israel by YHWH. Recall that "mountains" and "earth" appear among the witnesses to Hittite treaties. V 3 is an accusation, although phrased in the reverse of what we expect. YHWH asks Israel if she has a complaint to file against him. Apparently, the mountains and the earth will adjudicate between the parties to the proceedings. In vv 4–5, the divine plaintiff recites some of his benefactions to the defendant, in a compelling reflex of the historical prologue of the covenant formulary. Surely Israel has no claim upon her deliverer, but just as surely he has a claim upon her, as the witnesses summoned in vv 1–2 know full well. In vv 6–7, where we might have expected to hear the defendant state his case, we find, instead, a guilty plea. The only issue is how to make restitution. The prophet savages a theology that is the reverse of the liberal preference for ethics over ritual. Israel thinks first not of justice and covenant-loyalty, but of sacrifices, as if ritual action can atone for injustice. In v 8, God, who is

46   See Hillers, *Treaty-Curses and the Old Testament Prophets* (Rome: Pontifical Biblical Institute, 1964).

now both plaintiff and judge, announces that it cannot. What is needed instead is justice (law) and loyalty/walking with God (covenant).[47] This last verse of the oracle is a kind of sentence. It tells what the defendant, now that he has pleaded guilty, must do in compensation for his misdeed. In sum, Mic 6:1–8 is not only a divine lawsuit, but more specifically, a trial for breach of covenant.[48] It reflects the integration of legal forms and covenant forms which is the hallmark of Israelite morality.

The curses and blessings of the covenant formulary enables the prophets of Israel to provide a theology of history. Adversity—drought, famine, epidemic, defeat, or whatever—could be accounted for by reference to a violation of covenant obligations. Conversely, the prosperity and tranquility of either the past or the coming age could be seen as a consequence of faithful partnership with God (prophets did not see the present as blessed). In other words, the last item of the covenant formulary enables Israel to make sense—moral sense—of historical experience. To be sure, the notion that suffering must be owing to a misdeed and happiness to proper action is well-nigh universal. It lies at the base of much superstition, ancient and modern. Through covenant theology, however, Israel was able to develop a coherent correlation between experience and morals, especially public morals, the relationship between man and his neighbor. What covenant theology could not tolerate was the inability to correlate the two, the observation that the just suffer and the wicked thrive and that Israel may indeed have a just claim against God. Awareness of

47 On "walking" as a term to designate covenantal fidelity, see Weinfeld, "The Covenant of Grant in the Old Testament and in the Ancient Near East," *JAOS* 90(1970) 185–86.

48 On the structure of this and other lawsuits, see Huffmon, "The Covenant Lawsuit in the Prophets," *JBL* 78 (1959) 285–95; and Wright, "The Lawsuit of God: A Form-Critical Study of Deuteronomy 32" in *Israel's Prophetic Heritage*, ed. B. W. Anderson and W. Harrelson (London: SCM, 1962) 26–67; and J. Harvey, *Le Plaidoyer prophetique contre Israël après la rupture de l'alliance* (Bruges and Paris: Desclée de Brouwer; Montreal: Bellarmin, 1967).

this possibility, which flourished during and after the Exile, was to deal a deathblow to the classic prophetic theology and to alter radically the Israelite "feeling for history." But consideration of that would take us beyond the limits of this study.

8. ONE GOD OR ONE LORD?

Not so long ago, the great revolution manifest in the religion of Israel was seen to lie in the idea of monotheism. Israel gave the world the belief in one God, a belief that was supposed to testify to the genius of Israel. "The religion of the unity of God was a new cultural creation," wrote the Israeli scholar, Yehezkel Kaufmann, ". . . and since it was born and grew up only in Israel, we must add this: it was born of the creative spirit of the people Israel."[49] The problem is that the world seems to have rejected the fruit of this genius, for most people in it today are atheists or agnostics or polytheists of some sort. They do not believe in any god, or are unsure of the existence of the divine, or they believe in many gods. And, in fact, monotheism is a doctrine with problems. For the monotheist must see a principle of unity beneath the diversity of experience, and, if he is a Jewish or a Christian or a Muslim monotheist, he must believe that ultimate reality is not only a unity, but a benevolent one: one God wills what is good. But when everyone can see that experience is multifarious, it is difficult to understand how the monotheist dares to attribute everything ultimately to one principle. For monotheism obligates one to see the work of God not only in the splendor of a summer sunset or the majesty of a snow-capped mountain, but also in the birth of a deformed child or in the multiplication of cancer cells in an innocent person. Thus, monotheistic religions have had to confront head-on the issue of theodicy, the justice of God, while other worldviews have sometimes been able to evade it or to face it with

49   Y. Kaufmann, *Twldwt H'mwnh Hyśr'lyt* (Jerusalem: Bialik; Tel Aviv: Devir, 5720/1960) 1: 32. The translation is mine.

less at risk. Of course, one can save his monotheism by postulating that God is indeed benevolent, although we cannot understand his benevolence in the light of our experience—in other words, by an act of faith. But when the issue comes down to one of faith, we can no longer speak of Israel's "creative spirit," only of the appearance in her of a mysterious revelation, beyond anything the mind of even a genius can fathom.

But there are reasons to doubt whether the religion of Israel was really monotheistic. Consider an illustration: Once there were two gods. One held high hopes for creation and would not tolerate evil in it; the other was more a realist and was prepared to bear with man, even though the latter's impulses were evil from his youth on. The first god brought a flood to destroy the world with the exception of one family of righteous people, for he regretted having created the world. But, after a while, he was overcome by the second god, who caused the flood to subside and swore that he would never allow such a thing to recur, even though man is still evil. Now this story is surely polytheistic; there are two gods. But is it essentially different from the story of Noah in Genesis 6–9? In the latter, God determines to destroy the whole world, except for Noah and his family, because of its corruption (6:13), but then he promises that he will not bring a flood again, even though man has not reformed. "The inclinations of man's mind are [still] evil from his youth" (8:31). In other words, God changes his mind twice in the story of Noah. First, he regrets having created the world (6:7), and then he decides that he will not bring another flood even though man's evil, the cause of the flood, continues. My question is this: Is this one God or more than one? Does one relate to God differently before and after he changes his mind? If so, then in what sense is this one God and not two? Wherein lies the continuity of identity? Here is another example, more troubling. In 1 Kings 22, YHWH convenes his "host of heaven" (v 19), and sends out one member of it, who becomes a "lying spirit" (v 22), whose false message will bring about King Ahab's death. The problem is that another prophet,

Micaiah ben Imlah, delivers an oracle from YHWH, in which he discloses to the king what has happened in heaven (vv 19–23). In other words, YHWH here authorizes simultaneously two messages, one true and one false, and it is the false one whose acceptance he decrees in advance and accomplishes (vv 22, 29ff.). Is this monotheism or dualism? It is monotheism in that both messages come from YHWH, but it is dualism in that the messages clash. The "lying spirit" wins this one, although not without being exposed. Is there an essential difference between saying there are two gods within one pantheon ("paganism," polytheism) and two conflicting spirits subject to one God (1 Kings 22)? When a psalmist calls upon YHWH to "remove [or cancel] your anger from us" and, instead, to "show us your favor" (Ps 85:5, 8), is he not recognizing a plurality within his one God akin to the plurality within one pantheon of a polytheistic religion?

My point is not that Israelite monotheism and polytheism were the same; they were not. Rather, I stress the need to look beneath the surface of terminology and to examine the underlying spiritual experience of the worshipper. When we do so, we see that the two were not so distant as they are usually portrayed. And, more importantly, we become aware of the possibility that there may be elements in Israel's environment which helped develop her monotheism. Not that there was a revulsion against the culture of the other peoples, as Jewish tradition has tended to think for thousands of years, but that Israelite religion was, in part, a continuation of it.

Did Israel recognize the existence of other gods than YHWH? It is surely true that she called her God by names other than YHWH. Now whether these different names were thought to denote different gods, at least in the earliest period, is difficult to say. When Exod 6:2 tells us that YHWH is El Shaddai, it is reasonable to suspect that there had been cause to think otherwise. In the deep prehistory of this verse may lie an effort to subsume El Shaddai into YHWH. Henceforth, these words will be treated as two names for the same God.[50] In short, the question of whether Israel was monotheistic cannot be answered until another question has been answered: Of what period is one speaking?

The idea that YHWH is the only God appears unambiguously many times in the Hebrew Bible, for example:

> You shall know this day and keep in mind that it is YHWH who is God in the heaven above and on the earth beneath; there is no other! (Deut 4:39)

There are other passages, however, which speak just as plainly of "other gods." Best known among them is what Jews count as the second of the Ten Commandments:

> You shall have no other gods before me. (Exod 20:3)

The commandment forbids Israel to "have" other gods or, at least, to have them "before" YHWH, whatever this enigmatic expression means. But does it deny the *existence* of the rival deities? In what realistic sense can one put them before YHWH if they have no reality? If they are purely imaginary, then why not say so? In another passage from Exodus, one can deny the reality of the other gods only by depriving a moving hymn of its power:

> Who is like you, YHWH, among the gods,
> Who is like you, majestic in holiness,
> Worthy of awe and praise,
> Wonder-worker? (Exod 15:11)

The question, of course, is rhetorical. No one is like YHWH, not even the other gods. But if the latter do not exist, then what force does this great verse of praise have? It is like telling someone that he is more brilliant than a unicorn. But if one believes that the Torah is a monolith, with no historical development or doctrinal variety, and if he is a monotheist himself, then he must interpret

50 On this, see F. M. Cross, *Canaanite Myth and Hebrew Epic* (Cambridge: Harvard University, 1973) 44–75.

this verse in light of the affirmations of monotheism of verses like Deut 4:39. Thus, there is a long history in Judaism of providing verses like Exod 15:11 with translations far removed from the plain sense.[51] For example, an ancient Aramaic translation, which came to attain an authoritative status among Jews, renders as follows:

> There is none beside you. It is you who are God, Adonai. There is no God beside you. You are majestic in holiness, worthy of awe and praise, a wonder-worker.[52]

In the repetition of the assertion of monotheism here, one can detect something close to panic at the thought that the verse might be taken to mean what it says. The denial of the plain sense continued into the Middle Ages, when to give only one example, the great commentator Rashi (1040–1105) rendered "gods" here as "the mighty." In fact, it continues today. The new Torah translation of the Jewish Publication Society (1962) reads "the celestials" in place of "the gods," although with a note drawing attention to another reading, "the mighty," as if that were the most significant alternative. The New English Bible (1970), which is less constricted by doctrine, renders the word "the gods," but notes that "in might" is also possible. And, in fact, "the mighty" (or "in might") *is* a possible translation. My point is that the Jewish preference for this possibility over the other is owing not to philology, but to theology, specifically the theology that says the Torah is homogeneous and self-referential and is to be interpreted, even translated, everywhere according to the monotheism that became the only legitimate Jewish way of viewing divinity. In the process, as I hope to show, something of the power and the dynamism of the earlier, biblical faith has been lost.

It can be argued that, although parts of the Hebrew Bible acknowledge the *existence* of other gods, all the power remains in

---

51 See C. H. Gordon, "'lhym in Its Reputed Meaning of *Rulers, Judges*," *JBL* 54 (1935) 139–44.
52 T. Onq. to Exod 15:11.

the hands of YHWH. From a logical point of view, of course, it does not make much sense to speak of a powerless god. Isn't God almighty? And if he is, then there can be only one; two entities cannot each be endowed with omnipotence. Here, logic provides an argument for monotheism, just as the experience of innocent suffering provides an argument against it. Whatever the implications of logical analysis, however, there is ample support in the text of the Hebrew Bible for the notion that YHWH is ruler of the gods:

> For a great God is YHWH,
> The great king over all gods. (Ps 95:3)

There are texts, moreover, which tell how YHWH became the unchallenged ruler of the gods. One psalm, for example, speaks even of his having decreed the deaths of the others. "God takes his stand in the asembly of El" (Ps 82:1) and then procedes to indict the gods for injustice (vv 2–4). Finally, he sentences them to death (vv 6–7).[53] Is this psalm polytheistic or monotheistic? It is polytheistic for two reasons. First, it is by no means certain that the "God" ('ĕlōhîm) who takes his stand is the same as the "God" ('Ēl) in whose assembly he speaks (v 1),[54] nor is it at all clear that these two are identical to the "Most High" ('elyôn) whom v 6 identifies as the father of the gods.[55] In fact, the context is redolent of the polytheism that we see in a scene from a Canaanite poem from not later than about 1400 B.C.E., when mighty Baal takes his stand in the divine assembly and spits in defiance.[56] The second

---

53 On Psalm 82, see J. Morgenstern, "The Mythological Background of Psalm 82," *HUCA* 14 (1939) 29–126. With much of Morgenstern's thinking I cannot agree, although I do accept that the background is mythological. His suggestion (pp. 122–23) that behind *ûk'aḥad haśśārîm* in v 7 lies something like *kĕ'Hēlēl Ben Šaḥar* (Isa 14:12) is quite intriguing.

54 It has long been noted that very often in the "Elohistic Psalter" (Psalms 42–83) one must see the name YHWH where the word *'ĕlōhîm* is now found. Cf. Psalm 14 with Psalm 53. "El" is both a general term for deity and the name of the patriarch of the Canaanite pantheon.

55 K. Budde, "Ps 82⁶," *JBL* 40 (1921) 41–42.

56 *ANET*, 132.

reason to think Psalm 82 is polytheistic is that God plainly acknowledges in v 6 that those upon whom he pronounces sentence are divine. In short, Psalm 82 is witness to a plural concept of divinity.

The problem is that in the very next verse (v 7) God is depicted as stripping the others of their divinity and immortality. Once again, it will do no good to attempt to harmonize this idea with logic. It is surely true that one cannot *lose* his immortality; if he dies, he was *never* immortal. But Psalm 82 is not a treatise in philosophical theology, but a document from the history of a living community of persons, and one which seems to reflect the transition from polytheism to monotheism. The psalm that begins with a scene familiar to any student of (polytheistic) Canaanite religion ends with the death of the other gods and the assertion that "God" will take possession of all the nations, whoever it is they worship. Psalm 82 thus opens in polytheism and closes in monotheism.

The trajectory in the theology of ancient Israel that Psalm 82 represents is one which portrays the kingship (or uniqueness) of God not as something postulated, but as something won. God humiliates the gods. If they had never posed a challenge to him, his humiliation of them would be sadism. Instead, it is the pivotal stage in his assumption of universal dominion. In this particular theology—and I do not say it is the only one in the Hebrew Bible—monotheism is seen as dynamic rather than static, as more like a drama than a treatise in logic. Everything is at stake here. The very foundations of the earth quake as God pronounces his verdict (v 5). The simple statement that Israel was monotheistic or polytheistic cannot do justice to the spiritual dynamics at work in the Hebrew Bible. Nor will the old cliché about Israelite monotheism as a revolution in consciousness do justice to the relationship between this dynamic monotheizing drama and the literature of the rest of the ancient Near East, the culture from which Israel is supposed to have effected an absolute break. "Paganism" is not quite so simplistic as the proponents of the Israelite "revolution"

tend to assume. Herbert Farmer points out an element of monotheism in the religious experience of one whom we may classify as
a polytheist:

> ... there is, in the act of prayer and worship, an inherent tendency
> towards what may be called concentration ... We may surmise that at
> moments of living prayer and worship there is in primitive man a
> turning to *a* god as if he were in fact the one and only God, though
> without any expressly formulated denial of the existence of others; for
> the time being, the god worshipped fills the whole sphere of the divine.
> ... [57]

I should add that the spiritual experience of one form of prayer,
praise, is especially akin to that of the monotheist. One's heart
moves one to attribute uniqueness to the object of praise. This
attribution of uniqueness need not be taken as an indication that
in a context other than one of praise, the speaker would still deny
the existence of others. A hymn does not speak in the same
language as a philosophical treatise. Thus, most of the statements
of the uniqueness or kingship of YHWH are actually affirmations of his incomparability; they tend to occur in a context of
hymnody. "Who is like you, YHWH, among the gods?" (Exod
15:11). Israel did not assert the oneness of her God with the
dispassion of a philosopher. She praised God for being unique,
incomparable, a source of embarrassment to his rivals, their
master. Something precious is lost when we convert this language
of hymnody into a matter of doctrine. That there comes a moment
in the history of religion when philosophical reflection is necessary cannot be gainsaid. But we generate grave misunderstand-
ings when we read that moment back into an era when it had not
yet occurred.

The hymnic affirmation of the incomparability of YHWH has
been found to be paralleled nicely in other literature of the ancient
Near East, for example, in this Old Babylonian hymn to the god
Sin:

---

57 H. H. Farmer, *Revelation and Religion* (London: Nisbet, 1954) 105.

> Lord, who surpasses thee? Who can equal thee?
> Great hero, who surpasses thee? Who can equal thee?
> Lord Nanna, who surpasses thee? Who can equal thee?[58]

And of the god of the sun and justice, Shamash, we read:

> Thou shinest, thou alone! None among the gods equals thee.[59]

In Egypt in the fourteenth century B.C.E., the worship of the solar disc Aton attracted a theology that has been regarded as monotheistic:

> O sole god, like whom there is no other!
> Thou didst create the world according to thy desire,
> Whilst thou wert alone.[60]

We also find, again in Mesopotamia, strong parallels to the notion that one God came to be supreme in what had been a more "democratic" pantheon. For example, the god of Babylon itself, Marduk, acquired kingship over the (other) gods through his defeat of Tiamat, the sea monster who had cowed the rest of the pantheon. His praise sounds a note familiar to any student of the Hebrew Bible:

> Who restored all the ruined gods, as though they were his own creation.

> Who is highly exalted among the gods, his brothers, the lord of them all.

> The utterance of his mouth no god can change.[61]

In short, if one wishes to define monotheism as the idea that one god is supreme over the others, one must still acknowledge that in this Israel was not unique. To be sure, I have not established that

---

58 Quoted in C. J. Labushchagne, *The Incomparability of YHWH in the Old Testament*, Pretoria Oriental Series 5 (Leiden: Brill, 1966) 34.

59 Labushchagne, *Incomparability*, 36.

60 *ANET*, 370. The translator of "The Hymn to the Aton" is J. A. Wilson.

61 A. Heidel, *The Babylonian Genesis*, 2nd ed. (Chicago: University of Chicago, 1951) 53; 94; 152.

Israel borrowed the language of incomparability. If Farmer is right about the unitive element in even the rankest polytheism, and if I am correct in positing a monotheizing dimension to praise, then one can easily speak of a parallel development between Egypt, Mesopotamia, and Israel. Either way, it is clear that the ascription of supremacy and incomparability to YHWH was not a revolution in consciousness in the ancient world.

There are, however, dimensions to Israelite "monotheism" that are not (yet) documented elsewhere. Chief among these is the fact that Israel developed prohibitions upon the worship of the other gods. Generally, the other cultures of the biblical world were, by comparison to Israel, remarkably tolerant. Their pantheons absorbed gods with ease. Even where one god was hymned as incomparable and supreme, the others were still worshipped. With the possible exception of the Aton cult, the supremacy of one god was not regarded as a derogation of the others or a judgment upon service to them. But Israel, as we have seen, was to "have no other gods before me" (Exod 20:3). In fact, some passages make it clear that Israel was to have no other gods at all:

> He who sacrifices to a god other than YHWH alone shall be proscribed. (Exod 22:19)

Laws such as this bespeak a worldview incompatible with the free and easy attitude to divinity and cult that obtained generally in the rest of the ancient Near East. YHWH was intolerant of the gods to the point that he continually warns his votaries against situations in which they might be led away from him. For example, Deut 13:2–19 warns against following a prophet or diviner, even one who works miracles, if he advocates the service of any deity other than YHWH. Note that nothing in Deuteronomy 13 suggests that the other gods do not exist. The fear is not that Israel will be led into philosophical error, but that another deity will claim her *service,* and the assumption is that, if this occurs, she will have abandoned the service of YHWH, which is concretized and realized only in observance of his commandments. What is striking here is precisely the unstated assumption that one cannot combine the service of YHWH with that of the other gods; the two are mutually exclusive. This is the element for which we cannot account by comparison with the monotheizing tendencies within the pantheons of Israel's neighbors. On the other hand, parallels to the ideas and even the language of the chapter do appear in extra-biblical literature. Moshe Weinfeld draws attention to a section of a Hittite suzerainty treaty in which the vassal is obligated to report and to extradite anyone guilty of sedition against the emperor.[62] The goal of such stipulations is the suppression of insurrection. Like the vassal of the Hittite suzerain, the Israelite is required to report the apostate charismatic (Deut 13:10).[63] To fail to do so is to breach covenant and thus to undermine the value of whatever stipulations are still observed. In each case, the Hittite and the biblical, the great king obliges his ally not only to observe the terms himself, but to act affirmatively against any situation which weakens the alliance. The implication for the Israelite prohibition upon worshipping other gods is evident: YHWH the suzerain cannot tolerate rivals. His famous jealousy is the jealousy of a liege lord who demands, as all lords do, the exclusive loyalty of his vassals. It is this which underlies the prohibition upon covenant-making, joint worship, and intermarriage with Gentiles, as in Exod 34:12–16. In this passage, we find all the ingredients of the covenantal component of Israelite monotheism. A covenant with the Canaanites, presumably of the parity kind, will oblige Israel to recognize the pantheon of these new allies. But to do so is to grant legitimacy to the other gods, in fact, to absorb them into the institution of covenant, which until now has involved only one deity, the suzerain YHWH. To the nation whose God is its suzerain, every god is a potential suzerain, a potential paramour with whom the slightest contact harbors the

---

62   See Weinfeld, *Deuteronomy and the Deuteronomic School* (Oxford: Clarendon, 1972) 91–100. The text in question is on p. 93.

63   Read here *haggēd taggîdennû* with LXX for the reasons splendidly argued in Weinfeld, *Deuteronomy*, 94.

ominous capacity to destroy the covenant. Hence, the fear of "whoring" after the other's gods, a fear certain to be realized where one brings the others into his home through intermarriage. The prohibition on polytheism is a corollary of the exclusivity of the suzerain-vassal relationship.

My interpretation of the biblical view of polytheism finds confirmation in an observation by a scholar with some very different views. Yehezkel Kaufmann argued that Israel's religion was so utterly discontinuous with the traditions of her neighbors that she literally did not understand the nature of polytheism. In support of his position, he noted that the Hebrew Bible reported no myth about any god. Instead of polemicizing against the myth, Israel polemicized against the gods themselves. The war on myth and the war on the gods were entirely separate.[64] Kaufmann's observation is largely correct, but his conclusion is not. It is true that Israel attacked the gods more than their mythologies. But why? The reason is that, as regards the covenant theology, the myth is neutral. It will not raise a serious challenge against YHWH's suzerainty. The god, however, might; every god is a potential suzerain, who might displace YHWH. Therefore, the brunt of the polemic falls upon the other deities. They must be shown to be unworthy of lordship.

This need to discredit the other gods is the last component in Israelite monotheism. Central to it is the assertion that the other gods are not real. A fine example is Jer 10:2-10.[65] In these verses, we do not hear the covenantal proscription of polytheism, but, rather, an attack upon the gods that centers upon an identification of the deities with their images. In Kaufmann's thinking, this view of the gods as fetishes was proof positive that Israel's religion was so distant from that of her neighbors that she could not even understand theirs. In Part 2, I shall argue that statements made in the heat of interreligious polemic cannot bear the weight which

64 Kaufmann, *Twldwt,* 1:255-85, esp. pp. 283-85.
65 See M. Margoliot, "Jeremiah X 1-16: A Re-Examination," *VT* 30 (1980) 295-308. Margoliot dates the passage no later than 605 B.C.E.

Kaufmann places upon them.[66] Even here in Jeremiah 10, we must not miss both the atmosphere of fevered polemic against the gods and that of praise for YHWH, a praise that, again, stresses his incomparability (vv 6–7). Still, it is imperative to note that the hymnic assertion of YHWH's incomparability here entails a savage derogation of the rest of the pantheon, as it does not in Mesopotamia or in texts like Exod 15:11. Jeremiah 10 has its being in a world of either/or, either YHWH or the gods. In that sense, it recalls Deuteronomy 13, with its interpretation of the worship of other gods as a defection from YHWH. The precise connection between the prohibition of practical polytheism and the attack upon the gods as unreal is unclear. I suggest, however, that it is the need to discredit other deities who might be imported into a status of suzerainty which leads from the one to the other.

To summarize: we have examined three aspects of Israelite monotheism. The first is the statement of YHWH's incomparability, which seems connected with his emergence into a commanding position in the pantheon. This element is nicely paralleled in the hymnic and epic literature of Mesopotamia. The second element is the prohibition upon the worship of the other gods and upon any situation that might lead to such service. The Near Eastern source for this lies in the suzerainty covenant, which demands of the vassal exclusive allegiance to his suzerain. Finally, we have examined the polemical identification of the gods and their icons. Texts like Jeremiah 10:2–10 are the closest to genuine monotheism, the belief in the reality of only one deity, although we noted that the hyperbolic tone of such polemics inhibits our ability to say much about what the author believes about the gods he here insults.

This discussion has shown that, although no other religion has been discovered with the same "monotheism," almost all the elements of Israel's belief in the oneness/uniqueness of YHWH show convincing parallels in the Gentile world. The most impor-

66 See pp. 109–11, and Levenson, "Yehezkel Kaufmann and Mythology," *CJ* 36 (1982) 36–43.

tant of the parallels in my opinion, the one that sheds light on the most biblical texts, is the covenantal proscription on intercourse with other suzerains and their agents. Why, precisely, Israel should have taken one of the gods as her suzerain, thus dooming the others, is unclear. C. B. Labuschagne suggests that the answer lies in the uniqueness of Israelite historical experience:

> By his intervention in history, of which the deliverance from Egypt is the example *par excellence,* YHWH did something that no other god ever did: He delivered a nation for himself in a miraculous manner.[67]

Labuschagne is surely correct that YHWH's control of history often appeared to Israel as the decisive difference between him and the gods (e.g., Isaiah 44). But I doubt whether we can go farther and claim that it was Israel's unique experience of deliverance that *generated* her exclusive fidelity to YHWH as the one lord among the gods. For one thing, the historical experience of Israel could have been explained within the mechanism of a thorough-going polytheism. The Exodus, for example, could have been presented in terms of a theomachy, a war among the gods, in which one side freed the other's slaves. Historical events are mute. They do not bespeak any given metahistorical interpretations; the interpretation explains the event, not *vice versa.*[68] Israel's belief in the incomparability/lordship/exclusive reality of YHWH does not derive from her theology of history; her theology of history follows from her "monotheism." There is another reason why it is unlikely that a reflection on history generated Israel's "monotheism." The truth is that historical consciousness was to be found in Mesopotamia as well. There it was less central and less developed than in Israel, but the fact remains that the Mesopotamians also believed that their gods intervened in history. They even celebrated such interventions in their cults.[69] In short, the

67 Labushchagne, *Incomparability,* 136.
68 See V. A. Harvey, *The Historian and the Believer* (Philadelphia: Westminster, 1966) 281–83.
69 See B. Albrektson, *History and the Gods,* ConBOT 1 (Lund: Gleerup,

sense of history as open to the divine is not a sufficient explanation of the rise of Israel's covenantal faith. How the idea of God as exclusive suzerain was born thus remains cloaked in mystery. Historians may never pierce that cloak.

What is clear in light of the covenant theology is the connection between the profession of the uniqueness of YHWH and the performance of his commandments. To believe that he alone is lord is to do his will; to do his will is to enthrone him in lordship. The belief in the one God, the love of God, and the observance of his commandments are inextricable; they are all ways of stating one fact, his suzerainty. The Near Eastern material sheds light on the roots of what is perhaps the central affirmation of Judaism, that the Torah is the way to life with God, and God, the source of the Torah.

9. THE KINGSHIP OF GOD
AND THE KINGSHIP OF MAN

In our analysis of Israelite monotheism, we identified two themes that can be termed royal in nature, a general one and a specific one. The general theme is that YHWH is king and that all other beings, including the other gods, are therefore subordinate to him. The comparative materials suggest that nothing in this notion of the kingship of YHWH, of divine *sovereignty,* conflicts with the idea of human kingship. On the contrary, just as the story of Marduk's assumption of sovereignty did not undermine the kings of his city, Babylon, so did YHWH's sovereignty offer no critique of the institution of human kingship in Israel. In fact, we shall see in the next chapter that some texts present the sovereignty of the world as a kind of unequal diarchy, in which YHWH has invested the Israelite monarch with the authority to rule a global domain in the name of YHWH (e.g., Psalm 2). The perception of YHWH as sovereign is modelled upon the familiar

1967); and J. J. M. Roberts, "Myth *versus* History: Relaying the Comparative Foundations," *CBQ* 38 (1976) 1–13.

image of human sovereigns, but without the demand to choose one or the other. YHWH's temple, for example, is termed a palace (see Ezra 3:6), his prophets are viewed as royal envoys (Isaiah 6), and one of his sacrifices is termed "tribute" (*minḥâ*).[70] The analogy between divine and human sovereignty was known in Israel; it is explicit in a post-exilic polemic (fifth century B.C.E.) against the priesthood, in which a prophet asks rhetorically whether the governor will accept maimed sacrifices of the sort the Jews are bringing to YHWH (Mal 1:7-9). In this passage, there is no tension between divine and human sovereignty.

The second royal theme derives from the Near Eastern suzerainty treaty of the sort that we have been examining. What brought this theme into the discussion of monotheism was the proscription of other suzerains which is essential to the alliance. This proscription is the ultimate source of the prohibitions upon the worship of other deities in Israel, and, I have suggested, it underlies the depiction of them as unworthy, even, finally, unreal. We may call this second royal theme YHWH's *suzerainty*. It is a more specific theme than the one of sovereignty in that, in origin, it is limited to the relationship between states and thus cannot be predicated of every king. A king is sovereign by definition, but suzerain only if he is an emperor, that is to say, a master of vassals. In fact, they must acknowledge only one suzerain, the *great king* of their alliance. In the case of the treaty of Mursilis and Duppi-Tessub, the suzerain confers sovereignty upon his vassal or at least affirms that he will uphold his vassal's kingship, if Duppi-Tessub proves faithful in covenant. I drew a parallel between this and the statement in Exod 19:6 that Israel will, if she observes the covenant (v 5), become YHWH's "kingdom of priests and a holy nation." In short, all of Israel is endowed with sovereignty, for the nation as a whole has become royal in character. Thus, it is hardly surprising that the *mitsvot*, the covenant

70 *Minḥâ* in the secular sense can be seen in Judg 3:15; in the sacred sense, in Leviticus 2. See J. Tigay, "On Some Aspects of Prayer in the Bible," *AJSR* 1 (1976) 363-79.

stipulations of the Sinaitic pact, are as often couched in the second person singular as in the plural. Both Israel as a nation and the Israelite as an individual stand in the position of royal vassals of the divine suzerain.

Unlike the sovereignty of God, his suzerainty does place a limitation upon the potential for a human counterpart. If there can be only one suzerain, how can Israel enter into a covenant with any other lord? Hence, we find, especially in those books in which the covenant idea is prominent, an unqualified rejection of *Realpolitik,* since all (human) alliances are equated with apostasy. Hos 7:10-13, for instance, contrasts Israel's overtures to Egypt and Assyria with fidelity to YHWH their God. "I am their redeemer," YHWH complains, "but they have plotted treason against me" (v 13). This is the plaintive cry of the grieving and spurned suzerain. His vassal appeals to the conventional suzerains, the lords of politics, and in the process proves herself not only mindless, but rebellious and treasonous. YHWH has redeemed them. That is his claim to suzerainty. And yet Israel dishonors that claim and consorts with other lords, the great powers, in hopes of obtaining that of which YHWH has already proven himself supremely capable: deliverance. The radicalism of this aspect of covenant theology must not be missed. The covenant with YHWH is here presented as the alternative to conventional political relations. Israel (Ephraim) must choose one or the other. It is either Egypt/Assyria or YHWH, but not both, for the divine suzerain will not tolerate a human competitor any more than he will a divine one. This proscribing of international politics is thus the political equivalent of covenantal monotheism. In each case, Israel's special identity demands a radical separation from the ways of the nations. The whole world is YHWH's, but Israel is to be his "treasured possession ... a kingdom of priests and a holy nation" (Exod 19:5–6), a sacral state, not a political one.

What are the implications of divine suzerainty for Israel's internal governance? If all Israelites are vassals of the great king, then it follows that one Israelite may not be set up over his fellows as king. There is no such thing as a "vice-suzerain" to whom vassals in covenant may do homage without harming their relationship with the great king. In short, the directness of the two-party relationship of YHWH and Israel, including even the individual Israelite, precludes human kingship. YHWH is her suzerain, YHWH alone. Even within Israel, therefore, the covenantal institution undermines the basis for politics. Hence, in some biblical texts, the institution of human kingship, which lay at the very center of the religions of many other ancient peoples,[71] was denounced as an act of treachery against God. As an example, consider this exchange between the victorious general ("judge") Gideon and the men of Israel:

[22]The men of Israel said to Gideon, "Rule over us—you, your son, and your grandson as well, for you have rescued us from the power of Midian."
[23]But Gideon replied, "I will not rule over you, and neither shall my son. YHWH will rule over you." (Judg 8:22–23)

And when the people demand a king from Samuel, last of the "judges," YHWH answers him with these words of dejection and grief:

Heed everything the people say to you, for it is not you whom they have rejected, but me whom they have rejected as their king. (1 Sam 8:7)

Here, "king" is to be read in the light of suzerainty, for the demand for a human king is a rejection of the divine king. The two cannot coexist. In the theo-politics of this stream of tradition, there is no room for earthly government. The state is not part of the solution to the problems inherent in human society, but itself one of the problems.

The difference between sovereignty and suzerainty should not be overdrawn. After all, the two concepts are expressed in biblical Hebrew by the same word, "king" (*melek*). Just as law, the

71 See H. Frankfort, *Kingship and the Gods* (Chicago: University of Chicago, 1948).

proper concern of kings, and covenant, the concern of suzerains, combined into an indissoluble mesh in Israel from an early date, so did the concepts of YHWH as king and YHWH as lord in large measure merge. We usually do not know which nuance lies behind the term *melek*. The issue is further complicated by the fact that early Israelite kingship was elective in character, a fact reflected in the continuing ceremony in which the people acclaim the new king as their sovereign, even though YHWH designated him.[72] In the case of David, the king responds to his election by making a *covenant* with his subjects (2 Sam 5:1-3). It is quite possible that in some instances in which the Hebrew Bible speaks of a covenant with YHWH, the reference is to a royal one like that between Israel and David in 2 Samuel 5 and not to a suzerainty treaty along the lines of the Hittite exemplars. It is impossible to know for sure. I have stressed the distinction between sovereignty and suzerainty in order to shed light on the bifurcated attitude towards human kingship in ancient Israel. In some texts, on the one hand, the divine and the human monarchs appear together, with no tension between them. This model we shall examine in Part 2. On the other hand, there are texts, such as those we saw from Judges 8 and 1 Samuel 8, in which divine and human monarchy are mutually exclusive. Any king other than YHWH is an intruder into the pristine covenant relationship; his establishment derives from an act of defection.

In this theology, Sinai serves as an eternal rebuke to man's arrogant belief that he can govern himself. The state is not coeval with God. Rather, it was born at a particular moment in history and under the judgment of a disappointed God. In a better world, one in which man turns to God with all his heart, it would not exist. Moreover, this antimonarchical stream in Israelite religion served to inhibit a simple identification of the people Israel with

72 See R. de Vaux, *Ancient Israel* (New York and Toronto: McGraw-Hill, 1965) 1:106; and B. Halpern, *The Constitution of the Monarchy in Israel*, HSM 25 (Chico: Scholars, 1981).

the states they evolved. For the theological tradition maintained that Israel had been a people before she was a worldly kingdom, a people to whom laws and even a destiny had already been given. She owes neither to the state. Thus, it is of the utmost significance that the Torah, the law of the theo-polity, was, for all its diversity, always ascribed to Moses and not to David, to the humble mediator of covenant and not to the regal founder of the dynastic state. In Israel, law was not coterminous with the state; the latter found its justification only within the context of Torah, and the Davidic dynasty itself, as we shall see in Part 2, was established through a variation of the idea of covenant, which affirmed in its own way the suzerainty of YHWH. Israel was a sacral state before she was a political state, she had her law (according to the canonical theology) before she raised up a king, and what is perhaps unparalleled in human history, she survived the destruction of her state and even dispersion into the four corners of the world without the loss of that essential identity conferred at Sinai. She was "a kingdom of priests and a holy people" both before and after she was a kingdom of a more mundane kind.

10. THE WEDDING
OF GOD AND ISRAEL

We have seen that the relationship of Israel to her God was conceived in the covenant theology along the lines of a contract between states and that one stipulation of such a contract was the requirement to love the lord in covenant. At the heart of Israel's relationship with YHWH lay a dialogue of love. There was another realm in the life of ancient Israel in which one finds a relationship of love sealed by contract, the realm of marriage. In the ancient Semitic world, marriage was a matter of contractual obligation; a trace of this remains in the Jewish wedding ceremony, in which the *ketubbah,* or marriage contract, is still read. Unfortunately, no *ketubbot* are preserved in the Hebrew Bible. But we do have Jewish marriage contracts from late biblical times preserved in scrolls.[73] The structure of these *ketubbot* is not that of the covenant formulary that applied to international contracts. Nonetheless, the two types of relationship, the international and the marital, were sufficiently similar that the language of covenant could be applied to both:

> You ask, "Because of what?" Because YHWH is a witness between you and the wife of your youth, with whom you have broken faith, even though she is your partner and the woman with whom you are in covenant. (Mal 2:14)

Here, the prophet views the institution of marriage as an instance of covenant. YHWH is the witness, and divorce is a form of treason.

In fact, so great was the overlap between the two realms that prophets often presented Israel's relationship with YHWH as a marriage. The prophet Hosea, for example, a man of the eighth century B.C.E., believed that YHWH had commanded him to marry a prostitute in order to exemplify the apostasy and promiscuity of Israel. Gomer, the prostitute, bore Hosea children with such names as "Unloved," to signify that God no longer loved Israel (Hos 1:6), and "Not-my-people," a name that indicated that the bonds of covenant had been severed, "for you are not my people, and I will not be your God" (v 9). The career of Hosea testifies to a tradition in Israel to the effect that what happened on the mountain in ancient days was the consummation of a romance, a marriage in which YHWH was the groom and Israel (although a man's name) was the bride. Thus, a book like Deuteronomy, which is saturated with the idiom of covenant, sees in the selection of Israel to be YHWH's treasured possession, the fruit of a passionate affair (Deut 7:6–8). The special status of Israel rests not upon her merits, her strength or numbers or intelligence or honesty, but upon something irrational, a passion, an affair of the heart, not the mind, in short a love. All the efforts

---

73   See E. G. Kraeling, ed., *The Brooklyn Museum Aramaic Papyri* (New Haven: Yale University, 1953).

to explain the special destiny of Israel in rational terms only dissolve its power. For Israel is singled out by and for the love of God:

> [12]And now, what does YHWH your God demand of you? Only this: to hold YHWH your God in awe, to walk in all his paths, to love him, and to serve YHWH your God with all your heart and all your soul, [13]to observe YHWH's commandments and his laws, which I enjoin upon you this day, for your own benefit. [14]Mark well, the heavens to their uttermost reaches belong to YHWH your God, the earth and everything on it! [15]Yet it was only for your forefathers that YHWH took a passion, loving them, so that he chose their descendants after them—you!—from among all the peoples, as is the case today. (Deut 10:12-15)

This passage makes it clear that at the core of the covenant relationship lies a twofold love, the mysterious love of YHWH for Israel and the less baffling love of Israel for YHWH, her benefactor. Covenant-love is mutual; it distinguishes a relationship of reciprocity. On God's side lies an obligation to fulfill the oath he swore to the Patriarchs, to grant their descendants the promised land, to be their God. Israel, for her part, is to realize her love in the form of observance of her master's stipulations, the *mitsvot*, for they are the words of the language of love, the fit medium in which to respond to the passionate advances of the divine suzerain. It is not a question of law *or* love, but law conceived in love, love expressed in law. The two are a unity. To speak of one apart from the other is to produce a parody of the religion of Israel.[74] The love of God moves Israel to embrace the norms of Sinai.

In the book of Hosea, the great divorce is never finalized. The impassioned groom cannot endure without his bride, although she had whored with his Canaanite competitor Baal (2:15). Unable to tolerate her being in the arms of his rival, YHWH reinitiates the romance and coaxes his wayward spouse back to the spot where their first love was consummated, the desert (2:16-25). In vv 16-19, YHWH restores his relationship with Israel to the point at

---

74 See Moran, "The Ancient Near Eastern Background."

which it stood when he first impressed his claim upon her with his redemption of her from Egypt, when she had not yet broken faith to chase after the god of fertility, Baal. And so, in the desert, the marriage is reinstituted (vv 21–22), only this time without mention of the word "Baal," which also served as one of two terms for husband (v 18). Now, to make things clear, only the other term will be licit. The word "know" in v 22 is, of course, a *double entendre;* the term is both covenantal and sexual. We have already seen the covenantal context of the verb.[75] The vassal is to "know" (i.e., recognize) only one suzerain. But the term also indicates sexual union, as in the statement that Adam "knew Eve, his wife, and she conceived" (Gen 4:1). To us, the two meanings seem distinct, but in Israel's vocabulary, they pertain to either kind of passionate relationship, that of suzerain and vassal or that of groom and bride. The romance of God and Israel is tempered by lawfulness and animated by eros, love purified in law, law impelled by love.

In Hos 2:20, YHWH makes a new covenant, not one between himself and Israel, but between Israel and the beasts and birds and creeping things. In other words, God assumes the Mosaic office of covenant mediator,[76] in order to extend the peace and security of the covenant relationship beyond the confines of the divine-human dialogue. Now even nature will participate. All threats, whether from nature or from war, will vanish. Lurking behind these great promises are the blessings of the covenant formulary. But we hear nothing of the curses, for the vision is one of redemption through covenant, and the assumption seems to be that, where God mediates and thus guarantees covenant, the stipulations will be fulfilled as a matter of course.

In the last stanza of Hosea's prophecy (vv 23–25), all creation joins in the wedding ceremony. Sky responds to earth, and earth responds by bringing forth her bounty. What happens here is that the covenant with the living God comes to account for fertility, displacing the worship of the dying-and-rising deity, Baal. The real source of bounty lies in faithfulness and obedience to the God who redeemed Israel from Egypt. Baal has been bested on his own soil. And thus, in accordance with this vision of cosmic renewal, the three children of Hosea—Jezreel ("God-will-sow"), Unloved, and Not-my-people—are restored together with the covenant/marriage contract whose revocation their names symbolized.

In Hos 2:16–25, the making of a covenant moves beyond the limits of the juridical function in which it originated and becomes the stuff and substance of a vision of cosmic renewal. The entire universe takes part in the sacred remarriage of YHWH and Israel. Covenant is not only something lived, but something hoped for, the teleological end of creation and of history. Sinai is the model of cosmic harmony, and the relationship of Israel and YHWH, the prototype of redeemed life. Redemption is not "liberation" from law; that would be, in Hosea's eyes, relapse into licentiousness. Rather, redemption involves the gracious offer to Israel to reenter the legal/erotic relationship and the renewed willingness of Israel to do so.

The third paragraph of this passage, Hos 2:21–22, has entered the daily liturgy of Jewry. It is recited on weekday mornings as the male adult Jew finishes putting on his *tefillin,* the two little boxes containing scrolls of passages from the Torah, which are strapped to the arm and the head in conformity to the ordinance that these things "shall be a sign on your hand and frontlets between your eyes" (Exod 13:16). The implication is clear. By putting on *tefillin,* the Jew becomes engaged to God. He renews each weekday morning his fidelity to the ancient romance consummated on Mount Sinai. In an instant, the *mitsvah* of *tefillin* takes us back to the putative etymology of the word "religion," from the Latin verb *ligare,* "to bind," "to tie." "Re-ligion," from *religare,* "to tie again" or "to tie back," is to restore the bond, to tie oneself to the root that nourishes. In Judaism, the bond or band that ties man to God is a covenant. The Jew wakes each day to an old love affair beckoning to be renewed.

11. THE EVER-RENEWED COVENANT

The renewal of covenant was a central aspect of Israel's worship in biblical times. Psalm 81, chanted today on Thursday mornings, seems to have related the Sinaitic experience in some kind of regular liturgical celebration, also in its original setting. Although much of this psalm is obscure, v 4 would seem to locate its context in the celebration of the first day of the lunar month, on analogy with the celebration of New Year's Day (*Rosh Ha-Shanah*) so well known from later tradition, and comparable festivities for the day of the full moon, two weeks later.[77] What is most pertinent to us is that the liturgy for these holy days seems to have stressed the Decalogue. Vv 10-11 are a transparent restatement of the Second and First Commandments, according to the Jewish enumeration.[78] Vv 6b-8, in which YHWH becomes the speaker, perhaps through the mouth of a priest or prophet, and v 17 restate the historical prologue, with its emphasis upon all that the suzerain, in his graciousness, has done for his vassal. The curses of covenant can be heard in vv 12-13, in which YHWH disowns a disobedient people, but in vv 14-16, the blessings balance this with their promise of victory if only Israel walks YHWH's path.[79] In short, Psalm 81 evidences a regular liturgical occasion in which the Sinaitic covenant and the great choice it entails were re-presented to the Israelite congregation.[80]

77   See de Vaux, *Ancient Israel,* 2:469-70, 476.

78   Exod 20:2-3 and Deut 5:6-7. See also Exod 20:5 and Deut 5:9.

79   Cf. Lev 26:7-8 and Deut 28:7.

80   On the psalms and covenant renewal, see S. Mowinckel, *The Psalms in Israel's Worship* (New York and Nashville: Abingdon 1967) 1:155-61. On covenant renewal in general, see Mowinckel, *Le Décalogue* (Paris: Félix Alcan, 1927) 114-62; H.-J. Kraus, *Worship in Israel* (Oxford: Blackwell,

In the case of the book of Deuteronomy, the book of covenant *par excellence,* this insistence upon the relevance of the covenant of Sinai ("Horeb" in Deuteronomy) to the present generation reaches a pitch of intensity:

> [1]Moses called together all Israel and said to them: Hear, Israel, the laws and ordinances which I am proclaiming to you personally today. Study them, observe them, put them into practice. [2]YHWH our God made a covenant with us on Horeb. [3]It was not with our fathers that YHWH made this covenant, but with us—us!—those who are there today, all of us, the living. [4]Face to face YHWH spoke with you on the mountain, from the midst of the fire. (Deut 5:1-4)

The concern in this passage is that Israel may come to think of themselves as obliged in a distant way by the covenant of Sinai/Horeb, but not as direct partners in it. Lest the freshness of the experience be lost, v 3 hammers home the theme of contemporaneity in *staccato* fashion, with no fewer than six separate expressions: "with us"—"us!"—"those who are here"—"today"—"all of us"—"the living." The goal of this speech, as of the covenant renewal ceremony in which it probably originated,[81] is to induce Israel to step into the position of the generation of Sinai, in other words, to actualize the past so that this new generation will become the Israel of the classic covenant relationship (cf. Deut 30:19-20). Thus, life in covenant is not something merely granted, but something won anew, rekindled and reconsecrated in the heart of each Israelite in every generation. Covenant is not only imposed, but also accepted. It calls with both the stern voice of duty and the tender accents of the lover, with both stick (curse, death) and carrot (blessing, life) in hand. But it biases the choice in favor of life (Deut 30:19).

It is conventional to trace the influence of the covenant renewal ceremony and the formulary until the time of the disappearance

1966) 141-45.
  81 See von Rad, *Studies in Deuteronomy,* SBT 9 (London: SCM, 1953).

of the Dead Sea community (first century C.E.) and no further.[82]
The tacit assumption is that these institutions did not survive into
the next phase of Jewish history, the rabbinic era. In this, there is
a certain truth. The idea of covenant does not seem to have had in
rabbinic religion the centrality it had held since at least the
promulgation of Deuteronomy in the seventh century B.C.E.,
although its importance for the rabbis must not be minimized.[83]
There is no rabbinic ceremony in which the Jews are said explicitly to be renewing their partnership in the Sinaitic covenant, as
the eight day old boy is said, for example, to be entering the
covenant of Abraham (Gen 17:1–14) during his circumcision.
There is, however, a text which is central to the rabbinic liturgy,
in fact arguably *the* central text of the rabbinic liturgy, which is
composed of three Pentateuchal passages (Deut 6:4–9; 11:13–21;
Num 15:37–41)[84] expressive of the classical covenant theology.
The prayer is known as the *Shma,* after its first word. The first
verse of the *Shma* is correctly rendered, "Listen, Israel: YHWH is
our God, YHWH alone" (Deut 6:4).[85] It is manifestly an echo of

82   See Baltzer, *Covenant Formulary.*

83   See E. A. Urbach, *The Sages* ([Hebrew] Jerusalem: Magnes, 1975),
466–77.

84   The verse, "Blessed be the name of his glorious kingship forever and
ever," is whispered between Deut 6:4 and 5.

85   The verse is conventionally rendered into English as, "Hear, O Israel,
the Lord our God, the Lord is one," an interpretation that reflects the philosophical monotheism of a later tradition more than the covenantal monotheism of the Torah in its original setting. My translation essentially follows
that of the Jewish Publication Society new Torah translation (1962), which
draws attention to the commentaries of Ibn Ezra and Rashbam in support of
the rendering. The remarks of Rashbam (ca. 1080–1174, northern France)
are especially apt:

HaShem alone is our God, and we have no other god with him. Thus
the Book of Chronicles: "We will serve HaShem our God, and we
have not abandoned him," That is to say, HaShem is our God and
not the calves to whom you bow down. "HaShem alone": Him alone
we will serve, and we will not add any other god to serve with him.
. . .

the requirement of the old suzerainty treaties to recognize one lord alone. Since in the biblical case the lord is divine, the verse is a classic statement of covenantal monotheism, i.e., the prohibition upon the service of other suzerains.

In fact, we sense apprehension about the possibility of just such defection in each of the three paragraphs. In the second one, we hear of the danger of seduction, in language that recalls the career of Hosea (Deut 11:16–17), and in the last paragraph, such defection is termed "whoring" (Num 15:39). It is this passage from Numbers which establishes the ground of obedience to YHWH precisely where we expect it, in the redemption from Egypt (v 41). This verse, like the First Commandment of the Decalogue (Exod 20:2), is a condensation of the historical prologue. The central stipulation of the *Shma* is one familiar to any student of Near Eastern covenants, the obligation to love YHWH, which is inextricable from the requirement to carry out all his commandments. As we shall see, the rabbis, like the more ancient architects of covenant, saw in the acclamation of divine lordship and the love commandment of the first paragraph the basis for the acceptance of all other commandments. The second paragraph, which stresses performance of the stipulations, derives mostly from the blessings and curses of the covenant formulary. Fidelity to YHWH and the exclusive service of him will bring abundance; defection will result in drought, famine, and death. Finally, we should note that the insistence that the "words" be constantly recited, bound to one's body, written upon one's house, and the commandments symbolized in one's clothes, is also a reflex of part of the covenant formulary, the deposition of the text and the requirement for its periodic reading. In short, the idiom and the theology of covenant permeate the *Shma*.

What is interesting in light of the putative disappearance of the covenant renewal ceremony is that the rabbis selected these three texts to make up one prayer, for the three are not contiguous in the Torah, and the first of them there, Num 15:37–41, appears last here. What links the three paragraphs is that they constitute the basic affirmation of covenant. They confront us with the underpinnings of the entire Sinaitic dimension of the religion of Israel. The link between them is theological, and it is that theology that the rabbis considered basic to their own appropriation and adaptation of the biblical heritage. For they made the *Shma* a staple in the liturgy they wove for Jewry. In the requirement to "recite them . . . when you lie down and when you get up," they saw a *mitsvah* to recite the *Shma* twice daily, in the morning and evening every day of the year.[86] The *Shma* thus became one of the pillars around which those two services developed.

What, precisely, did the rabbis think happened when one recites the *Shma*? We find an anwer in the reply of the Tannaitic master Rabbi Joshua ben Korhah to the question of why Deut 6:4–9 is positioned before 11:13–21:

> so that one might accept upon himself the yoke of the kingdom of heaven first; afterwards, he accepts upon himself the yoke of the commandments.[87]

"Heaven" in Talmudic language is usually a more delicate way of saying "God." Rabbi Joshua sees the *Shma*, therefore, as the acclamation of God's kingship. Only in light of such an acclamation do the *mitsvot* make sense. In light of the biblical ideas, we can say that one must first accept the suzerainty of the great king, the fact of covenant; only then can he embrace the particulars which the new lord enjoins upon him, the stipulations. If God is suzerain, his orders stand. But his suzerainty is not something irrational and threatening. It follows from his gracious character:

> *I am the Lord Thy God.* Why were the Ten Commandments not said at the beginning of the Torah? They give a parable. To what may this be compared? To the following: A king who entered a province said to the people: May I be your king? But the people said to him: Have you done anything good for us that you should rule over us? What did he do then?

86 *m. Ber.* 1:3.
87 *m. Ber.* 2:2

He built the city wall for them, he brought in the water supply for them, and he fought their battles. Then when he said to them: May I be your king? They said to him: Yes, Yes. Likewise, God . . .[88]

His past grace grounds his present demand. To respond whole-heartedly to that demand, to accept the yoke of the kingdom of heaven, is to make a radical change, a change at the roots of one's being. To undertake to live according to *Halakhah* is not a question of merely raising one's moral aspirations or of affirming "Jewish values," whatever that means. To recite the *Shma* and mean it is to enter a supramundane sovereignty, to become a citizen of the kingdom of God, not simply in the messianic future to which that term also refers (e.g., Dan 2:44), but also in the historical present. Thus, one can understand the horror a rabbinic Jew would have of failing to say the *Shma,* as exemplified in this story: There was a law that a bridegroom was exempt from the commandment to recite the *Shma,* probably because he was in no mental condition to give the prayer the concentration it required. But concerning one early rabbi, we read this exchange in the Mishnah:

It happened that Rabban Gamaliel got married and recited the *Shma* on the first night. His students said to him, "Our master, have you not taught us that a bridegroom is exempt from the recitation of the *Shma* on the first night?" He said to them, "I am not going to listen to you and annul the kingdom of Heaven from myself for even a moment!"[89]

In other words, one who neglects the *Shma* when its recitation is due is rebelling aginst the sovereignty/suzerainty of God. Or, to put it positively, the *Shma* is the rabbinic way of actualizing the moment at Sinai when Israel answered the divine offer of covenant with the words "All that YHWH has spoken we will do"

---

88 *Mek., Baḥôdeš,* 5. The translation is from *Mekilta de-Rabbi Ishmael,* ed. J. Z. Lauterbach (Philadelphia: Jewish Publication Society, 1933) 2:229–30.

89 *m. Ber.* 2:5. On the significance of the *Shma,* see Urbach, *Sages,* 348–70.

(Exod 19:8). In short, the recitation of the *Shma* is the rabbinic covenantal renewal ceremony. It is the portal to continuing life in covenant.

There is, therefore, no voice more central to Judaism than the voice heard on Mount Sinai. Sinai confronts anyone who would live as a Jew with an awesome choice, which, once encountered, cannot be evaded—the choice of whether to obey God or to stray from him, of whether to observe the commandments or to let them lapse. Ultimately, the issue is whether God is or is not king, for there is no king without subjects, no suzerain without vassals. In short, Sinai demands that the Torah be taken with radical seriousness. But alongside the burden of choice lies a balm that soothes the pain of decision. The balm is the history of redemption, which grounds the commandments and insures that this would-be king is a gracious and loving lord and that to choose to obey him is not a leap into the absurd. The balm is the surprising love of YHWH for Israel, of a passionate groom for his bride, a love ever fresh and never dulled by the frustrations of a stormy courtship. Mount Sinai is the intersection of love and law, of gift and demand, the link between a past together and a future together.

2

Zion,
the Mountain
of the Temple

I. THE EARLY HISTORY OF ZION
IN PROSE TRADITIONS

Sinai is the mountain of Israel's infancy, of the days of Moses, when the nation, as the story has it, was but a few generations old. Mount Sinai is the location of only one great event in Israel's history, the revelation of Torah, and although this event momentously and forever altered the nature of Israel's religion, with immense consequences for her daughter religions as well, still, the mountain itself had no ongoing significance for the people who believed their destiny was transformed there. In fact, some biblical traditions stress that the Sinaitic experience was not repeatable, at least not at Sinai. When, for example, the great prophet of the ninth century, Elijah, attempts to duplicate the experience of Moses on Sinai/Horeb, he fails utterly, for no longer does YHWH reveal himself in a pyrotechnic spectacle, with lightning, thunder, dense cloud, fire, and the blast of a trumpet, as he did in the days of Moses (Exodus 19):

> [11]He said, "Go and stand on the mountain in the presence of YHWH." For YHWH was passing by: there was a great and powerful wind, rending mountains and shattering boulders before YHWH, but YHWH was not in the wind. After the wind was an earthquake, but YHWH was not in the earthquake. [12]After the earthquake, there was a fire, but YHWH was not in the fire. And after the fire came the sound of a thin silence. (1 Kgs 19:11-12)

In the days of Elijah the prophet YHWH no longer revealed himself, this passage seems to be saying, in atmospheric phenomena (unlike his rival, the Canaanite storm-god Baal), but in the word, the voice, the oracle.[1] The prophetic address has replaced

1 See F. M. Cross, *Canaanite Myth and Hebrew Epic* (Cambridge: Harvard University, 1973) 191-94; and R. B. Coote, "YHWH Recalls Elijah" in *Traditions in Transformation,* ed. B. Halpern, and J. D. Levenson

the fixed theophany on Sinai, the apparition of God on that mountain of ancient tradition. Elijah must learn to heed the almost imperceptible signal within and not to rely on the dramatic intervention of God which defined the career of Moses and of Elijah himself in his contest with the prophets of Baal on Carmel in the previous chapter (1 Kings 18). The Mosaic era was different from anything that followed:

> Never again has there arisen a prophet in Israel like Moses, whom YHWH knew face to face. (Deut 34:10)

In fact, so unavailable is that Mosaic mode of revelation that even the site of the grave of the great prophet is unknown (v 6). It is surely no coincidence that the site of Mount Sinai is similarly unknown. The legacy of Mount Sinai, what Jewish tradition calls Torah in the broadest sense, endured. But the mountain itself long ago vanished from the consciousness of Israel.

How did the mountain of Israel's transforming vision come to be forgotten? Specifically, how could the covenant theology attributed to Sinai be so pervasive in the developing religion of ancient Israel when the mountain itself ceased to play any role? Here it is important to remember that however much Deuteronomy and texts written under its influence (such as 1 Kings 19) may wish to isolate the Sinaitic theophany from the continuing tradition, other texts made it evident that an experience like that of Moses was still possible, but on a different mountain. An example is Psalm 97. Here, as in Exodus 19, the account of the Sinaitic theophany, the atmospheric phenomena and pyrotechnics are stressed, rather than played down, as in the experience of Elijah at Horeb. Here we see again the cloud, the fire, and the lightning (vv 2–4), and we hear again of YHWH's assumption of universal kingship and his humiliation and subjugation of the other gods (vv 6–9), which, as we have seen, are major themes of the book of Exodus in its present form and central aspects of the covenant theology. We

(Winona Lake: Eisenbrauns, 1981) 115–20.

hear even of the divine decrees or "judgments," which are so important in the Sinaitic materials. In Psalm 97, however, Sinai is not the focus, but a new mountain, Mount Zion (v 8). The traditions of YHWH's theophany, his earthshattering apparition to man—even, to some extent—his revelation of law, have been transferred from Sinai to Zion. In short, Sinai has not so much been forgotten as absorbed.

In the early poetry of Israel, as we have seen, one common theme is the march of YHWH, conceived as a warrior, from Sinai in an earthshattering apparition (e.g., Ps 68:8-9; Deut 33:2).[2] But in most passages it is not from Sinai, but from Zion that he comes:

> [2]From Zion, perfect in beauty,
> God shone forth.
> [3]Our God came;
> He did not fail to act.
> Before him was a devouring fire;
> Around him it stormed fiercely! (Ps 50:2-3)

The transfer of the motif from Sinai to Zion was complete and irreversible, so that YHWH came to be designated no longer as "the One of Sinai," but as "he who dwells on Mount Zion" (Isa 8:18). More than merely the name of the mountain abode of YHWH is involved in the change. Zion, unlike Sinai, was a known site in Israel. The transfer of the divine home from Sinai to Zion meant that God was no longer seen as dwelling in an extraterritorial no man's land, but within the borders of the Israelite community. This, in turn, means that the anarchistic tendencies associated with the Sinaitic traditions, which we discussed in the last part, will be somewhat mitigated or altered in the Zion traditions, which will see YHWH as less remote from the ordinary governance of human society. Within the complex of

2 See Cross, *Canaanite Myth,* 99-105; and P. D. Miller, *The Divine Warrior in Early Israel,* HSM 5 (Cambridge: Harvard University, 1973) 74-128.

Zion traditions, there will emerge something almost unthinkable in the case of Sinai, a pledge of divine support for a human dynasty.

Mount Zion was a hill in Jerusalem between the Tyropoean and Kidron valleys, on the eastern side of the city. What is called "Mount Zion" today is a hill to the southwest of the ancient Zion and across the Tyropoean Valley from it. The identification of this mountain with the Zion of the Hebrew Bible is very late, in fact Byzantine, and generally regarded today as inaccurate. It must be noted, against the impression of so many contemporary tourists, that the walls of the Old City of Jerusalem date only to Turkish times; they were built four and a half centuries ago— yesterday, by the standards of biblical historians. The Jerusalem of the monarchies of the Hebrew Bible lay essentially to the southeast of the Old City, where one nowadays finds the village of Silwan. It is not clear that "Zion" always referred to the same spot in ancient times. In any event, most of the biblical references to Zion have in mind what is today known as the Temple mount, on which sits the spectacular mosque, the Dome of the Rock.[3] A further complication is that the city has changed names over the centuries, in accordance with shifts in politics and demography. What the Jews call Jerusalem, the Arabs call *Alquds* after their word for "holy." According to 2 Sam 5:7 (=1 Chr 11:5), the name in use just before King David's conquest (ca. 1000 B.C.E.) was Stronghold of Zion. We know, nevertheless, that the name Jerusalem long predates the Israelite conquest of the city. We have, for example, letters from the king of Jerusalem in the fourteenth century B.C.E., over a hundred years before the conquest, to his liege lord, the Egyptian pharaoh.[4] The diplomatic messages make it very clear that Jerusalem—with that name—was one of a handful of important city-states in Canaan in the Late Bronze

---

3   On the archeology of ancient Jerusalem, see K. Kenyon, *Jerusalem* (n.p.: Thames and Judson, 1967); and H. Shanks, *The City of David* (Washington: Biblical Archeology Society, 1973).

4   These are known as the Amarna letters. See *ANET*, 483–90.

Age. From Ps 76:3—"In Judah God has made himself known, /
In Israel his name is great; / Salem became his tent, / Zion, his
abode"—it is clear that Jerusalem was also known as Salem. In
fact, the last two syllables of Jerusalem constitute the same word
as Salem, originally the name of a Canaanite deity.[5] It is interesting that a patriarchal narrative presents Salem as the name of
the city in the time of Abraham, who is blessed by its priest-king
(Gen 14:18), perhaps in adumbration of the priestly and royal
significance of the city from David's time on.

It appears that the Canaanites in Jerusalem successfully re-
sisted the social and military movement that put most of Canaan
into the hands of Israel in the thirteenth century. Although
Joshua 10 speaks of Joshua's humiliation of the king of Jerusalem, Adoni-Zedek, it is evident from Josh 15:63 that the Canaanite inhabitants of the city, the Jebusites, continued to live there.
Josh 19:28 places Jerusalem (under the name "Jebus") in the
patrimony of the Israelite tribe of Benjamin, but it is quite
doubtful that this verse indicates an actual Israelite settlement of
Jerusalem in the time of the conquest. The fact is that Jerusalem
passed definitively into the hands of Israel only in the lifetime of
King David, a few centuries later:

'The king and his men set out for Jerusalem to attack the Jebusites,
who lived in the area. The Jebusites said to David, "Never will you
come in here. Instead, even the blind and the lame will turn you
away"—as if to say, "David will never come in here." 'But David did
capture the Stronghold of Zion, which is now the City of David. (2 Sam
5:6–7)[6]

V 6, above, is obscure and ambiguous, so much so that it seems to
incorporate at the end some ancient commentator's gloss. What is
unclear is whether the blind and the lame are said to be able to
turn away David's attack, as I have translated it, with the support

5 See J. Gray, "The Desert God 'Aṭtr in the Literature and Religions of
Canaan," *JNES* 8 (1949) 72–83.
6 Textual note on 2 Sam 5:6–7. In v 6, read *wayyō'měrû yôšěbê yěbûs
lědāwîd* with 1 Chr 11:5.

of an ancient Greek rendering, or whether the verse means that David will be unable to take the city until he has removed even the blind and the lame. This latter translation would then indicate the dogged determination of the Jebusites to resist David to their last man.[7] If my rendering above is correct, the verse would seem to indicate a belief on the part of the Jebusites in the inviolability of their mountain city. Even its handicapped can successfully thwart David's army. Whence did they derive this seemingly foolhardy confidence? The answer must remain uncertain, but it is interesting to note that this theme of confidence in the face of attack is one that will dominate Israel's view of Zion as well. As we shall see, the note of absolute security in the face of the grimmest military facts becomes a central theme of the hymns of Zion that were sung in the days of the Judean monarchy. 2 Sam 5:6 may hint that this great motif has been taken over from the Jebusites.

The rabbis of the post-biblical era identified Mount Zion with the Mount Moriah on which Chronicles locates Solomon's Temple and hence with the land of Moriah in which Abraham proved willing to sacrifice his promised son, the one he loved, Isaac, as a burnt offering in obedience to the mysterious command of God (Gen 22:2).[8] The Hebrew Bible presents both Abraham and David as having undergone a visionary experience on that spot (Gen 22:14; 2 Chr 3:1). The passage in Chronicles refers to 2 Samuel 24, wherein David is permitted to see the angel of YHWH, just as Abraham, after passing the test of the binding of Isaac, was addressed by an angel and accordingly named the site after his vision. In both cases, there is a play on Moriah and the verb rā'â, "to see," and its derivative nouns, mar'â and mar'ê,

---

7 The issue is whether the suffix on hĕsîrĕkā is subjective or objective. See also the interpretation in Y. Yadin, *The Art of War in Biblical Lands* (Jerusalem and Ramat Gan: International, 1963) 2:267–70. Yadin sees here an instance of dramatic symbolism: if David and his men attack, they will be like the handicapped.

8 E.g., *Yalqut Shimoni, Wayyērā'* 22; 2 Chr 3:1.

meaning "sight, spectacle, vision." The visionary experiences of Abraham and of David here serve as authorizations for the inauguration of the Temple on Mount Zion/Moriah. The theophany authenticates the sanctuary. This is a common idea in the religion of ancient Israel. The patriarchs set up shrines at the place where they had witnessed a divine apparition,[9] and one of the "judges," Gideon, is said to have built an altar at Ophrah, where he was privileged to see the angel of YHWH face to face (Judg 6:22-24). In other words, the sanctuary serves to perpetuate a visionary experience of God, for there is a very real sense in which the deity is visually available in the Temple, this in spite of all the insistence that one cannot see God and that his reality cannot be captured in an image.[10] As we shall have occasion to note at length,[11] this concept of the Temple as a primarily visual (as opposed to auditory) vehicle for the knowledge of God is central to the very idea of the shrine on Zion and appears in several important instances in biblical poetry. Once again, we see in what is ostensibly historiographic prose a major theme of the hymns of Zion, the theme of vision. As the narrator remarks in his gloss to the speech of Abraham in Gen 22:14, "On the mountain of YHWH, he can be seen." Mount Zion is a place of visionary experience.

King David, renaming the Jebusite stronghold "City of David" (2 Sam 5:9), made it his personal capital and, later, the seat of his dynasty. In fact, it was the first real capital Israel had known. As we saw, David bought the land upon which the Temple was to stand from one Araunah (or, Ornan) the Jebusite (24:15-25), who had used it as a threshing floor, a place of cultic significance in those days. The tradition that dominates is that David built no temple, in other words, that the structure his son and successor Solomon erected was the "First Temple." In point of fact, how-

9   See R. de Vaux, *Ancient Israel* (New York: McGraw-Hill, 1965) 2:288-94.

10   E.g., in Exod 19:21 and Deut 4:15-16.

11   See Pp. 148-51.

ever, it is clear that a temple stood at Shiloh in the time of Samuel's youth (1 Sam 3:3), more than a generation before David, and one can wonder whether there really was no structure housing the tent-shrine which David moved to his new city (2 Sam 6:17), in an effort to make the political capital also the religious capital of the fledgling monarchy. In fact, one passage does mention that David worshipped in the "house of YHWH" (12:20),[12] which may have been a temple that he, and not Solomon, built. At all events, given the force of Solomon's personality and the probable origin of much of the literature in the cultural florescence that took place in his reign, we should not be surprised to find that any tradition about a Davidic Temple has been suppressed. What is interesting are the theological rationales offered to account for David's ostensible failure to erect a permanent structure. In 1 Kgs 5:17–19, for example, Solomon claims that David was too preoccupied with war to build a temple. In 1 Chr 28:2–3, a passage from a later book, one sees the effects of a humanizing tendency. It was not that war consumed too much of David's time, but, rather, as a man of war, he was unfit to build a temple for YHWH, the God of peace. Underlying this humanism is the assumption that the Temple is above the realm of ordinary politics, with its wars and bloodshed. It was, in fact, a place of asylum,[13] and an old law forbids the altar in any shrine to be made of dressed stone, "for you have struck your sword against it and thus profaned it" (Exod 20:25). In the passage from Chronicles, we detect, then, a certain unease with ascribing the better part of the institution of a temple to the reformed terrorist, David. The Temple on Mount Zion was to be, from its very inception, a palace of peace. Once again, in the hymnody that centered upon Zion, this theme of peace unthreatened by the reality of war on earth will be central.

---

12   See also Psalm 30, "A Psalm of David," which is labelled also "A song for the dedication of the House" (v 1).

13   See 1 Kgs 1:50–53; 2:28–31; and de Vaux, *Ancient Israel* 2.276.

2. THE HOUSE OF YHWH
AND THE HOUSE OF DAVID

We have found that in the mind of Israel Jerusalem was inextricably associated with King David. It was he who conquered the city for Israel, who brought the Ark of the Covenant—the most potent symbol of YHWH—into the city, who made Jerusalem his capital, and laid the groundwork for the Temple which his son built on Mount Zion. That Temple was thus different from the other shrines throughout the land; it was a royal sanctuary, close to the king's palace, with which it shared a destiny. From the tenth century on, for the next four hundred years, until the destruction of the kingdom of Judah and the razing of Solomon's Temple by the Babylonians in 587 B.C.E., the fortunes of Jerusalem and of the house of David were to rise and to fall together.

This growing centrality of a religious institution so closely linked with monarchy is indeed remarkable. In Part 1, we saw that the theology implicit in the covenant formulary is a theology at odds with the idea that the state is central to the relationship of God and the people Israel.[14] On the contrary, the Sinaitic covenant casts the authority of the state into doubt by presenting the suzerainty of YHWH as exclusive of all comparable relationships. YHWH is king, YHWH alone. We saw that a source discernible in the books of Judges and of Samuel attributes the late emergence of monarchy in Israel to precisely this theological idea: if God is king, then the establishment of a human king is at least superfluous and probably idolatrous. And so how did it happen that the religion came to focus increasingly upon a royal dynasty and a state sanctuary, the house of David and the house of YHWH on Mount Zion?

There is no need here to review the social and political changes that brought about the institution of kingship in Israel; rather, the

14 Pp. 71–75.

present interest is in the theological rationale that was offered for what was, by the standards of some of the traditions current then, a major revolution in the structure of the religion of Israel. To understand the basis of the Davidic entitlement to dynastic kingship, one must first examine the oracle of the court prophet Nathan to King David that appears in 2 Samuel 7.[15] Nathan offers this prophecy in response to David's intention to build a permanent shrine for YHWH (v 2). The oracle revolves around play on the word "house." David will not build a "house," i.e., a Temple, for YHWH, but YHWH will build a "house," i.e., a dynasty, for David (v 11). His successor, who will be his son, as was not the case with his tragic predecessor Saul, will then build a "house," i.e., a Temple, for YHWH (v 13). In this fashion, Nathan's oracle weaves the existence of the dynasty and of the Temple together. The first dynast, Solomon, is also the Temple builder. He is the common side of the two dimensions of the oracle. The dynasty, however, like the Temple, will long survive Solomon. In fact, God here promises David eternal kingship, an everlasting dynasty (v 16). In a sense, although David remains the biological ancestor of the royal line, YHWH has adopted the house of David, regarding the incumbent king of any generation as his son, to be corrected but never disowned (vv 14–15), as Saul was, according to Davidic tradition, disowned for his sins (1 Samuel 15).

Upon what basis does this far-reaching, in fact extravagant promise, rest? To answer this question, we must discuss a poetic adaptation of the oracle of Nathan in the Psalter, Ps 89:4–5, 20–38. It is clear from vv 4, 29 and 35 that the tradition behind this poem sees the burden of Nathan's oracle in 2 Samuel 7 as a covenant between YHWH and David. But the statement of this Davidic covenant does not follow, even loosely, the formulary

15 On 2 Samuel 7, see D. McCarthy, "II Samuel 7 and the Structure of the Deuteronomistic History," *JBL* 84 (1965) 131–38; Cross, *Canaanite Myth* 229–65; and J. D. Levenson, "Who Inserted the Book of the Covenant?," *HTR* 68 (1975) 203–33.

characteristic of the suzerainty treaty upon which so many of the texts dealing with the Sinaitic covenant are modelled. Here, there is, to be sure, an oath (v 36) and a witness (v 38), but no preamble, historical prologue, deposition of the text, blessings and curses, or, most importantly, stipulations. The absence of some of these items can be explained by noting that we have in Psalm 89 a poetic adaptation of the Davidic covenant, which is cited for the poet's own purpose, rather than a well-rounded account of how that covenant was concluded. But the absence of stipulations, of terms that David and his descendents must fulfill, is more serious. For the fact is that the psalm, like Nathan's oracle, states distinctly that God will uphold David's posterity at all cost, even— and here the contrast with Sinai could not be sharper—if they break the commandments and desecrate divine law.[16] In other words, the obligations involved in this covenant fall upon one party only, YHWH the suzerain, who therein swears to maintain the covenantal relationship under all conditions. Let us clarify immediately a point that is often missed: nothing in either of these two statements of the covenant with David implies in any way that he or his house is exempt from the stipulations of the Sinaitic covenant.[17] Far from it. The assumption of vv 31–33, which speaks of their punishment in the event they violate God's "Torah," "rules," "laws," and "commandments," is that they remain under the obligation of the directives of Sinai. Failure to discharge those obligations will result in the rod and lashes. In short, as Israelites, the Davidids are bound by the Sinaitic Torah, or Mosaic covenant. There is no text in the Hebrew Bible that holds that the Davidic *replaces* the Sinaitic. But within the national covenant lies another, restricted to one family, the royal house of David. Presumably, the king could even be executed for his violations of the earlier pact.[18] But, if he were, his successor

16 Vv 31–35; cf. 2 Sam 7:14.
17 See Levenson, "The Davidic Covenant and Its Modern Interpreters," *CBQ* 40 (1978) 210–15.
18 Levenson, "The Davidic Covenant," 211.

would be another Davidid, for God will not betray his oath to David. In other words, it is the ancestor who is the human partner to the covenant. His descendants are an afterthought. They are mentioned only as a token of God's enduring fidelity to David. He is God's ally; their moral record is no way essential to the validity of the covenant.

This type of covenant, no less than the suzerainty treaty, has parallels elsewhere in the ancient Near East. Moshe Weinfeld identified over a decade ago a type of covenant which he calls the "covenant of grant," to distinguish it from the type we saw in Part 1, which Weinfeld terms the "treaty." " . . . While the grant is a reward for loyalty and good deeds already performed," he writes, "the treaty is an inducement for future loyalty."[19] In the case of the grant to David, the ancestor has already satisfied what claims YHWH might wish to make upon his line. YHWH reciprocates by granting David an endless dynasty. It is the suzerain (God) who is now under oath. He swears to reward David with the gift of a continuing dynasty. The same pattern appears elsewhere in the Bible as well, especially in the cases of Noah, Abraham, Caleb, and Phinehas.[20]

This Davidic covenant, then, is distinct in kind from the Sinaitic. The focus of the Mosaic covenant sealed at Sinai is twofold: history and morality. God there formalizes a longstanding relationship of love and benevolence (on his part, at least) into a pact through which Israel might come to reflect back to God some of the grace she has known. The historical prologue establishes the claim upon Israel which the latter discharges only through observance of the *mitsvot*. The dynamics of Sinai, which are the dynamics of the treaty, metamorphose history into morality, or in rabbinic language, *aggadah* into *halakhah*, lore into law. In the case of the Davidic covenant, history and morality are no

19   M. Weinfeld, "The Covenant of Grant in the Old Testament and in the Ancient Near East," *JAOS* 90 (1970) 185.

20   Genesis 9; 17; Numbers 14; 25. On this type of covenant, see also Levenson, "On the Promise to the Rechabites," *CBQ* 38 (1976) 508–14.

longer the focus, for any claim God might make peculiarly upon the house of David has already been satisfied by its founder. Rather, the Davidic covenant, a covenant of grant, looks beyond the vicissitudes of history, since they cease to be critical. This covenant fixes attention to that which is constant beneath—or perhaps I should say, above—the flux of history. That supra-historical constant is God's commitment to the Davidic dynasty: it shall always rule. And since the focus is upon the constancy of God rather than the changeability of man, it brings to light what is secure and inviolable, whereas the Sinaitic texts tend to emphasize the precariousness of life and the consequent need for a continuously reinvigorated obedience. Thus, in the book of Kings, God bears with one corrupt Davidic king after another, punishing but never deposing, for a reason given so many times it rings as a refrain throughout the book:

> Because for David's sake YHWH his God had given him a fief in Jerusalem . . . (1 Kgs 15:4)

> YHWH refused to destroy Judah, for the sake of David his servant, as he had promised him to grant a fief to his descendents forever. (2 Kgs 8:19)[21]

Hence, Davidic possession of Jerusalem—which God has granted as a familial fiefdom—is seen not merely as a curiosity of history, but rather as a visible token of divine fidelity, of the faithfulness and trustworthiness of God, and, conversely, of the relativity and limitedness of ordinary history, history not guaranteed by the divine promise. Jerusalem and, as we shall see, especially Mount Zion, are a sign that beneath and beyond the pain and the chaos of the realm we call history, there is another realm, upheld by the indefectible promise of God. Dynasty and Temple, the house of David and house of God, function within the order of history, but are rooted in that other order of things.

21 See the list and discussion in Cross, *Canaanite Myth*, 281- 83, esp. p. 281 n. 30.

3. THE VITALITY OF MYTH
IN BIBLICAL ISRAEL

This faith in the perpetuity of the dynasty and the Temple flies in the face of any kind of political prudence. The wise observer of history knows now and knew in antiquity that cities and king-doms rise and fall in response to conditions that no one can control. In Israel in the tenth century B.C.E., the era of David and Solomon, the rapid pace of historical change in recent times alone should have sufficed to make men wary of the claims of the new royal theology on behalf of the immunity of the Temple on Zion and the house of David, its patron. Clearly it is not a meditation on history in a simple sense which gave birth to the new theology.

To find a word that expresses this nonhistorical way of relating to experience is not easy. It is probably best to stay with a term which is admittedly amorphous and vulnerable to misuse, the word *myth*. What is unfortunate about this choice of words is that myth is used to cover a wide range of things. "In both scholarly and popular usage," writes a contemporary student of mythology, "myth has acquired a variety of meanings; we throw together traditional tales, magico-religious beliefs, theology, false beliefs, superstitions, ritual formulae, literary images and symbols, and social ideals into a common pot and call the mixture mythology."[22] In light of this bewildering latitude of usage, it is quite unlikely that anyone will devise a single definition that will prove satisfactory to all possible uses of the word; the radical opposition of the numerous theories of myth makes such a defini-tion all the less likely to appear. Instead, the most for which one can hope is that scholars will define the term in a way appropriate to the material which they are interpreting and that they will employ it with a fair measure of consistency.[23] In this book, I shall

22   J. E. Fontenrose, *The Ritual Theory of Myth* (Berkeley: University of California, 1966) 53.

23   Cf. J. W. Rogerson, *Myth in Old Testament Interpretation, BZAW* 134 (Berlin and New York: de Gruyter, 1974) 173: "Modern scholarship has

use the term myth to refer to a cast of mind that views certain symbols in terms of an act of unlimited scope and import that occurred, in Brevard Childs' words, in "a timeless age of the past."[24] It was in that "age" that "the foundation of the world occurred," writes Mircea Eliade,[25] an age that precedes even the creation of time as we know it—if such temporal terms can be invoked to describe a situation in which ordinary temporality did not obtain. This era of mythical time Eliade terms *illud tempus,* Latin for "that time." The primal event occurred/occurs/will occur *in illo tempore,* "in that time."

These great founding acts, which order reality, we shall call *protological,* that is to say, partaking of the nature of the beginning of things, on analogy with the term *eschatological,* which is commonly used by biblical scholars to describe the "last things," which occur at the "end of time." According to Childs, "the present world order established by a victory in the past does not continue automatically. It must be constantly reactivated in the drama of the cult."[26] Although we do not need to posit an immediate connection to the cult for all mythical symbols, Childs' observation about the continuing relevance of the protological "events" to every moment does seem constitutive of the usage of myth adopted here. Mythic symbols are thought to be by their very nature invulnerable to obsolescence. On the contrary, they are more "real" than the flux and change of history.

Before leaving this bedevilling question of terminology, let me stress four points. First, note again that much material quite

been more concerned to find and sustain a definition of myth than to look at particular problems which scholars have tried to elucidate over the years with the help of the notion of myth, variously defined. It is more important that the problems should be solved than that the impossible task of finding an adequate and all-purpose definition of myth should be persisted in."

24   B. S. Childs, *Myth and Reality in the Old Testament,* SBT 27 (London: SCM, 1960) 20.

25   M. Eliade, *The Myth of the Eternal Return, or, Cosmos and History,* Bollingen Series 46 (Princeton: Princeton University, 1971) 20.

26   Childs, *Myth and Reality,* 20.

legitimately termed "mythic" for other purposes will not fall under the definition with which I am working here. It is not my intention to propose an overall interpretation of myth or even of myth in the Hebrew Bible. Second, the definition I propose is not so remote from other scholarly usage as to be idiosyncratic. The concentration upon the perception of time in the definition of myth builds upon the work of such scholars as Childs, whose book on the subject has met with approval in the very comprehensive and analytically keen study of *Myth in Old Testament Interpretation* by J. W. Rogerson.[27] In fact, timeless events as a key ingredient in myth have been recognized in a recent study by a leading classicist;[28] the usage is not peculiar to biblicists and semitists. We shall soon see that it is preeminent among some phenomenologists of religion (although their efforts to apply it comprehensively are too ambitious). Third, since it is impossible to isolate the perception of time from other aspects of consciousness and worldview, one should not be surprised to see in the ensuing discussions mention of concepts of space, for example, that are more congruent with the mythic than with other modes of thinking. The perception of time cannot be disengaged from the perception of space. In fact, the mythic symbols to be analyzed exist in radically different modes both of space and of time. No definition can be expected to be more than a reliable generalization about usage; words in a given context always mean more than the dictionary would lead us to believe. Hence, the concept of time is central to this definition of myth, but not exhaustive of it. My final point is perhaps obvious by now: myth does not mean "untruth" or "falsehood," in spite of such usage in ordinary discourse. One should not allow this pejorative use of the word to prejudice oneself against the Aristotelian position that poetry is truer than history. One implication of this discussion will be that *mythopoesis*, "the making of myth," is a means by which man discerns and conveys

27 Rogerson, *Myth*, 165.
28 M. J. Finley, "Myth, Memory and History," in *The Use and Abuse of History* (New York: Viking, 1975) 11–33.

truths otherwise inexpressible. If this implication is correct, then the familiar interpretation of the religion of Israel as radically demythologized,[29] besides being factually inaccurate, obscures great spiritual treasures. If there is a sense in which myth is true, then divine revelation and myth need not be seen as incompatible, and those who are disposed to view this literature as sacred will ask themselves why God chose certain mythic symbols and not others as the vehicle to mediate revelation. The reader must determine for himself whether the mythic interpretation of these symbols enhances or vitiates the spiritual power of the Hebrew Bible.

I turn now to a few instances in the Hebrew Bible in which mythic consciousness can be detected in order to compare it with another mode of perception, which we may call *history*. To the historian, David died at a particular moment (1 Kgs 2:10). But to a prophet, living nearly four centuries after David's death, but speaking in the evocative tones of myth and poetry, David is still available; the moment of his death is not definitive:

> Then I will raise up a single shepherd over them,
> He shall tend them—My servant David;
> He shall tend them,
> And he shall be their shepherd (Ezek 34:23)

Now, it may be the case the "David" here refers to any king of the Davidic line. If so, however, the verse still testifies to a perception of the boundaries between past and present—the old David and the new—which is different from the modes of perception of time called *historical*. Or, to give another example, the historian presents Solomon as the builder of the Temple (1 Kgs 6:1). The chronological detail—the year, the month, and the regnal year in 1 Kgs 6:1—fix the event in historical time, just as the name of Solomon attaches it to a known historical figure. Now contrast this allusion to the same event in the mouth of a psalmist:

29 As in G. E. Wright, *The Old Testament Against Its Environment*, SBT 2 (London: SCM, 1950).

> [69]He built his sanctuary like the heights,
> Like the earth which he founded for all eternity.
> [70]He chose David his servant
> And took him from the sheepfolds. (Ps 78:69–70)

Who is the Temple builder here? The subject of v 69 is YHWH; he, not Solomon, built the Temple. Or, to put it more precisely, the flat historical fact that Solomon built the Temple is not denied by the psalmist; it is of no importance to him. The deeper meaning of the Temple is such that God is to be seen as the one who constructed it. And when, according to Psalm 78, was this shrine built? Again, what interests the poet is something other than the historical sequence perceived through the ordinary concept of time. He presents the construction of the Temple as *preceding* the selection of David. In contrast to what we read in Samuel and Kings, Psalm 78 describes the divine choice of Zion (in the tribe of Judah) as lying before the rise of David. This is not because he has a different historical tradition about the Temple from that of the author of 1 Kgs 6:1, but, rather, because to the psalmist, the essential meaning of the Temple lies in its foundation in primal times, *in illo tempore,* in other words, in its protological character.

Of course, the contrast between these two modes of presenting reality must not be overdrawn. The construction of the Temple, for example, is an item both in passages narrated from a historian's point of view and in passages where the perspective is closer to that of mythology. There is no reason that historical data cannot be absorbed into the mythic mind as I have tried to define it. Furthermore, in the Hebrew Bible itself, history is almost always presented as something meaningful. But history becomes meaningful by dint of its relationship to something else. A mere agglomeration of uninterpreted facts is meaningless. The biblical historian tends to see the meaning of history as located in the fact that certain institutions such as the house of David and the Temple on Zion are eternal. At this point, meaningful history is beginning to sound like mythology, inasmuch as both focus on what is timeless. Or, to put the issue differently, the philosophy or theology of history—and the latter is what most of the Hebrew Bible is about—will always involve an interpretive framework which is outside flat historical fact. Mythic thought, as understood here, imparts meaning to history. In short, the contrast between myth and history is useful, but should not be understood to mean that the two need always stand in opposition.

As we have noted, the idea that myth was a vibrant force in the religion of ancient Israel, as presented in the Hebrew Bible, has not been generally popular with scholars. In part, the problem is one of definition. If, as has often been the case, myth is defined as stories about the gods, then the monotheizing tendencies in the Hebrew Bible exclude myth by definition. Today, this position seems excessively narrow and static and commands little support.[30] A weightier objection to the presence of myth in the Hebrew Bible has been lodged by Yehezkel Kaufmann (1889–1963), a scholar whose influence upon Jewish biblical scholarship has been so pervasive that his argument merits special attention. Kaufmann maintained that since the biblical presentation of foreign religion is so far from the reality which modern discoveries have disclosed, this very fact demonstrates that the Israelites did not understand their neighbors and, therefore, were possessed of a radically different way of thinking.[31] Since, like most scholars, Kaufmann was not always precise in his definition of myth, one might argue that he did not mean to deny the ongoing significance of protological symbols in ancient Israel, but only the presence of stories about the gods, or the like. In that case, the interpretation of Zion/David that we have seen would not have offended Kaufmann. The truth is, however, that Kaufmann advanced a bold denial of the mythic character of kingship in

30 See the discussion of Hermann Gunkel and of the contrasting position of G. Henton Davies in Rogerson, *Myth*, 57–67; 170–71.

31 See Y. Kaufmann, *History of the Religion of Israel* ([Hebrew] Jerusalem: Bialik, 5720/1959) 1:9; 2:255–285. The same idea appears in Wright, *The Old Testament Against Its Environment*, esp. p. 29.

Israel, understanding myth, at least in this passage, very much as it is used here:

> Pagan kingship aspired to be anchored in cosmic-mythological symbols of creation: in the symbols of the rule of divine kings from the distant past, in the priestly service of primordial temples, in which the gods themselves had committed the secret of destiny to the hands of a divine priest-king. But Israelite kingship is not anchored in cosmic-mythological symbols of creation, but rather seeks out symbols of election, new historical symbols, symbols of the grace of YHWH which was disclosed in Israel.[32]

In this passage, Kaufmann seems close to our definition of myth. He writes of "symbols of creation," of "the distant past," and of "primordial temples"—all of which will be central to the rest of this discussion of Mount Zion. In light of this, his effort to make a hard distinction between Israelite and "pagan" kingship is all the more indefensible. First, the notion of the gracious election of the king is not unique to Israel.[33] But more fundamentally, Israelite kingship is not divorced from "cosmic-mythological symbols of creation." We shall see at length that the enthronement of the human monarch upon the mountain of God, Mount Zion, was essential to an important current in the theology of Israelite kingship.[34] One might note this promise of YHWH to David as an indication of the protological character of the dynastic institution:

> I will set his hand upon the sea,
> His right hand upon the rivers. (Ps 89:26)

The sea was the great enemy of order both in Mesopotamia and in Canaan. Its defeat was the essential element in creation and

---

32 Kaufmann, *History*, 2:181. The translation is my responsibility. See also Levenson, "Yehezkel Kaufmann and Mythology," *CJ* 36:2 (1982) 36–43.

33 See H. Frankfort, *Kingship and the Gods* (Chicago: University of Chicago, 1948); and H. W. F. Saggs, *The Encounter with the Divine in Mesopotamia and Israel*, Jordan Lectures (London: University of London/Athlone, 1967), 81–85.

34 Pp. 154–56.

won the victorious god kingship and the right to a palace (or temple) of his own.[35] Creation, kingship, and temple thus form an indissoluble triad; the containment of the sea is the continuing proof of their eternal validity (e.g., Psalm 93). The promise of the divine king to commit the sea/rivers to the charge of his human vassal is surely "anchored in cosmic-mythological symbols of creation."[36] To be aware of this mythic dimension is not to deny the importance of the "historical symbols ... of the grace of YHWH which was disclosed in Israel" or the possibility that the two sets of symbols can come into tension. But to speak of a complete displacement of myth by history in Israel is indefensible.

On one point, Kaufmann was surely correct: the Hebrew Bible does present foreign religion as fetishism, the worship of mindless matter (e.g., Ps 115:4–8). It identifies the god with his or her icon. But no one with an acquaintance with Mesopotamian or Canaanite religion can accept that we have in this identification a sensitive or even perceptive understanding of the role of iconography in those traditions.[37] It is precisely the fact that the non-Israelite did not conceive his icon as inanimate matter and identify it as such with his god *in toto* which makes the polemic inaccurate. But we cannot conclude from the inaccuracy of the Israelite poet's satire

---

35 See A. Heidel, *The Babylonian Genesis*, 2nd ed. (Chicago: University of Chicago, 1951); *ANET*, 129–42; Cross, *Canaanite Myth*, 112–44; and O. Kaiser, *Die mythische Bedeutung des Meeres in Ägypten, Ugarit und Israel*, BZAW 78 (Berlin: Töpelmann, 1959) 44–47; 140–54.

36 The connection of human kingship to cosmogony in Israel is nicely stated in R. J. Clifford, "Psalm 89: A Lament Over the Davidic Ruler's Continued Failure," *HTR* 73 (1980) 35–47.

37 See H. Ringgren, "The Symbolism of Mesopotamian Cult Images," in *Religious Symbols and Their Functions*, Scripta Instituti Donneriani Aboensis 10, ed. H. Beizais (Stockholm: Almqvist and Wiksell, 1979) 105–9; and Saggs, *The Encounter*, 14–17; 89–91. The polemical misrepresentation of Canaanite and other "pagan" religion in the Hebrew Bible parallels the polemical misrepresentation of Pharisaism (or Judaism) in the New Testament. My impression is that American Christian scholars are now more willing to concede the latter than Jewish scholars are to concede the former. See Levenson, "Is There a Counterpart in the Hebrew Bible to New Testament Anti-Semitism?" *JES* 22 (1985) 242–260.

that he had no understanding of the spiritual life of his Canaanite neighbor and nothing in common with it. To do so would be to miss entirely the situation out of which interreligious polemics grow. Polemic is by nature reductionistic. Its goal is to present the opposition as ridiculous. It therefore cannot concede dignity or even good intentions to its target. Its roots, after all, lie in that moment when one closes oneself off to the appeal of the alternative and polarizes one's sensibility in such a way as to conceive of the options as diametric opposites. One is either an idiot who prays to statues, or an aniconic YHWHist. But polemic endures precisely because that act of closure is never so final as the polemic says it ought to be. The appeal of the alternative survives the effort to cast it in the most reductionistic terms. The proof of the idea that "pagan" religion struck a responsive chord in Israelite consciousness is the fact that the prophets continually polemicized against a syncretism of the two.[38] Syncretisms do not form between things that have nothing in common. The prophetic assertions that YHWH and Baal are totally different must not be taken at face value. They must be seen within the rhetorical intents of interreligious polemic.

A modern analogy may show the fallacy in Kaufmann's argument. If one were to ask an unenlightened Jew or unenlightened Calvinist about the role of iconography in Roman Catholicism, he might well hear a response very reminiscent of the verses in Psalm 115 cited above. But it would be an obvious blunder to conclude from this that Judaism and Calvinism have nothing in common with Roman Catholicism. In fact, it would not be correct to assume even that the spiritual experience associated with iconography in Roman Catholicism is unparalleled in Judaism and Calvinism. It is the appeal of the alternatives and the frightening fact that that appeal threatens to reopen the fundamental question of identity that calls forth polemic. The presentation of

38 As in 1 Kings 18 and Hosea 2.

"pagan" religion in the Hebrew Bible is not evidence for Kaufmann's proposition that mythic symbols had lost their power in Israel. Rather, it indicates that they were vital enough to pose a threat to a different component of Israelite religion, the historical component, which Kaufmann mistakenly saw as sovereign and self-sufficient.

4. ZION AS
THE COSMIC MOUNTAIN

The particular mythic symbol that unlocks much of the power of the image of Zion is that of the *cosmic mountain*. A recent study by Richard J. Clifford compares this myth as it appears in the Hebrew Bible and in the culture of Ugarit, a city-state on the coast of Syria from which we have a remarkable collection of tablets dating from the fourteenth century B.C.E., the infancy of Israel. These tablets, discovered about half a century ago, are written mostly in a Canaanite language closely akin to Hebrew, and, in fact, many central biblical ideas can be identified in Ugaritic literature. In the case of the cosmic mountain, it should be noted at the outset that the term "cosmic" can be misleading. Clifford's point is not that the cosmos is envisioned in ancient Canaan as a mountain, but rather that a mountain is given characteristics and potencies of cosmic, that is, of an infinite and universal scope. Four characteristics of the cosmic mountain that Clifford delineates will prove essential to the present analysis of the traditions about Zion. First, one of the most important aspects of the cosmic mountain is that it is "the meeting place of the gods," like the Greek Olympus. Second, it is also "the battleground of conflicting natural forces." Third, and most significantly, the cosmic mountain is the "meeting place of heaven and earth," the tangent of celestial and mundane reality. And since it is the meeting place of heaven and earth, it follows that the mountain is also "the place where effective decrees are issued," in other words, the moral as well as the physical capital of the universe, a place "involved in the government and stability of the Cosmos."[39] To these points of Clifford's, it should be added that from the cosmic mountain there frequently is thought to issue a miraculous stream, whose waters teem with supernatural significance.

The Canaanite god, Baal, for example, appears in the Ugaritic texts as the inhabitant of the mountain *spn,* the same word as "Zaphon" in the Bible, which came to be an epithet of Mount Zion. In one Ugaritic text that Clifford translates, we hear some other characteristic epithets of Baal's mountain:

> Come, and I will seek it,
> In the midst of my mountain, divine Zaphon,
> In the holy place, the mountain of my heritage,
> In the chosen spot, on the hill of victory.[40]

In addition to the term Zaphon, we see in this Ugaritic text other undeniably close parallels to the biblical idiom. For example, "the mountain of your heritage" is cited in Exod 15:17 as the goal of the Exodus. The idea of a "holy spot" or "holy mountain" is common to the traditions about Zion (e.g., Ps 48:1–2). And a synonym for the Ugaritic expression "hill of victory" we have already seen in Ps 89:27, in which the psalmist terms YHWH "the mountain of my victory." Clearly, there is a vocabulary common to the mountain of Baal and to that of YHWH. A similar commonality of language and concept can be seen in connection with another Ugaritic deity, El, whose name becomes one of the names of the God of Israel (e.g., Gen 33:20), in short, a synonym of YHWH. El, too, dwells on a mountain,[41] on which he presides over the council of the gods (cf. Psalm 82). This mountain is

39 Clifford, *The Cosmic Mountain in Canaan and the Old Testament,* HSM 4 (Cambridge: Harvard University, 1972) 3; see also A. Ohler, *Mythologische Elemente im Alten Testament* (Dusseldorf: Patmos, 1969) 154–73.

40 Clifford, *Cosmic Mountain,* 68.

41 See the discussion in Clifford, *Cosmic Mountain,* 35–57. For our purposes here, it is not essential to determine whether El's cosmic mountain was infernal or celestial in character.

apparently the source of a river whose significance, at least to judge by biblical parallels, is also cosmic and supernatural:

> Then they set face
> Toward El at the sources of the Two Rivers,
> In the midst of the pools of the Double Deep.[42]

The association of YHWH with a miraculous stream issuing from his mountain abode, the Temple on Zion, is one that colors markedly the perception of the mountain and the city in the literature of psalmists and prophets. What is essential to note is that some of these cosmic mountain ideas have been carried over from Canaan into Israel. An acquaintance with the literature of Bronze Age Ugarit has proven essential to an understanding of Zion.

Clifford's study of the cosmic mountain corroborates a point already clear from the examination of the covenant formulary in the last part: despite the anxiety of biblical literature to dissociate Israel from her neighbors and to proclaim her radical uniqueness, the various cultures of the ancient Near East exhibited a substantial measure of overlap, even in their thinking about God/gods, the area in which the Hebrew Bible is most insistent upon the distinctiveness of Israel. It is clear that some of the historical roots of the religion of Israel lay in the Canaanite world, for which the literature of Ugarit is at present our best evidence.

It is fair to say that the only criticism of the historical-comparative approach on theoretical grounds (disputes on individual points are endless and often correct) comes from fundamentalists, Jewish or Christian, whose prior religious commitments make them unable to concede the obvious parallels and to accept the notion of important common ground between Israelite religion (revealed truth) and "paganism" (human error). More controversial than this approach is one which compares symbols of cultures that, unlike those of Canaan and of Israel, are not in historical

42 Clifford, *Cosmic Mountain*, 48.

contact, in other words, a comparative method that does not necessarily posit diffusion of basic symbols, but analyzes them according to their own inner reality and as the revelation of elements basic to the human spirit. These *phenomenological* comparisons are less convincing, since the symbols are often extracted and abstracted from context and compared in a way that the historian is inclined to deem subjective. Furthermore, since no scholar can hope to control cultures so remote from each other in history and language, any essay at phenomenological comparison will tend to seem facile and careless to the historian and philologist (and most of modern biblical study has been history and philology). Such studies often *are* facile and careless. The fact remains, however, that it is myopic and pedantic to limit to *historical* investigation phenomena which seem to be almost universal, occurring in cultures which never stood in historical contact. For example, the phenomenologist Mircea Eliade finds more or less the same notion of a cosmic mountain in cultures as far afield as those of India, the Ural-Altaic peoples, the Laotian Buddhists, the Finns, the Japanese, and the Sumerians and Babylonians.[43] Even if Eliade is in error on some of his examples and even if he has overstated the degree of parallelism in general, it is still dangerous to ignore the evidence that he adduces, in a discussion of the cosmic mountain as a theological concept in ancient Israel. This is not to say that one can assume that the symbol is identical in every culture, that each of its aspects in one context must have existed in all contexts. It is to say, however, that we may be able to isolate and identify certain features of the cosmic mountain in Israel by comparison with other, distant cultures. No general formula can be given for determining when such a comparison is cogent and when it is farfetched. Only by the fruit it bears on specific points can we ascertain the success of the method.

43   Eliade, *Patterns in Comparative Religion* (Cleveland and New York: Meridan, 1958) 367-87; see also W. B. Kristensen, *The Meaning of Religion* (The Hague: Martinus Nyhoff, 1960) 106-9; 368-75.

Let us now examine five principal attributes of the cosmic mountain in order to see how, if at all, they appear in Israel. Perhaps the most important of these everywhere is its centrality. The mountain lies at the center of the world; everything else takes its bearings from that mountain.[44] Geography is often, to the "primitive" mind, simply the physical representation of transcendent reality. What is most important must stand at the center, as any artist knows. The biblical scholar immediately thinks of Ezekiel:

> Thus spoke the Lord YHWH:
> This is Jerusalem.
> In the midst of the nations I have set her,
> And all around her are countries. (Ezek 5:5)

> You expect to despoil and plunder, to turn your hand against repopulated ruins, against a people gathered from among the nations, a people acquiring cattle and goods and dwelling at the very navel of the earth. (Ezek 38:12)

Each of these two verses seems to offer support for the centrality of Jerusalem/Zion or of the land or people of Israel, with which it was increasingly identified. Ezek 5:5 appears to imply that Jerusalem lies at the center of the community of nations, and Ezek 38:12 goes further and identifies Israel or perhaps specifically Jerusalem as the *ṭabbûr* of the earth, the "navel." To be sure, each of these interpretations can be impugned. Shmaryahu Talmon maintains that Ezek 5:5 does not speak of Jerusalem's geometric position, only of its importance. Similarly, he interprets the term *ṭabbûr,* which occurs only in Judg 9:37 and Ezek 38:12, not as "navel," as do many scholars, but as a "high plain." *Ṭabbûr,* according to Talmon, acquires the meaning "navel" only in post-biblical times. In fact, he sees the idea of the navel of the world, which is well attested in rabbinic literature, as a borrowing into

44 See Eliade, *The Sacred and the Profane* (New York: Harper and Row, 1961) 36–47.

post-biblical Judaism from the Greeks.[45] One senses from Talmon's lexicographic objection just how little we have to work with when we seek to explicate the mythological conceits of biblical Israel. His reasoning is, in my opinion, plausible, but not convincing. It is difficult to imagine, for example, that ancient Israel possessed such a highly developed empirical geography that she could imagine Jerusalem as spiritually central, but geometrically peripheral. The notion that something can be spiritually central but physically peripheral is quite modern; it was vigorously attacked only four centuries ago, in the age of Copernicus and Galileo. In short, a much more literal reading of Ezek 5:5 is possible. The experience of travellers could, of course, easily falsify the notion that Jerusalem lay at the center of the earth, with nations arranged around her on all sides. After all, the Mediterranean Sea was only a few miles to the west, whereas to the east one had to travel hundreds of miles to reach a roughly equivalent body of water, the Persian Gulf. The point is that we must not understand biblical geography as a statement of a scientific nature. Rather, to the unscientific mind of Israel (and to the persecutors of Galileo as well), geography is simply a visible form of theology. Since Jerusalem was, as Talmon concedes, central to Israel's world view, it may well have been central also to her cartography, if we may use the word. God does not dwell at the periphery of his creation any more than he dwells at the periphery of the religious person or community's life.

As for the translation of *ṭabbûr* as "navel" in Ezek 38:12, this is

45 Sh. Talmon " *Ṭbwr h'rṣ whṣyth hmṣwwh,*" *Tarbiz* 45 (5736/1976) 163–77. Note Talmon's survey of post-biblical references on pp. 166–67. See also his "HR/GB'H," *TWAT* 2, 472, 475; and "The 'Comparative Method' in Biblical Interpretation—Principles and Problems," VTSup 29, Göttingen Congress volume, 1977 (Leiden: Brill, 1978), esp. pp. 348–51. On the other hand, if Talmon is right that the idea was a borrowing from the Greeks, it was a borrowing that certainly found fertile soil all over the west semitic world. See A. J. Wensinck, *The Ideas of the Western Semites Concerning the Navel of the Earth* (Amsterdam: Johannes Müller, 1916). In Jewish sources other than Judg 9:37 and Ezek 38:12, its first attestation would seem to be Jubilees 8:19.

even more problematic, for the word occurs in only one other place in the Bible, and there its meaning is also obscure.[46] It is true that, without the post-biblical evidence for the translation "navel" (which is certain), we should not have known to propose such a reading for the biblical attestations. On the other hand, the translation "high plain" is also speculative; any number of sensible (but erroneous) meanings can be attached to a word that occurs only twice. The fact is, however, that if *ṭabbûr* had any other meaning in the Bible than "navel" (or, by metaphor, "center"), then that other meaning was lost by Talmudic times. It is, therefore, not irresponsible to suggest that the Talmudic definition existed even in the biblical period.[47]

The rabbinic texts that develop this notion in connection with Zion/Jerusalem exhibit a profound parallelism with the many examples Eliade adduces:

46 See R. G. Boling, *Judges*, AB 6A (Garden City, 1975) 178–79, where the *omphalos* interpretation is defended.

47 Another interpretation of Ezek 38:12 appears in D. Sperling "Mount, Mountain," *IDBSup*, 622: "The intended victims are as unprotected as the human navel in the center of the body. ... All that is described is an incursion through the outer defenses into the center. Needless to say, we learn nothing of the victim's cosmology. ... Apparently, then, we should see nothing more than poetic personification in the Ezekiel passage." What Sperling has not explained is how those "as unprotected as the human navel" could prove to be immune to the fierce attack about to be launched upon them. All that he has shown is that the navel is indeed an appropriate image for the mythological/cosmological idea underlying the passage. "Poetic personification" this certainly is, but why personify Israel as—of all things—the navel?

Still another discussion of this myth appears in S. Terrien, "The Omphalos Myth and Hebrew Religion," *VT* 20 (1970) 315–38. Unlike Sperling, Terrien sees the idea of the navel as "the determining factor" in the Temple worship (p. 317), which ties together these five aspects: "snake-worship, chthonian rites, the solar cult, male prostitution and bisexuality" (p. 320). Our interest here, however, is not in these "deviant" expressions of the notion of the cosmic center, but in the more "normative" expressions, those which passed through the priestly/prophetic filter and made their way into the Hebrew Bible as we have it. See Also T. H. Gaster, *Thespis: Ritual, Myth, and Drama in the Ancient Near East* (New York: Harper and Row, 1950) 183, n. xxviii.

The Holy One (blessed be he) created the world like an embryo. Just as the embryo begins at the navel and proceeds onwards from there, so the Holy One (blessed be he) began to create the world from its navel and from there it spread out in different directions.[48]

And lest there be any doubt where exactly the rabbis located this navel:

The world was created beginning from Zion.

Rabbi Eliezer the Great says: "These are the generations of the heavens and the earth when they were created on the day the Lord God made earth and heaven." (Gen 2:4) The offspring of heaven were created from heaven, and the offspring of the earth were created from earth. But the sages say, Both were created from Zion ... as the Bible says, "From Zion, perfect in beauty, God shone forth" (Ps 50:2). That means, from it the beauty of the world was perfected.[49]

These two passages from the Talmudic tractate *Yoma* posit Mount Zion as the point from which creation proceeded, the only place of a genuinely primordial character in our world. This conceit is elaborated and embellished in the following midrash:

Just as the belly-button is positioned in the center of a man, thus is the Land of Israel positioned in the center of the world, as the Bible says, "dwelling at the very navel of the earth" (Ezek 38:12), and from it the foundation of the world proceeds ... And Jerusalem is in the center of the Land of Israel, and the Temple is in the center of Jerusalem, and the Great Hall is in the center of the Temple, and the Ark is in the center of the Great Hall, and the Foundation Stone is in front of the Ark; and beginning with it, the world was put on its foundation.[50]

In sum, Zion is first in beauty, first in order of creation (a point we shall develop at length), and first in importance, not only to Israel, for whom it held precious historical memories, but for all nations, in fact, for the entire cosmos.

48 Midrash *Haššēm Běḥokmâ Yāsad 'Āreṣ*, A. Jellinck, *Bet ha-Midrasch*, vol. 5, 2nd ed. (Jerusalem: Bamberger and Wahrmann, 1938) 63.
49 *b. Yoma* 54b.
50 *Tanḥuma: Kedoshim* 10.

What of the contention that this rich vein of rabbinic folklore was an import from the Greeks? The question is impossible to answer with any certainty. It does seem unlikely, however, that the force of the Greek mythos would have been so great that it obliterated the original meaning of *ṭabbûr* in the two biblical passages in which it is found and caused the word to assume a radically different meaning, "navel." Furthermore, if I have interpreted Ezek 5:5 correctly,[51] it, too, testifies to a conception of Jerusalem as central, and without any involvement of the controversial word *ṭabbûr*. In Ezekiel 48 that prophet (or his school) envisioned a future rearrangement of tribal lands in such a way as to make the centrality of the Temple city a literal reality, rather than an item of folklore only. Finally, it should be noted that the concept of a navel of the world is so ubiquitous that there is no need to see Greece as the source of diffusion into Israel. In fact, since analogous ideas are attested in the Near East, and in civilizations older than Israel,[52] the likelihood is that, even in a scenario of diffusion rather than of independent development, both Israel and Greece received the notion of the navel from

---

51 The most comprehensive commentary on Ezekiel offers the same interpretation: W. Zimmerli, *Ezekiel* 1, Hermeneia (Philadelphia: Fortress, 1979) 174–75.

52 An example is the name of the temple in the Sumerian city Nippur, *Dur-an-ki*, "the bond of heaven and earth," in other words, the point at which the god Enlil had separated the two (cf. Gen 1:7–8). This is also the spot from which mankind springs up from a hole left when Enlil breaks away a clod with his pickax. See Th. Jacobsen, *Toward the Image of Tammuz and Other Essays on Mesopotamian History and Culture*, ed. W. L. Moran, HSS 21 (Cambridge: Harvard University, 1970) 112–13. An Egyptologist has related Judg 9:37 and Ezek 38:12 to the Egyptian concept of the primeval hillock which the temples replicated. S. Morenz, *Ägyptische Religion*, Die Religionen der Menschheit 8 (Stuttgart: Kohlhammer, 1960) 44–45. It is quite plausible that such ideas were displaced or suppressed in the circles that produced the Hebrew Bible. But to argue that they were unknown in Israel until Hellenistic times strains the imagination. On the significance of the various images of centrality in the Bible, see M. A. Fishbane, "The Sacred Center: The Symbolic Structure of the Bible," in *Texts and Responses*, ed. Fishbane and P. A. Flohr (Leiden: Brill, 1975) 24–43.

elsewhere. If so, there is no necessity to see the process as exclusively post-biblical.

What is certain is that the expression of the idea of Jerusalem as a cosmic center, the navel of the world, is fuller and more developed in rabbinic literature than in the Hebrew Bible. It is this fuller expression that leads scholars like Talmon to see the idea as a borrowing from the Greeks. To be sure, there were many such imports into rabbinic folklore and theology. Not every item in rabbinic religion existed in biblical Israel, and even when the rabbinic idea justifies itself by attachment to a biblical verse (in the process known as *midrash*), one cannot assume the rabbis had an accurate understanding of the biblical text. Still, there are reasons why the biblical authors and editors would have exercised a critical scrutiny amounting even to censorship upon the Temple mythos, whereas the rabbis could be freer with the same materials. For the great struggle of biblical times was to preserve the identity of Israel in a world in which she was a small people (Deut 7:7) and in an extremely vulnerable political situation, one in which autonomy was often *de jure,* but not *de facto*. Much of the biblical law, especially from the Priestly sources, evidences a desire to establish a clear and durable border between the Israelites and the Canaanites among whom they lived (e.g., Lev 20:22–26).

In other words, all the social pressure in biblical times encouraged Israel to stress what set her apart from her neighbors, for example, the experience of the Exodus, rather than what she shared with them. This latter category certainly included the Temple, which was executed by Phoenician craftsmen (1 Kgs 7:13–14) and whose design and decoration, as described in the Bible, are familiar to archaeologists from the excavation of the temples of other peoples in the area.[53] It is therefore not sur-

53 See Wright, "The Significance of the Temple in the Ancient Near East: III The Temple in Palestine-Syria," *BA* 7 (1944) 66–77; and W. F. Albright, *Archaeology and the Religion of Israel* (Baltimore: Johns Hopkins, 1956) 14–55. On the *realia* of the Temple, see Th. A. Busink, *Der Tempel*

prising that the text of the Hebrew Bible is so taciturn about the theology of the Temple. It does not tell us the meanings of the iconography; we have to reconstruct them. It does not specify the prayers that must have accompanied the sacrifices; we have to reconstruct them, mostly from the Psalms, as best we can. And it does not elaborate upon the idea of a cosmic center; this, too, we must reconstruct from hints the text has left and from comparative materials. But to take this taciturnity at face value, to take it as an indication that the idea of the center was absent in Israel, or that the decorations in Solomon's Temple held no symbolic significance, or that the sacrifices were a dumb show because Leviticus supplies no words,[54] is to miss the social dynamics at work. It seems more probable that it was precisely the vitality of the Temple mythos which accounts for the fragmentary character of the references to it. It was too well-known, too much part of the common cultural landscape, to be allowed free and independent expression.

In the communities to which the rabbis of the Talmudic era addressed themselves, the Jews were already, in Muhammad's terms, "the people of the book" and thus radically and visibly distinct from their neighbors. They dressed differently (Num 15:37–41), abstained from foods others consumed (Leviticus 11), and observed a radically different rhythm of life (ch. 23), all of which perplexed and annoyed those around them, even as it does today. In a world in which the difference of Israelite identity was so elementary, so palpable, and so comprehensive, and in which it commanded canonical authority, those elements which Israel shared with her neighbors could be expressed more openly. A people who placed their book before their Temple did not need to fear that their own elaboration upon a common Temple mythos

von Jerusalem, 2 vols. (Leiden: Brill, 1970).

54 This is in fact the Kaufmannian position. See the critique of it in N. M. Sarna, "The Psalm Superscriptions and the Guilds," in *Studies in Jewish Religious and Intellectual History*, ed. S. Stein and R. Lowe (University, AL: University of Alabama, 1979) 282–83.

would threaten their survival. Once the mechanism of internal censorship fell away, then the presentation of the theology of the Temple could move from the compactness of the biblical text to the differentiation of rabbinic literature.[55] The elaborateness of the rabbinic materials about the cosmic center is the result of learned reflection upon the Hebrew Bible in a more relaxed atmosphere. The biblical hint that the Temple was central, a notion undoubtedly opposed by some in biblical times, could be developed into an important item of rabbinic theology.

The second major characteristic of the cosmic mountain to concern us is that, in Eliade's words, it or "the temple or sacred city, in turn, as the place through which the Axis Mundi [the axis of the world] passes, is held to be a point of junction between heaven, earth, and hell."[56] The cosmic mountain is a kind of fulcrum for the universe; it is on the line to which all the regions of the universe are referred, and it is somehow available to each of them. The base of the mountain lies in the chaotic underworld, and its head reaches into the heavens. On it, messages can be passed from heaven to earth and *vice versa*. It is the prime place of communication between transcendent and mundane reality. Consider, for example, the account of Isaiah's great vision of God enthroned in Isa 6:1–8. The relevant point about this justly famous passage is that it occurs in the Temple, in other words, on the cosmic mountain, Zion. Isaiah is privileged actually to see the divine council, YHWH and his attendants, in session. The Ark within the holiest room in the Temple, the *sanctum sanctorum* (*děbîr*), was thought to be either the throne or the footstool of the deity.[57] That chamber was therefore the throne room of God,

55 The notion of history as involving a movement from compactness to differentiation is developed in E. Voegelin, *Order and History: 1. Israel and Revelation* (Baton Rouge: Louisiana University, 1956). The idea is a very fertile one for the analysis of the relationship of the Hebrew Bible to Rabbinic Judaism.

56 Eliade, *Patterns*, 375.

57 On the Ark as the throne of God, see R. E. Clements, *God and Temple* (Oxford: Blackwell, 1965) 28–30. On the Ark as footstool, see M.

wherein he held court with his cabinet. In it appeared two cherubim carved of olive wood (1 Kgs 6:19-28). What happened to Isaiah the year King Uzziah died is that glyptic representation became immediate spiritual experience. Art became the reality to which it pointed. The Temple mythos came alive. In Isaiah's ecstatic experience, he sees and hears a session of the divine council; moreover, he is enabled to take part in it by bearing its message simultaneously down from heaven and out of the Temple (which are, in fact, the same thing[58]). The earthly Temple is thus the vehicle that conveys the prophet into the supernal Temple, the real Temple, the Temple of YHWH and his retinue, and not merely the artifacts that suggest them. This Temple is an institution common to the heavenly and the terrestrial realms; they share it. It is the place where a mere mortal, even a man who had uttered slander (Isa 6:5), can make contact with the realm of overpowering holiness, where he can hear the language of angels and respond to it.[59] Thus, Isa 6:1-8 shows that the Temple could serve as both the "meeting place of the gods" (with allowances for Israel's monotheizing tendencies) and the "meeting place of heaven and earth." One should note as well that the immediate agendum of the divine council is to find a messenger to bear its verdict "down" to earth (as we would say, although spatial terms are problematic when predicated of the *axis mundi*), to preach it to the people of Israel: "Whom shall I send,/And who will go for us" (v 8). In short, like the cosmic mountain of Ugarit, the

Haran, *Temples and Temple-Service in Ancient Israel* (Oxford: Clarendon, 1978) 246-59. Haran sees the *kappōret* (cover of the Ark) as the throne. The difference between these two positions is negligible.

58 See G. W. Ahlström, "Heaven on Earth—at Hazor and Arad," in *Religious Syncretism in Antiquity*, ed. B. A. Pearson (Missoula: Scholars, 1975) 67-83.

59 This is not to say that the Temple was the *only* possible locus of communication between heaven and earth, but that this intermediary function was central to the theology of the Temple in Israel, as in the rest of the ancient Near East and elsewhere. The same notion of the shrine as the locus of divine communication can be seen in the old Tent of Encounter ('*ōhel mô'ēd*, e.g., Num 7:89) and in the Temple at Shiloh (1 Sam 3:1-18).

Temple on Zion is also, in Clifford's terms, a "place where effective decrees are issued."[60]

The Temple on Mount Zion may have been conceived as what Eliade calls the "point of junction between heaven, earth, and hell"[61] in a more literal sense as well. Consider, for example, the oracle against the Babylonian emperor in the book of Isaiah (Isa 14:12-15).[62] It obviously reflects an old story in which an astral deity mounts a rebellion against the head of the pantheon ("the Most High") and pays for his hubris by ejection from heaven and banishment to hell, Sheol. This myth is clearly the ancestor of the Lucifer story, which figures prominently in post-biblical tradition. For present purposes, the essential point is that this oracle presents "the utmost peak of Zaphon" (v 13)[63] as not only the mountain upon which the gods assemble, the Hebrew Olympus, but also as a place higher than the heavens, above the clouds, the mirror image or opposite pole to deepest hell, "the lowest depths of the abyss" (*yarkĕtê bôr*, v 15). Now the expression *yarkĕtê ṣāpôn*, "the utmost peak of Zaphon," appears in Ps 48:3 as an epithet of Mount Zion, the whole expression being in synonymous parallelism with "the city of the great king." Zaphon, we have already seen from Clifford's study of the Ugaritic material, was the mountain of the Canaanite god, Baal. If the epithet can be transferred to Mount Zion, it is not too much to suggest that the imagery associated with this epithet similarly migrated. In that event, Zion would also be perceived as reaching into the highest heavens, above the clouds and the stars. But the other side of this dizzying height is the depth of the base of the mountain in the chaotic abyss here called Sheol, to which the Babylonian emperor is hurled with frightening suddenness. The shortest distance

---

60 Clifford, *Cosmic Mountain,* 3.

61 Eliade, *Patterns,* 375.

62 See Childs, *Myth and Reality,* 67-71; B. Alfrink, "Der Versammlungsberg im Äussersten Norden," *Bib* 14 (1933) 41-67.

63 On the translation, see A. Robinson, "Zion and Saphon in Psalm XLVIII 3," *VT* 24 (1974) 121.

between the utmost peak of the cosmic mountain and the lowest reaches of the abyss beneath it is a straight line along the *axis mundi*.

As the junction between heaven and earth, Zion, the Temple mount, is a preeminent locus of communication between God and man. We have already seen one highly dramatic instance of such communication in the experience of Isaiah in chapter 6. It must not be thought, however, that the availability of God in his shrine atop Mount Zion was limited only to divinely designated clairvoyants. On the contrary, the centralization of the sacrificial liturgy, its limitation to one shrine only, is consistently phrased in terms of the presence of God experienced there (e.g., Deut 12:5). Here it is not the case that YHWH dwells in the sanctuary in a literal anthropomorphic sense, but that he places his "name"— i.e., his essence, his nature, his signature—there. His "name" dwells (*škn*) there in the sense of setting up a tent (*miškān*). His presence is not gross and tangible, but subtle and delicate, like the presence of a traveller at his favorite camping spot. In the Exile (587–539 B.C.E.), when the Temple was in ruins, the Israelite could still direct his prayers to the place upon which it stood (and was destined to stand again) in the assurance that YHWH would still be available, that prayers could still ascend on that sacred mountain (1 Kgs 8:28–29).[64] Thus the legendary savant Daniel, even when an exile in Persia, prays in the direction of Jerusalem in the hope that his supplications will ascend from there into the heavenly court (Dan 6:11). In short, Jerusalem retains its sanctity regardless of whether the Temple happens to be standing in it and regardless of whether the supplicant can approach it physically. The sacred city is the conduit through which messages pass from earth to heaven, no matter where, in a geographical sense, they originated.

---

64 On 1 Kings 8, see Levenson, "From Temple to Synagogue: 1 Kings 8," in *Traditions in Transformation,* ed. B. Halpern and Levenson (Winona Lake: Eisenbrauns, 1981) 142–66. In that study, I find that the language of 1 Kgs 8:23–61 is drawn consistently from a distinctly exilic stratum of

Isaiah's experience (ch. 6) is one such exchange of messages. Another, which, unlike Isaiah's, was routine, is the work of the Temple priesthood, of whom the main characteristic is that they have special access to the mind of God, on the one hand (Deut 33:8), and offer up the sacrifices of his worshippers, on the other (v 10). In other words, the priest is a mediator in each direction. He bears the will of God down to earth through the manipulation of sacred lots, Urim and Thummim, and he sends the offerings of men aloft to God at the altar. He instructs Israel in the name of God and petitions God in the name of Israel. It is this intermediary function that earns the priest the epithet "messenger" (it is also the word for angel) of YHWH:

> ⁶A Torah of truth he spoke,
> No word of injustice was on his lips;
> In complete loyalty and integrity,
> He walked with me,
> And he turned many back from sin.
> ⁷For the lips of a priest guard knowledge,
> And men seek Torah from his mouth;
> For he is the messenger of the Lord of Hosts. (Mal 2:6–7)[65]

Later, this instruction in Torah which emanates from the Temple on Zion will come to be projected onto the age-to-come, when the nations stream to the cosmic mountain in Jerusalem, now visibly elevated above the rest of the world, and mundane existence comes to be radically transfigured according to a vision of cosmic peace.[66] But this eschatological vision is not different in essence from what was held to take place at the Temple all along—the enthronement and glorification of YHWH in his cosmic abode, the pilgrimage of his worshippers, and his instruction of them in his sacred law, which transforms and elevates them.

Deuteronomistic redaction.
65 Torah refers here to revealed instruction, oracles, and not to the Pentateuch. See J. Begrich, "Die Priestliche Torah," *BZAW* 66 (Berlin: Töpelmann, 1936) 63–88.
66 Isa 2:2–4; Mic 4:1–5.

The third attribute of the cosmic mountain that I wish to discuss deals with the issue of time and the perception of time on the mountain. As we saw in our discussion of the difference between myth and history, mythic consciousness, as the term is used here, conceives time as nonlinear. In linear time, each moment succeeds its predecessor with a certain finality. The past does not return. It may have an afterlife in its influence upon the present, but the world can never regress to the point when what is now present had never been. This notion of time as a succession of moments along a line in which motion is in only one direction Eliade calls "profane time." In contrast with profane time, there is another way of perceiving existence in which temporality is not a factor. It will be recalled that the *moment* "when the foundation of the world occurred," is termed by Eliade *illud tempus.*[67] In some manner, at the cosmic mountain, the axis of the world, the act of creation is shielded from the ravages of time and of the decay time measures. On that mountain the divine creative energy endures intact. The cosmic mountain is a *place,* that is to say, a point in the dimension of space, in which temporality as we know it does not exist, but only "sacred time [which] *by its very nature ... is reversible,* in the sense that properly speaking, it is a *primordial mythical time made present.*"[68]

In the Hebrew Bible, it is clear that the Temple precincts are perceived as radically and qualitatively different from the rest of the world. Between the Temple and ordinary reality lies a barrier of *holiness,* a palpable energy or force which resists the intermingling of the two modes of reality. The sanctuary itself, whether the Temple on Zion or the Tent of Encounter ('ōhel mô'ēd) that foreshadowed it during the period of wandering in the wilderness, is a place that guards the perfection of the divine presence. The laws that regulate the liturgy there are expressly designed to thwart the irruption of profane experience into the zone of the sacred (e.g., Lev 21:21–23). The sanctuary then, is a place in which reality is

---

67 Eliade, *The Myth,* 20.
68 Eliade, *The Sacred and the Profane,* 68 (his italics).

perceived as a whole, as fresh and untarnished, where the costs exacted by the harshness of normal life are not paid. The animals offered there, like the clergy who present them, are unblemished (22:20); the materials used in the very construction of the shrine are precious and pure (Exodus 25–30). Once something has been designated for the realm of the sacred, once it has passed into that zone of perfection, it cannot be easily withdrawn (Lev 22:12–16; Num 6:9–20), for the sanctuary is an enclave of ideal reality within the world of profanity.

Words like "ideal," "perfection," and "unblemished," suggest that the Temple was, in fact, a paradise. A biblical tradition, in common with the stories of origins found in many cultures, maintained that human experience began in a paradise, called the "Garden of Eden," the last word denoting in Hebrew "luxury" or "delight." What caused man's banishment from the Garden of Delight was his unwillingness to accept a status inferior to that of God (Gen 2:4b–3:24). The prophet Ezekiel applied this ancient story to the king of Tyre (Ezek 28:11–15), a poem which will go on to predict the fall of the Tyrian monarch in language strikingly reminiscent of the taunt against the Babylonian emperor which we have already examined (Isa 14:12–15). What is most revealing about Ezekiel's oracle is that it makes an identification of "Eden, the garden of God" (Ezek 28:13) with "God's holy mountain" (v 14). In Ezekiel (or his school), the vocabulary of the Temple mount, Zion, is common to the old story of the Garden of Eden.[69] This becomes clear in the companion piece to the oracle against Tyre in 28:2–5. Here, the riches of vv 4–5 are in parallel with the wondrous gems of vv 13–14. The prophet is in both instances making an analogy between the opulence of the port city, Tyre, and the fabulous wealth which is characteristic of both Eden and the mountain of the gods. In fact, the description of the solitary resident of Eden in 28:12, the king of Tyre, is taken from the description of Zion in older literature. He is the "seal of

69 See Levenson, *Theology of the Program of Restoration of Ezekiel* 40–48, HSM 10 (Missoula: Scholars, 1976) 25–36.

perfection" (*ḥôtam taklît*), and Zion is "perfect in beauty" (*miklal-yōpî*, Ps 50:2). The king is "flawless in beauty" (*kĕlîl yōpî*), as is the Temple city (*kĕlîlat yōpî*, Lam 2:15), and as is the fame of Jerusalem, which, according to another oracle of Ezekiel's, became widespread "because of your beauty, which was perfect" (*bĕyopyēk kî kālîl hû'*, Ezek 16:14). The same language describes life in Eden, the Garden of Delight, and Zion, the Temple mount, in which the primal perfection of Eden is wonderfully preserved.

The similarity between Zion as the garden of God and Eden in the same role appears very clearly in the description of the Garden of Eden in what is known as the "J" account of creation (see Gen 2:4b–14). V 12 speaks of precious stones in the vicinity of Eden, just as do Ezek 28:4–5 and 13–14 in connection with Eden or the mountain of God. More fundamentally, Eden is the place from which the primordial river appears, dividing into four great branches. Since rivers flow downstream, it must be the case that the Garden of Eden is here conceived as elevated, certainly at least a high plateau.[70] The river Pishon appears to come from the root *pwš*, "to jump," and thus the name probably means "Bubbler." It is otherwise unattested. Two of the rivers, however, the Tigris and the Euphrates, are very well known even today; they define what the Greeks called "Mesopotamia", the land "between the rivers." Since these two streams flow generally northerly from sources which are now in eastern Turkey (Armenia), the Garden of Eden in which their common source originates must be in the north. Note also the parallelism of Jer 46:10, which speaks of YHWH's preparing a slaughter "in the land of Zaphon/by the river Euphrates."[71] In other words, the Garden of Eden, like

---

70 H. Gunkel, *Das Märchen im Alten Testament* (Tübingen: Mohr, 1921) 45; and *Genesis*, 6th ed. (Göttingen: Vandenhoeck and Ruprecht, 1964) 36.

71 J. Morgenstern ("Psalm 48," *HUCA* 16 [1941] 61) held that Jer 46:10 and Zeph 2:13 "locate Safon, or the land of Safon, at the headwaters of the Euphrates." He also noted (p. 65) that Job 37:22 attributes gold to Zaphon, a point that may also bear upon the identification of Eden and the Temple

Baal's Zaphon (*ṣpn*) lies in the far north. Ugaritic and Mesopotamian tradition (from which the account is derived) agree in basic outline on this point.[72] But is there an equation between Zaphon proper and the Garden of Eden in a distinctly Israelite mode? In other words, does the Hebrew Bible apply the two stories to a common referent within Israelite experience, or does it simply inherit from its antecedents an item of folklore that now has no life, but only antiquarian significance? Here the fourth river, the Gihon, is of the utmost relevance. Like Pishon, Gihon comes from a root that one might predict would be the name of a river *gwḥ* or *gyḥ*, "to burst forth" or "to draw forth." One might regard the Gihon here, with Clifford, as "artificaly formed [like the Pishon] to bring the number of rivers to four," four being the symbol of "totality, as, for example, the four winds, the four corners of the world."[73] The problem is, that unlike Pishon, Gihon is attested elsewhere in the Hebrew Bible. It was a spring on the eastern side of the City of David which served as the principal source of water for Jerusalem. As we shall see in our discussion of Isaiah 7–8 below, the water system of Jerusalem held transcendent significance in the religious consciousness of those who lived there. In the case of the Gihon itself, it is a telling

mount. See Gen 2:11.

72   But Speiser ("The Rivers of Paradise," in *Oriental and Biblical Studies*, ed. J. J. Finkelstein and M. Greenberg [Philadelphia: University of Pennsylvania, 1967] 23–34) argues that Gen 2:10–14 is basically accurate geographically and deals with real rivers, which it locates at the confluence of the Tigris and the Euphrates, far south of where I argue the Garden was thought to be situated. The Gihon he sees as the Dyala, and the Pishon, as the Kerkha (p. 31); the names have been "etymologized" (p. 26). But if the account is so historical and so unmythological, why does it change the names of two of the rivers? And why change one of them to the name of the sacred spring in Jerusalem? Finally, Speiser's reading of *rōʾš* in v 10 as meaning "upstream rather than down" (p. 28) is quite forced. It is possible, of course, that a very different tradition lay behind the account of the four rivers of paradise of 2:10–14, but, if so, the old tradition is quite remote from the present text. On this problem, see also Kaiser, *Die mythische Bedeutung,* 107–12.

73   Clifford, *Cosmic Mountain,* 101.

fact that King David instructs his servants to take Solomon to that spring to be anointed into kingship.[74] Apparently, the spring, even in David's time, served in a sacramental capacity. It is true that a river that "winds through the whole land of Kush" (Gen 2:13), which is, according to E. A. Speiser, the land of the Cassites (in Western Iran), not Ethiopia, as generally believed, can hardly have originated as a spring in Jerusalem.[75] That would necessitate its flowing across the Syrian desert, crossing the Euphrates and the Tigris, and flowing steeply uphill into the Cassite homeland! On the other hand, it is naive to read a description of the primordial paradise in terms of scientific cartography. One might as well argue that the Zion that will be elevated above the mountains in the eschatological vision of Isa 2:2–4 and Mic 4:1–5 is not the mountain in Jerusalem, since the latter is so low. The point is that the mythic mind makes associations according to a logic of its own, which is impressionistic and not scientific. To say that the mind of ancient Israel did not make an equation between the Gihon of Gen 2:13 and the Gihon of 1 Kings 1 is indeed to strain the imagination, especially if Speiser is correct in his hesitant dating of the source J to the tenth century, that is, the century of David and Solomon.[76] In sum, it is reasonable to assume that some in Israel saw in Zion the cosmic mountain which is also the primal paradise called the Garden of Eden. The sacramental spring which is the source of Jerusalem's miraculous waterworks was conceived as the cosmic stream which issues from that mountain and sheds its fertilizing waters upon the face of the whole earth.

The equation of Temple mount and paradise, then, did not begin with Ezekiel. The two have common roots in the mythopoetic mind of the ancient Near East. After all, like the Temple, paradise is a place in which God/the gods are forever present in an intensely palpable sense, a place therefore of beatific existence,

74   1 Kgs 1:33, 38, 45.
75   Speiser, "The Rivers," 25–26.
76   Speiser, *Genesis,* xxviii.

of perfection. No wonder the psalmists at times waxed rhapsodic in their descriptions of life inside the Temple precincts:

> ⁸How precious is your faithfulness, O God;
> Mankind takes shelter in the shadow of your wings.
> ⁹They are filled with the rich plenty of your Temple,
> And you give them drink from the stream of your delights.
> ¹⁰For with you is the Fountain of Life;
> By your light do we see light. (Ps 36:8–10)

In these verses, the Temple is seen as a place of refuge from the harshness of ordinary life. In it, God shares his food with his worshippers; the reference is to the shared offerings in which the congregation and God participated in a common meal (Leviticus 3). The "stream of God's delight" in Ps 36:9 is probably the wadi which some traditions placed within the garden/Temple city. Note that the word translated as "delights" (*'ădānêkā*) is simply the plural of Eden. Most likely, the reference is to the Gihon or to one of the conduits which in various periods of the history of Jerusalem bore its water to the other end of the city. Here, "the stream of [God's] delights" is identified with the "fountain of life," a spring (probably also the Gihon) a draft from which was perhaps believed to confer enhanced vitality, even immortality.[77] In short, it is that cosmic spring which makes life possible; it is the "Fountain of Life" in a quite literal sense. But what of the light which makes vision possible? If we keep to the assumption of a Temple/paradise context, that light must be from the great lamps (*mĕnōrôt*) in the Temple (2 Chr 13:11). No wonder the Priestly source in the Torah (P) made so much of the Tabernacle lampstand.[78] The assertion that it is by that light that we see light (Ps 36:10) is a reflection of the primordial or protological

77   See G. Widengren, *The King and the Tree of Life in Ancient Near Eastern Religion*, Uppsala Universitets Arsskrift 1951:4 (Uppsala: Lundequistka; Leipzig and Wiesbaden: Harrassowitz, 1951) 5–41.

78   Exod 25:31–40; 37:17–24. See C. L. Meyers, *The Tabernacle Menorah*, ASOR Diss Series 2 (Missoula: Scholars, 1976).

dimension of the Temple. The light in the Temple, like its priesthood, its food, and its water, is pure and unblemished, the light of creation preserved in the paradisical garden. In rabbinic times, this connection between the light of creation and the Temple on Zion is developed explicitly:

> Rabbi Berechiah said in the name of Rabbi Isaac: From the place of the Temple, light was created, as it is written, "The glory of the God of Israel came from the east . . . and the earth shone from his glory" (Ezek 43:2). "Glory" can be only the Temple, as you read, "O throne of glory, exalted from the beginning, the place of our Temple." (Jer 17:12)[79]

As Raphael Patai comments on this midrash, "it was from the spot on which later the Temple was erected that the first ray of light issued and illuminated the whole world."[80] In light of Ps 36:8–10, he might have added that that primordial ray may still be glimpsed in the ideal realm within the Temple precincts on Mount Zion. In short, the Temple is intimately associated with creation. It is, in a sense, the gateway to life as it was meant to be, unlimited by death, eternal life, life *in illo tempore*, sacred time, always new, always just created.

As we have already seen, the notion of Zion as the first of God's creations, which is not explicit in the Bible, is reflected in rabbinic literature, as in the statement of the sages that, "Both [heaven and earth] were created from Zion."[81] More fundamentally, in rabbinic cosmology, Mount Zion is the capstone which keeps in place the waters of chaos whose subjugation made creation and hence all civilization possible. Were it not for the Temple on Zion, those angry waters would surge from the abyss in which they are imprisoned, undo the work of creation, and return the world to the primordial chaos which is described in Gen 1:2. In fact, some rabbinic sayings mention moments when precisely such a reversion threatened to become reality:

79 *Gen. Rab.* 3:4.
80 Patai, *Man and Temple* (New York: KTAV, 1967) 84.
81 *b. Yoma* 54b.

> At the time that David dug the foundations, [for the Temple], the watery abyss [těhômā'] came to the surface and sought to flood the world. David recited the fifteen [songs of] ascent [Pss 120–34] and brought them [i.e., the waters] down.[82]

In fact, a late Aramaic translation of the Torah speaks of a rock, the "rock of foundation," 'eben šětîyâ, on which the ineffable four-letter name of God was engraved, and with which God "sealed the mouth of the great abyss in the beginning."[83] Hans Schmidt argued that the rock in question was the podium for this inner-most *sanctum*, although the more conventional view is that it supported the outer altar.[84] In any event, the rock may have been the one from which the great mosque, the Dome of the Rock, which dominates the landscape of the Old City of Jerusalem, takes its name. The underlying assumption of the rabbinic refer-ences seems to be that this boulder restrained the abysmal torrents so that they emerged instead downhill from the Temple, at the Gihon spring in the Kidron Valley, where, as a consequence, they appeared in a way that is benevolent and enhances creation.[85] As we shall see later in this part, the contrast between the waters of chaos and the water system of Jerusalem appeared in psalmody and prophecy long before rabbinic times. The *aggadah* of the rabbis again renders explicit and prosaic what is implicit and poetic in the Hebrew Bible.

In Genesis, the work of creation which replaced a watery chaos with a world of order and goodness was undone ten generations

82 b. *Sukk.* 53a. See Patai, *Man and Temple*, 55–57, for a discussion of other rabbinic texts attesting the same notion.

83 Targ. Pseudo-Jon. to Exod 28:30.

84 See H. Schmidt, *Der Heilige Fels in Jerusalem* (Tübingen: Mohr. 1933), esp. p. 59.

85 The Mesopotamian analogies are numerous. See E. Burrows, "Some Cosmological Patterns in Babylonian Religions," in *The Labyrinth*, ed. S. H. Hooke (London and New York: Macmillan, 1935) 43–70. "Elsewhere we learn, writes Burrows (p. 50), "that Babylon was founded on the *bāb apsî*, the Gate of the Apsu—which may suggest that the temple was thought to stand in a central position upon the *apsu* as keeping ward over the waters subdued in the cosmogony."

later in the time of Noah, when God regretted the high hopes he held for man at the beginning (Gen 6:5–7). And so "all the springs of the great abyss broke through and all the windows in the skies were opened" (7:11). Anti-creation threatened; as the restraints on the primeval waters gave way, the world was inundated. In the midrash, however, there is a legend to the effect that Jerusalem (or the land of Israel) was not submerged by the great deluge, for it was from the Mount of Olives that the dove took the olive branch to bring to Noah (8:11). But another midrash, in the name of Rabbi Berechiah, attributes that olive branch to the Garden of Eden.[86] Jerusalem (=land of Israel=Garden of Eden) is an impregnable bulwark against ultimate disorder; it stood when all else collapsed into chaos. Similarly, in the Talmud, we find a discussion which claims to establish exegetically the reason by which Zion might be expected to survive a deluge that submerged the rest of the world: "the Temple was higher than all the rest of the Land of Israel and ... the Land of Israel is higher than all the rest of the lands."[87] In short, Zion as the place from which the world was created, as the point from which the primal ray of light emanated, and as the only mountain to stand above the deluge, is also the highest point in the highest land, the center of the center, from which all the rest of reality takes its bearings.

We have seen that Mount Zion registers in the Hebrew Bible and even more so in rabbinic literature, Talmud and midrash, many of the qualities found in cosmic mountains almost everywhere. It is the center (or navel) of the world, the junction of heaven, earth, and the underworld, and the point at which communication between at least the first two passes. On Mount Zion itself is a paradise in which the primal reality of creation survives intact, untarnished by the passing of time and unaffected by the threats of an aggressive chaos. It may have been noticed that in this discussion we have moved easily from talk of Zion to talk of Jerusalem and even of the land of Israel in its entirety.

86 *Lev. Rabb.* 31:10.
87 *b. Qidd.* 69a–b.

This is not sloppiness, but rather another characteristic of the cosmic mountain, for, as Eliade puts it, "every temple or palace, and by extension, every sacred town and royal residence, is assimilated to a 'sacred mountain' and thus becomes a 'centre.'"[88] In the Bible, it is not unusual to find the mountain and the city in synonymous parallelism (e.g., Ps 48:2-3). It is evident that Zion and Jerusalem were not distinguished in the hymnody that centered upon them. In fact, as one might imagine from the last midrash at which we looked, Zion comes to signify the land of Israel as well. This is true in the Hebrew Bible as well (e.g., Isa 57:13). Given this synonymous usage of "land" and "mountain," we should not be surprised even to find that an old hymn refers to the destination of those redeemed in the Exodus as "the mountain of your [i.e., God's] patrimony, your dais ... the Temple, YHWH, which your own hands established" (Exod 15:17). Originally, this may have referred to Mount Sinai. But it is the land of Israel which becomes the sacred mountain, God's throne and his palace, from which he exercises cosmic sovereignty. In fact, the idea of a holy land, which is so startlingly dominant in the religion of Israel at all periods, is most likely an extension of the universal idea of the holiness of the Temple or mountain. It may not be the case that Israel conceived of the world as a mountain, but Exod 15:17 testifies to their conception of the land of Israel in terms of its hills, perhaps because of their initial settlement in the central mountain range, while the Canaanites and Philistines retained the coastal plain. Hence all the references to coming "up" out of Egypt, from the lowlands of the Nile Valley and Delta into the highlands of the Sinai and Canaan. It is interesting that one text portrays the area outside of Israel as "profane" or "unclean" and therefore unfit for the altar the Trans-Jordanian tribes have built there (Josh 22:19). The verse speaks in a cultic context. It assumes, in good Deuteronomic and Priestly fashion, the existence of only one legitimate altar and therefore denounces the

88 Eliade, *Patterns,* 375.

Trans-Jordan tribes for building a rival. What is curious, however, is not that an oracle with the biases of the Jerusalem priesthood would consider a rival altar "unclean" (*ṭāmēʾ*), but that it would apply this same language of cult, the language of purity and impurity, to a description of territory. The focus of Temple language is, by its very nature, broad enough to include the dichotomy of holy land/profane land within the universally attested dichotomy, sacred space/profane space. Trans-Jordan is profane and hence unfit for an altar to YHWH.

There is an even more far-reaching extension of Temple language in Israel. Not only Jerusalem and the land of Israel, but even the people Israel can be designated as Zion:

> I have put my words in your mouth,
> And in the shelter of my hand I have kept you safe,
> That I might fix the heavens and establish the earth,
> And say to Zion:
> You are my people. (Isa 51:16)

Here, the people of Israel have been identified with the Temple mount; the restoration of the one goes hand in hand with that of the other.[89] The divine choice of the Israelites is more than a fact of history in this oracle from the exilic period. It is a cosmic reality, as fundamental as the establishment in their proper places of heaven and earth. By virtue of Zion, Israel has become the cosmic people.

5. THE TEMPLE
AS SACRED SPACE

We have seen that the most central aspect of the cosmic mountain, that which implies the others, is the presence of God or the gods. That presence insures that those privileged to dwell in the Temple atop the mountain will enjoy the beatific life. They will be blessed in every way. The idea of the presence of God,

89 Note also Zech 2:11, which speaks of "Zion . . . dwelling in Babylon."

however, is problematic, especially to modern minds, for it implies a spatial dimension to divinity which seems hopelessly primitive to anyone of philosophical sophistication. If God is present, he must be present somewhere and, in turn, absent, at least to a degree, somewhere else. But a God who is spatially limited is, in some minds, no God at all, or at least one of whom the term "cosmic" seems inappropriate. Within the Israelite tradition itself, what appear to be critiques of the notion of God's being present spatially can be detected:

> YHWH is near to all who call upon him,
> To all who invoke him in truth. (Ps 145:18)

> For what great nation is there whose God is near to it as YHWH our God is whenever we call upon him? (Deut 4:7)

The psalmist appears to be saying that the presence of YHWH does not depend upon one's location, but upon one's willingness to call to him from a stance of truth. The Deuteronomistic homilist goes further. He implies that YHWH's ubiquity differentiates him from the would-be gods of the nations, who, in his thinking, are not able to draw near in answer to the call of the heart because they are somehow spatially confined. The question is, do these passages attack the essence of the Temple mythos?

The fact is that the Temple and the world, God's localization and his ubiquity, are not *generally* perceived in the Hebrew Bible as standing in tension. On the contrary, the Temple is the epitome of the world, a concentrated form of its essence, a miniature of the cosmos. This notion of the Temple as a model or representation of the world underlies the symbolism executed by the Phoenician king Hiram for King Solomon (1 Kgs 7:23–26). We have already had occasion to note a general story in the ancient Near East, which describes the creation of the world and the establishment of cosmic order as a consequence of a god's defeat of the sea.[90] The sea embodies chaos; its defeat and containment constitute order.

90 Pp. 108–9.

In fact, they do more than that: they also legitimize the victor's claim to kingship and initiate the construction of his royal palace, his temple. In light of this story, to which allusions are made in the Hebrew Bible, only with YHWH as the triumphant deity,[91] it is not surprising to find a model of the sea, now utterly tame, within the Temple precincts. YHWH is enthroned near the tangible symbol of the legitimacy of his cosmic sovereignty, established in protological times (Psalm 93). The rest of the symbolism in 1 Kings 7 is less amenable to secure interpretation, although a cosmic understanding seems likely here as well. The twelve oxen may symbolize the twelve months of the year. They are grouped into three in order to represent each of the four directions. The arboreal and vegetative symbolism along the rim of the sea recalls the primal paradise, with which, as we have seen, the cosmic mountain was identified. In fact, the association with the cosmic mountain becomes explicit in another blueprint for the Temple in Jerusalem, in which the name of the altar (*har'ēl*) seems to have been understood to mean "the mountain of God"; that altar rests upon a trench called "the bosom of the earth" (Ezek 43:13–17), just as the cosmic mountain in other cultures is identified explicitly with the navel of the earth and caps the underworld.[92] What all this suggests is that the Temple is not a place in the world, but the world in essence. It is the theology of creation rendered in architecture and glyptic craftsmanship. In the Temple, God relates simultaneously to the entire cosmos, for the Temple (or mountain or city) is a microcosm of which the world itself is the macrocosm. Or, to put it differently, the center (or navel or axis or fulcrum) is not a point in space at all, but the point in relation to which all space attains individualization and meaning. The center sustains the world, as the umbilical cord sustains the embryo, or as the seed sustains the seedling, except that the world does not

91 See Cross, *Canaanite Myth*, 112–44. Such passages include Pss 74:12–17; 89:9–11; 114; and Isa 51:9–11.

92 See W. F. Albright, *Archaeology*, 144–55; and Clements, *God and Temple*, 56–66.

outgrow its center as the baby outgrows the need for an umbilical cord or as a plant comes to shed its seed. It is for this reason that the Hebrew Bible is capable of affirming God's heavenly and his earthly presence without the slightest hint of tension between the two:

YHWH is in his sacred Temple,
YHWH's throne is in the heavens. (Ps 11:4)

In short, what we see on earth in Jerusalem is simply the earthly manifestation of the heavenly Temple, which is beyond localization. The Temple on Zion is the antitype to the cosmic archetype.[93] The real Temple is the one to which it points, the one in "heaven," which cannot be distinguished sharply from its earthly manifestation. Thus, when Moses is to construct Israel's first sanctuary, the Tabernacle in the wilderness, he does so on the basis of a glimpse of the "blueprint" or "model" of the heavenly shrine which he was privileged to behold upon Mount Sinai (Exod 25:9, 40). This notion of the revelation of a heavenly model or blueprint (*tabnît*) to the mortal Temple builder has deep Near Eastern roots. Perhaps the closest parallel dates from the second half of the third millennium, when the Sumerian king Gudea of Lagash was shown in a dream the plan for the sanctuary of Ningirsu which he was to build.[94] About two millennia later, in post-exilic Israel, the *topos* was still alive, for the chronicler speaks explicitly of a model or blueprint (*tabnît*) for the First Temple, which David presented Solomon. Its literal author, the narrator insists, was, of course, God, (1 Chr 28:11–19). Thus, we should hardly be surprised to find in rabbinic tradition the notion that Mount Zion was chosen as the Temple mount because it was

93   On the same idea in rabbinic literature, see Patai, *Man and Temple,* esp. the reference on p. 130.

94   See F. Thureau-Dangin, *Les Cylindres de Goudéa* (Paris: Geunther, 1925); Weinfeld, *Deuteronomy,* 246–50; A. S. Kapelrud, "Temple Building, A Task for Gods and Kings," *Or* 32 (1963) 56–62; and Levenson, *Theology,* 37–53.

uniquely oriented towards the ideal shrine. The Tanna Rabbi Shimon bar Yohai, for example, is quoted as punning on the name Moriah (Gen 22:14), which, as we have seen,[95] was identified with the Temple mountain (2 Chr 3:1): It was called Moriah (*Môrîyâ*) because it was located "appropriately" (*rā'ûy*) over against the heavenly Temple.[96] It is not that God grants his presence in the earthly Temple at the expense of other locations; rather, his presence there is an aspect of his universal presence. The earthly Temple is the world *in nuce;* the world is the Temple *in extenso.* Temple and world do not stand in dialectical tension, but in a relationship characterized by complementarity. Therefore, Isaiah, in his vision in the Temple, experiences the holiness and "glory" that characterize the shrine, but hears the heavenly chorus identify them, instead, with the entire world:

> Holy, holy, holy is the Lord of Hosts,
> The fulness of the whole earth is his glory. (Isa 6:3)[97]

The glory of God does not grow weaker as it is diffused.

When one speaks of an "earthly Jerusalem" and a "heavenly Jerusalem," as is frequent in rabbinic literature, and, we have argued, implicit in the Hebrew Bible, then it is clear that we are dealing with a world picture which is composed essentially of two tiers. The upper tier represents ultimate reality; it is the realm of God and his retinue. The lower tier is that of mundane reality, which is vulnerable to time, change, and flux, in short, open to history. Whereas Sinai, as we saw in Part 1, represents the possibility of meaningful history, of history that leads toward an affirmation, Zion represents the possibility of meaning above history, out of history, through an opening into the realm of the

---

95 P. 94.

96 *Ber. Rab.* 3:4. The idea is ubiquitous in both Hellenistic and rabbinic literature. For example, in Wis 9:8, the Tabernacle is seen as "prepared from the beginning," and, of course, these same ideas underlie much of the discussion in the Epistle to the Hebrews.

97 See Levenson, "The Temple and the World," *JR* 64 (1984) 275–98.

ideal. Mount Zion, the Temple on it, and the city around it are a symbol of transcendence, a symbol in Paul Tillich's sense of the word, something "which participates in that to which it points."[98] For the two tiers, the earthly and the heavenly, are not closed to each other, but open, and interpenetrating on Zion. Hence there is a philosophical dimension to this cosmology which must not be overlooked. As Eric Burrows observed nearly half a century ago:

> The interest is not so much in the terrestrial centre of the universe as in a world that is in some sort transcendent. There seems to be an imaginative approximation to a kind of idealism.[99]

The Temple and its rites, especially those of a purgative character, can be conceived as the means for spiritual ascent from the lower to the higher realms, from a position distant from God to one in his very presence. The ascent of the Temple mount is a movement toward a higher degree of reality, one from the world as manifestation to the world as essence, the world as the palpable handiwork of God and his dominion.

6. SACRED SPACE AND SACRED TIME

If the Temple is a form of the world, then the construction of the Temple, and of its predecessor, the Tabernacle, should mirror the creation of the world. In fact, exactly such a parallelism can be seen from a comparison of the language describing the two building programs.[100]

98   P. Tillich, *Dynamics of Faith*, World Perspectives 10 (New York: Harper and Row, 1958) 42.

99   Burrows, "Some Cosmological," 60.

100   See also J. Blenkinsopp, *Prophecy and Canon*, University of Notre Dame Center for the Study of Judaism and Christianity in Antiquity 3 (Notre Dame and London: University of Notre Dame, 1977) 56-69; Weinfeld, "Sabbath, Temple Building, and the Enthronement of the Lord" (Hebrew) *Bet Miqra'* (5737/1977) 188-93. The English version is "Sabbath, Temple, and the Enthronement of the Lord—The Problem of the Sitz im

A₁ ¹The heaven and the earth were finished, and all their array. ²On the seventh day God finished the work which he had been doing, and he rested on the seventh day from all the work he had done. (Gen 2:1-2)

B₁ And God saw all that he had made and found it very good. And there was evening and there was morning, a sixth day. (Gen 1:31)

C₁ And God blessed the seventh day and made it sacred, for on it God had ceased from all the work of creation which he had done. (Gen 2:3)

D₁ Same as C₁

A₂ All the work of the Tabernacle, the Tent of Encounter, was finished. The Israelites had done everything exactly as YHWH had commanded Moses: Thus had they done it. (Exod 39:32)

B₂ And Moses saw all the work and found that they had made it as YHWH had commanded: Thus had they made it. And Moses blessed them. (Exod 39:43)

C₂ Same as B₂

D₂ You shall take the anointing oil and anoint the Tabernacle and all that is in it, and you shall make it sacred, along with all its furnishings. It shall be sacred. (Exod 40:9)

In the case of Solomon's Temple, the presence of the cosmic symbolism that we discussed in the previous section compensates for the absence of precise verbal correspondences of the sort demonstrated above. There are, however, several features of Solomon's building program that recall its protological archetype. For example, it takes him seven years to complete the work (1 Kgs 6:38), just as it takes the divine king seven days to complete creation (Gen 2:2). That the correspondence is more than coincidence can be seen from the fact that Israelite agricultural law included a cycle of seven years, six of work and one of rest, which is called "Sabbath" (Lev 25:3-7). The cycles of seven days and of seven years share a common vocabulary and are of the same order.

Leben in Genesis 1:1-2:3," in *Melanges biblique et orientaux en l'honneur de M. Henri Cazelles,* ed. A Caquot and M. Delcor, AOAT 212 (Kevalaer: Butzon and Bercker; Neukirchen-Vluyn: Neukirchener, 1981) 501-12. The correspondences are noted also in M. D. Cassuto, *Commentary on the Book of Exodus* ([Hebrew] Jerusalem: Magnes, 5721 (1961) 338-39.

Furthermore, Solomon dedicates his Temple during the festival of Tabernacles, a seven-day feast (Deut 16:13) that occurs in the seventh month (1 Kgs 8:2). His speech on that occasion includes a carefully constructed list of seven specific petitions (vv 31–53).[101] In short, both the appurtenances of the Temple and the account of its construction reflect the character of the acts of creation narrated in Gen 1:1–2:4a.

Since the creation of the world and the construction of the Temple are parallel, if not identical, then the experience of the completed universe and that of the completed sanctuary should also be parallel. In fact, the two entities share an interest in *rest* as the consummation of the processes that produced them. In the case of creation, God "rested" on the seventh day, the primordial Sabbath, after he had completed his labors (*wayyānaḥ*, Exod 20:11), and he commands his servants to rest *in imitatione Dei* in similar language.[102] The same root (*nwḥ*) describes his experience in the Temple as well:

> [13]For YHWH has chosen Zion,
> He has desired it for his seat:
> [14]"This is my resting place (*měnûḥātî*) forever;
> Here I shall be enthroned, for I desire it." (Ps 132:13–14)

The book of Chronicles goes so far as even to say that Solomon, and not David, would build the Temple because the former is a "man of rest" (*měnûḥâ*) and of peace (*šālôm*), as his name (*šělōmōh*) would imply (1 Chr 22:9). The connection between the two forms of rest becomes explicit in Isa 66:1, in which a prophet invokes the cosmic dimension of the Temple theology in critique of the mundane Temple building program which produced the Second Temple about seventy years after the destruction of the first by the Babylonians:

101 See Levenson, "The Paronomasia of Solomon's Seventh Petition," *HAR* 6 (1982) 131–35.

102 As in Exod 23:12 and Deut 5:14, each with *yānûaḥ*.

Thus spoke YHWH:
The heavens are my throne,
And the earth, my footstool:
Where could you build a Temple for me,
A sanctuary in which to rest (*mĕnûḥātî*)? (Isa 66:1)

In other words, the world is God's Temple, and in it he finds rest,
just as in the miniature man makes of it, the earthly Temple atop
Mount Zion.[103] The Sabbatical experience and the Temple
experience are one. The first represents sanctity in time, the
second, sanctity in space, and yet they are somehow the same. The
Sabbath is to time and to the work of creation what the Temple is
to space and to the painful history of Israel which its completion
brings to an end, as God has at last given Solomon "rest from all
his enemies round about" (1 Chr 22:9). "The seventh day is," in
Abraham Joshua Heschel's splendid phrase, "like a palace in
time with a kingdom for all. It is not a date but an atmosphere."[104]

7. THE MEANING OF
THE COSMIC MOUNTAIN IN ISRAEL

We have established that many of the salient features of the
cosmic mountain known from foreign sources appear in the
religion of biblical Israel in connection with Mount Zion. How
the cosmic mountain functions in any given society must be
determined by the exegesis of specific texts in which it appears.

Psalm 48

Today, practicing Jews recite this psalm every Monday morning. In origin it probably also had a liturgical function. V 4 speaks
of some kind of event in which God has made his power and

---

103 Note also that some conceived of the return from the Exile as a
jubilee year. See Zimmerli, *Ezechiel*, BKAT 13 (Neukirchen-Vluyn: Neukirchener, 1969) 995–96, 1018.

104 A. J. Heschel, *The Sabbath: Its Meaning for Modern Man* (New
York: Farrar, Straus, and Young, 1951) 21.

reliability public knowledge. Vv 8–9 indicate the participation of a community in the experience of YHWH enthroned in his Temple, and vv 13–14 call upon the congregation to make a procession upon Mount Zion. The likelihood is that Psalm 48 served as a liturgy for pilgrims who undertook to fulfill an obligation to celebrate the festivals at the Temple in Jerusalem (e.g., Deuteronomy 16).

As we have seen, the mountain which is the goal of the pilgrimage or procession is identified with the city complex upon it, and, more importantly, with Zaphon, the cosmic mountain of Baal in Ugaritic tradition (Ps 48:3). It is true that "Zaphon" denotes the direction "north" in Hebrew, but it acquired this meaning because the mountain associated with Baal was to the north, just as the term "Negev", the name of the southern wasteland, came to mean "south" in biblical Hebrew.[105] No psalmist was so inept as to imagine that Jerusalem was in the north; rather, Zion as the sacred mountain of YHWH had attracted the name of the sacred mountain of his Canaanite arch-rival Baal. It is not only the name, but also many of the concepts associated with the Canaanite mountain that will appear in this psalm.

Vv 13–15 call upon the congregation to conduct a visual inspection of Mount Zion and its fortifications in order to learn the lesson that YHWH is Israel's God and leader forever. The notion of learning a lesson that can be passed on to the next generation is frequent in biblical literature. Psalm 78, for example, opens—in very similar language to Psalm 48—with a call to give ear to the lesson "our fathers told us," so that we might "tell the next generation."[106] The lesson of Psalm 78 is the great story of the history of redemption, the Exodus, the wandering in the wilderness, the conquest of the land, the selection of David, all of which is recounted in some detail. In Psalm 48, however, we hear no

105   But see also Alfrink, "Der Versammlungsberg," for some of the Mesopotamian lore behind this.
106   Ps 78:3–4; cf. Ps 48:14.

such story, but only the cryptic call to gaze upon Zion in order to be able to speak of the eternal guidance of God. But how does a visual examination of Zion impart such knowledge? The answer must be that the Temple city complex was thought to be a source of revelation in and of itself. The very sight of it yields knowledge of God, without the utterance of a word. Hence, the foreign kings of vv 5–8 panic when they merely *see* the spectacle described in vv 2–4, the sacred mountain of YHWH. In the very citadels upon it YHWH somehow discloses his strength (v 4). The foreigners see them and panic; the Israelite pilgrim sees them and draws strength from the same knowledge, that this is Israel's God for all eternity (vv 14–15). In each case, it is vision which is the medium of revelation. It is sometimes asserted that whereas the Greeks thought with the eye, the Hebrews thought with the ear. To be sure, there is considerable truth in the generalization. The Homeric epics are filled with acute visual description. In the Hebrew Bible, visual description is usually of little account: we do not know, for example, even the color of Abraham's hair or Moses' height. This is because in Israel, the focus is upon the word of God, not the appearance of man and his world (1 Sam 16:7). Thus, as is well known, Erich Auerbach set up the narrative methods of Homer and the narrative of Abraham's near sacrifice of Isaac (Genesis 22) as antithetical types:

> It would be difficult, then, to imagine styles more contrasted than those of these two equally ancient and equally epic texts. On the one hand, externalized, uniformly illuminated phenomena, at a definite time and in a definite place, connected together without lacunae in a perpetual foreground; thoughts and feelings completely expressed; events taking place in a leisurely fashion and with very little of suspense. On the other hand, the externalization of only so much of the phenomena as is necessary for the purpose of the narrative, all else left in obscurity; the decisive points of the narrative alone are emphasized; what lies between is non-existent; time and place are undefined and call for interpretation; thoughts and feelings remain unexpressed, are only suggested by the silence and the fragmentary speeches; the whole, permeated with the most unrelieved suspense and directed toward a single goal (and to that

extent far more of a unity), remains mysterious and "fraught with background."[107]

Auerbach's remark that in Genesis 22, "the decisive points of the narrative alone are emphasized," implies a worldview in which the ear dominated the eye, for it is characteristic of the ear to absorb only one message at a time, in other words, to perceive sequentially, whereas the eye is capable of a *panorama* in the etymological sense, "the sight of everything." The ear, which perceives meaning in the alternation between sound and silence, necessarily gives an account which is in Auerbach's term, "fragmentary," whereas the eye is able to sense an integral whole "without lacunae." It is quite true that there is more to Hebrew narrative than can be accomodated into the typology that Auerbach derives from a comparison of Homer and Genesis 22 alone. If we were to consider all of biblical Hebrew narrative, we should have to amend and expand his observations considerably.[108] Still, the dominance of ear over eye does seem to be characteristic of ancient Israelite sensibility.

There is, however, one area in which the relationship is reversed, the Temple. What was spoken in the Temple, the liturgy that accompanied the sacrifices and its other rites, must all be reconstructed. Ancient Israel's manual of worship, the book of Leviticus, gives us detailed descriptions of the sacrifical apparatus and the liturgical calendar, but offers, as we have noted, almost nothing of what was uttered in the Temple or the Tabernacle. Similarly, we have the most sustained visual description in the entire Hebrew Bible in 1 Kings 5–7, the account of Solomon's erection of the Temple. In other words, the Temple traditions,

---

107   E. Auerbach, *Mimesis: The Representation of Reality in Western Literature* (Princeton: Princeton University, 1953) 11–12.

108   See the criticism of Auerbach in Levenson, "1 Samuel 25 as Literature and as History," *CBQ* 40 (1978) 21–22. The comments are reprinted in revised form in *Literary Interpretations of Biblical Narratives,* Volume II, ed. K. R. R. Gros Louis (Nashville: Abingdon, 1982) 234–35.

unlike the traditions of the history of redemption which are so much better known, are addressed to the eye of the viewer, not to the ear of the auditor. Somehow, in a way which, for obvious reasons, we cannot explicate in words, the sight of the Temple conveys a revelation about God. It is, therefore, interesting to note the prominence of visual terminology in Psalm 48. Zion is "fair-crested," (v 3) and kings panicked when they "saw" her (v 6), "what we had heard, we have now witnessed" (or "seen," v 9): three visual terms in one short psalm. There may be two others. The idiom to "take careful note [of its ramparts]" (*šîtû libbĕkem*, v 14) clearly implies here a visual examination. The same expression is linked with two synonyms with the meaning "to see" in Prov 24:32:

> I saw and took careful note (*'āšît libbî*),
> I saw and learnt a lesson.

The term *dimmînû* in Ps 48:10 is more problematic, but potentially quite revealing of the underlying dynamics of the spiritual experience registered in this poem. The King James Version renders this word as "thought of," and the new Jewish Publication Society edition offers a similar reading, "meditate." The New English Bible here has "re-enact." There are defenses to be offered for each choice. But there is another point in the semantic range of the *pi'el* stem of the root *dmh* which, in my view, correlates best with the overall theme of the psalm, the visual revelation of God through the structures on Mount Zion. If one considers that the related noun *dĕmût* means "image," "resemblance," "likeness," then *dimmâ* may be a denominative verb meaning "to form an image," that is, "to imagine" in the etymological sense. Thus, the King James Version and new Jewish Publication Society version make sense, but it must be stressed against their translations that the word does not always signify a purely mental process, but can retain its more physical connotations (unlike "imagine" in English). For example, in the report of Ezekiel's inaugural vision, we read:

Like the sight of the rainbow which appears in the clouds on a rainy day was the sight of the encircling radiance. It was the sight of the image (dĕmût) of the glory of YHWH, and when I saw it, I threw myself on my face. . . . (Ezek 1:28)

In Second Isaiah, we find the noun (dĕmût) linked synonymously with the same verb (the pi'el of dmh) that we find in Ps 48:10:

[18]To whom will you "liken" (tĕdammĕyûn) God,
What image (dĕmût) will you set up for him?
[19]Is it an image that a craftsman has cast,
And a goldsmith covers with plate? . . . (Isa 40:18-19)

The continuation in v 19 makes it very clear that "liken" in v 18 means "to form a physical image, an icon." Whereas Ezekiel believes it is possible to see, if not God himself, at least the appearance of something like his refulgent "glory," Second Isaiah believes that God the creator immeasurably transcends any physical representations, which must of necessity be based upon his creation (vv 25-26). The pilgrims of Psalm 48 affirm not that they have seen God on Mount Zion, but that they have formed a mental picture of his faithful care (v 10) through their inspection of his Temple. They now know by sight what they had known before only through faith in an oral report—"What we had heard, we have now witnessed"—that Jerusalem has been founded as the *urbs aeterna* (v 9) and that God will guide Israel forever (v 15).

With five visual terms in a mere fifteen verses, Psalm 48 attests a different mode of spiritual experience from that associated with Mount Sinai. The traditions ascribed to Sinaitic revelation are militantly anti-iconic.[109] Revelation, they assert, was given through the ear, and it is oral recitation, based in the historical prologue of the covenant formulary, which is the Sinaitic mode of celebration and which leads to an affirmation through observance of the *mitsvot*. In Psalm 48, it is the eye which, to foe and friend alike, communicates the nature of God and his special relation-

109   E.g., Exod 20:3; Deut 4:9-19.

ship to Israel. In the religious traditions that derive from the Hebrew Bible, it is the Sinaitic rather than the Zionistic mode that dominates. In Rabbinic Judaism, for example, it becomes imperative to commemorate the Temple and to hope for its reconstruction and glorification, but it is no less imperative to avoid duplicating what went on in the Temple. One is not to build a Temple outside of Mount Zion (the synagogue is a different institution), and one is not to imagine that the final redemption associated with the coming Third Temple has arrived when the world daily attests its need of redemption. The fact that rabbinic religion centers upon the study of books, that is, the written word, further undermines its appreciation of the nonverbal mode of revelation. Nor does the Christian tradition, for the most part,[110] offer many resources for the reclamation of the visual component of revelation. The notion that the Temple was corrupt and cursed (e.g., Matt 21:12-13) and that the body of Jesus is the new Temple has also made an appreciation of the sort of theology represented in Psalm 48 less likely. Furthermore, the anti-iconic tendencies in Protestantism, combined with the latter's emphasis upon preaching (i.e., the spoken word), have only added to the difficulty, especially in light of the dominance of Protestants in the critical study of the Bible over the last century. But it may be the case that through the sort of study of the literary legacy of Zion that we have undertaken here, we can begin to acquire a sense of this lost dimension of spiritual experience.

Psalm 46

In Psalm 46, the magnitude of the threat to Zion and, consequently, of its inviolability comes to the fore. In this poem, we see a reflex of the theme Clifford called "the battleground of conflicting natural forces."[111] In vv 3-4, the image is of a cataclysmic reversion of creation to chaos: the dry land, even the mountains,

---

110 The Orthodox churches, with their emphasis upon iconography, constitute an important exception.
111 Clifford, *Cosmic Mountain*, 3.

the great symbols of eternity and fixity (Ps 90:2), topple into the raging waters. These verses recall the theme of the great deluge (Genesis 6–9), when an embittered YHWH ordained a process of violent anti-creation that briefly restored the world to its original status of watery waste. In Psalm 46, over against this picture of the powerlessness of the mountain fastnesses before an angry sea, lies the scene of the next strophe, vv 5–8. Suddenly the storm is over, the earthquake spent. The waters of these verses are those of a stream that dispenses joy, not fear and devastation. No longer is the scene that of a hostile and inhumane landscape, austere mountains and a relentless, demonic ocean. Now, as if by magic, we find ourselves in a city, the city of God, no less, of the "Most High" ('elyôn, v 5) who is quite literally "above it all." The fury and rage of the sea may tarry for the night, but by dawn God will have insured the rescue of his chosen dwelling (v 6), for the city of God is immune to the onslaught of nature. Within her, ideal nature, the immediate fruit of divine creation, reigns untarnished, and the wild, malevolent nature of ordinary human experience remains muzzled, in accordance with God's intention in the beginning. Thus, although mountains "topple" (v 3) and kingdoms "topple" (v 7), the city of God's presence can never be "toppled" (v 6). The verb changes to the passive, for what agent can overthrow God? With the mention of "nations" and "kingdoms" in v 7, a new note is struck. The assault on cosmic order and on the sovereignty of God, which sustains it, has two prongs. One is the attack of the sea against the earth. The other is the war of kingdoms and nations against the city of God's choice and of the gladdening waters. One may note here the ease with which the psalm slides from the realm of nature to that of history. Actually, nature as it appears in the first strophe is colored by an old story common in the Near East, and best attested in the Babylonian creation epic *Enuma Elish,* in which order derives from the defeat of chaos personified as the sea.[112] The primordial combat between

112   See n. 35.

God (Marduk, Baal) and the sea (Tiamat, Yamm, Lothan) established cosmic order (creation), the kingship of God, and his right
to a palace (temple). In Psalm 46, anti-creation, the rebellion
of chaos, has two dimensions, the natural and the historical (or
political), and it is impossible to call one preeminent over the
other. In fact, here it is not even true that "myth and history
[stand] in strong tension," in Frank Moore Cross's words.[113]
They are, instead, two indistinct dimensions of the alternative or
opposite of God. One does not have a sense here of a specific
historical event, which mythic thought endows with a cosmic
dimension, nor a specific natural catastrophe, which is attributed
to the malice of human enemies. Rather, nature and politics stand
together in their opposition to the one great fact of reality: that
YHWH is God. Civilization, like the waters of chaos, can refuse
to accept the given. That refusal takes the form of political deeds,
of involvement in nations and kingdoms and wars. In place of this,
the psalmist calls upon his listeners simply to "be still."

What, exactly, is the psalmist calling upon us to do? According
to Mitchell Dahood, he wants us to "do nothing, do not enter into
military alliances with other nations, since YHWH controls
history," and the theology should be related to that of Isa 30:15:[114]

> Through stillness and quiet you shall be saved,
> In calm and confidence shall be your heroism.

The radicalism of this theology must not be missed. What we see
here is nothing so banal as a denunciation of corrupt politics in
the hope for reform. Instead, the psalmist opposes *all* politics, for

---

113 Cross's view (*Canaanite Myth*, 90) that "in Israel, myth and history
always stood in strong tension . . ." is an overstatement. The unity of vision of
some currents of thought appears striking in this verse:

> Who stills the raging seas,
> The raging waves
> And tumultous nations. (Ps 65:8)

No hint of tension between myth and history is to be detected here.

114 Dahood, *Psalms II* (Garden City: Doubleday, 1965) 282.

he does not share the belief in the power of human initiatives to change fundamental reality. That belief and those initiatives are as doomed and as futile as the rebellion of the sea against the order that derives from creation. Those rebellions may prevail in ordinary experience, but in Jerusalem, the city of God, the water is that of a gentle river that spreads joy. The violence of the sea and the kings does not even register at the cosmic center. The likelihood is that we see here another reflex of the old Mesopotamian notion of the temple which is the capstone of the subterranean waters (*apsū*), a notion which, as we have seen, resurfaces vividly in Hellenistic and rabbinic times. The Temple mount (or the rock on top of it) is a bulwark and a guarantee against chaos. Only the waters of life flow there.

It is curious that we here arrive at an evaluation of politics very much like that implicit (and occasionally explicit) in the Sinaitic covenant, but by an utterly different route. In the case of Sinai, we saw that the exclusivity of the covenantal suzerainty of YHWH renders all earthly politics suspect. If God is suzerain, human suzerains are superfluous. If God is the lord of the covenant, then political alliances are of no utility and may prove to be a distraction from basic reality. The Zionistic traditions are not dependent upon the covenant formulary underlying the developing Sinaitic traditions, and, on occasion, they are even in tension with them. But Zion, too, speaks of the unconditional lordship of YHWH and the consequent deprecation of the rights and prerogatives of earthly political institutions of whatever quality. Only the "City of our God" is endowed with the security that derives from centrality; all else is peripheral and therefore vulnerable to chaos. "Nations rage, kingdoms topple" (Ps 46:7), but in Jerusalem, there is peace and bliss—if only man will "be still" and realize that God is God (v 11).

Psalm 2

In another psalm, the specifically political dimension of Mount Zion as the sacred mountain constitutes the main theme. In Ps

2:6-7 the speaker must be the king. It is he to whom YHWH addressed his decree recounted in vv 7-9. The effect of that divine ukase is to make the human monarch the adopted son of the divine monarch. "You are my son; this day I have become your father." In all likelihood, the king recited these words upon his coronation (or, to be more precise, his anointing), at which point he took his place as the son of God. The adoption formula harks back to the eternal covenant announced in Nathan's oracle.[115] Davidic kingship is an earthly manifestation of divine kingship. To attack the ruler from the house of David, as "the kings of the earth" are doing, is to violate an eternal decree. Thus, the scenario of Psalm 2 takes place upon a split set. God is "enthroned in heaven"; the Davidic king is enthroned on earth (vv 4, 6). But the two realms are linked. The lower is simply the human manifestation of the higher, Mount Zion being the common side of the two tiers of reality. Hence, the Davidic monarch's installation there lifts him above the arena of ordinary politics and renders his realm impervious to assault. Zion endows his reign with the inviolability of the cosmic mountain, an inviolability that fits nicely with the perpetual grant and the eternal covenant with David announced in Nathan's speech. Jerusalem is *in* ordinary history, the history in which "kingdoms topple" (Ps 46:7), but it is not *of* it. As the twelfth century Spanish commentator Rabbi Abraham Ibn Ezra remarked about Ps 76:3, Jerusalem is called "Salem" because it "corresponded in its entirety (*šělēmâ*) to the gate of heaven." Thus, the revolt against Davidic suzerainty declared in Ps 2:3 is an attack upon the rule of YHWH, which is here seen as universal (v 8), although exercised through the medium of Davidic conquest. The practical political corollary of this two-storied world picture is that the Israelite king is YHWH's vicar in the world of politics:

[1]YHWH said to my lord:
"Sit at my right hand,

115   2 Sam 7:14; cf. Ps 89:27.

While I make your enemies your footstool.
²YHWH will stretch forth your mighty sceptre from Zion;
Hold sway over your enemies!" (Ps 110:1-2)

In Psalm 2, the divine promise of Davidic rule, exercised from Zion, is given a cosmic scope not attested in Nathan's oracle (2 Samuel 7), but in plentiful evidence in the traditions about Mount Zion. Here we see a kind of syncretism of the Davidic tradition and the idea of the cosmic mountain. The latter endows Davidic imperialism with supernatural energy.[116] All politics are therefore futile—except that which emanates from Zion. Davidic kingship has a foot in each of two realms, the mythical mountain and terrestrial politics. It is the intersection of the eternal and the contingent.

In short, although Mount Zion symbolizes the revolutionary idea that God cannot be contained within politics, the implications of the politics of God's choice of Zion and the Davidic dynasty that holds court there are immense. The subjugation of the nations to the united Davidic monarchy of Israel and Judah is a facet of the subordination of David to YHWH. A passive stance toward the arena of politics is here, as in Psalm 46, a corollary of faith in God's providential rule over his universal kingdom.

Isaiah 7-8

This impact of the mythos of Zion upon the world of practical politics harbors the potential for great conflict, for it would appear to require political leaders to act according to mythic consciousness rather than the *Realpolitik* appropriate to the situation confronting them. It is one thing for a psalmist to sing a hymn of God's protection of David and Zion; it is quite another for a king to conduct his statecraft according to the same ideas. This conflict appears paradigmatically in the account of the Syro-Ephraimite War.

116 On the Near Eastern sources and analogues, see H. Frankfort, *Kingship and the Gods* (Chicago: University of Chicago, 1948). A. R Johnson, *Sacral Kingship in Ancient Israel* (Cardiff: University of Wales,

After the death of David's son and successor, Solomon, the united kingdom disintegrated into two states, a northern and a southern monarchy, Israel and Judah respectively. Israel was ruled by a succession of unrelated individuals and by a few dynasties, located at various capitals, whereas Judah continued under the house of David, whose seat remained Jerusalem. In the third quarter of the eighth century, the kingdom of Israel under King Pekah and the Aramean state of Damascus, under King Rezin, formed an alliance which subjected first King Jotham (2 Kgs 15:37) and then King Ahaz of Judah to severe pressure.[117] In fact, according to 2 Kgs 16:5 (and Isa 7:1), Pekah and Rezin advanced upon Jerusalem, apparently in hope of either deposing or subjugating a recalcitrant Ahaz. To compound the latter's miseries, the Edomites were, according to the chronicler, attacking in the southeast, and the Philistines, in the southwest (2 Chr 28:17). In short, Ahaz was in the most pressing of straits. There was, however, one source of hope, the resurgent and aggressive Assyrian Empire, which, under Tiglath-Pileser III, was beginning to put all the states of the Levant into grave jeopardy. It was during Ahaz' efforts to decide upon a response to the crisis that the prophet Isaiah approached with his counsel (Isa 7:2–9). It is clear from v 6 that Rezin and Pekah were planning to dethrone Ahaz and to replace him with one "Ben Tabeal," in other words, to depose the house of David, in contradiction to the divine decree we saw in 2 Samuel 7, Psalm 89, and Psalm 2. In fact, the situation seems to be almost identical to that of the latter psalm. The kings gather to besiege Jerusalem in violation of the putative decree of Ps 2:7–9, through which the king is rendered inviolable, like the mountain he inhabits. The major difference is that these two kings are not endeavoring to sunder the bonds of Davidic suzerainty over them, but rather to force the beleaguered kingdom of Judah into vassalage to themselves. One can appre-

1955) is the classic study of the Israelite phenomenon.

117 See B. Oded, "The Historical Background of The Syro-Ephraimite War Reconsidered," *CBQ* 34 (1972) 153–65.

ciate the agony of King Ahaz' situation. Under attack on all
flanks, one's natural reaction would be to concede, ignominious
though such a surrender would be in light of the mythos of the
Davidic house, henceforth the vassal not the subjugator. To hold
out against the coalition would make sense only if Assyria could
be relied upon to come to a faithful ally's aid, but even if this
happened, Judah would still be the underling, not the ruler. In
short, to ally with either side would be to negate the theology of
David and Zion by granting recognition to ordinary politics.

One can thus understand Isaiah's advice, which calls upon the
king to substitute faith for political action in his quest for survival:
be calm and the whole problem will vanish. In Isa 7:9 the prophet
turns a pun which is impossible to capture in English: "If you are
not firm in faith (ta'ămînû),/ You will not stand firm
(tĕ'āmĕnû)." Two different verbal stems of the same Hebrew root
are employed to express the delicate relationship between faith/
trust (the *hiphil* stem) and security/unshakeability (the *niphal*
stem). The implication is that to endure requires faith, which is
here, as usually in the Hebrew Bible, indistinguishable from
radical trust. However moving Isaiah's advice may have been as a
confession of faith, it must have been pronounced absurd from the
standpoint of politics. How can doing nothing avail against
armies? With an assault upon Jerusalem already under way,
what consolation is it to know that in the economy of salvation,
Aram and Israel have only sixty-five more years of life? If Ahaz
chooses the recommended course of neutrality, how will he
answer the domination of the Levant by Assyria once she has
eliminated the two firebrands? We should not be surprised to see
Ahaz choosing the course of political wisdom over Isaiah's vision:

> Ahaz sent envoys to Tiglath-Pileser, the King of Assyria, with this
> message: "I am your servant and your son. Come and save me from the
> hands of the King of Aram and the King of Israel, who are attacking
> me." (2 Kgs 16:7)[118]

118   Read *haqqāmîm*.

In other words, Ahaz, the Davidic king, the adopted son of YHWH, declares Tiglath-Pileser his father and accepts vassalage to him. Isaiah's reply is that because the people have rejected the calm waters of the Shiloah, YHWH will bring the torrential Euphrates against them, which will reach "up to the neck" (Isa 8:1–8). The Shiloah is one of the conduits that carried water from the spring of Gihon. The oracle contrasts its waters with those of the Euphrates, one of the two main rivers of Mesopotamia, which is presently under Assyrian domination. Here, the Euphrates symbolizes *Realpolitik,* power politics and the military might necessary to sustain it. Its waters are mighty, massive, swift, and uncontrollable, like a flash flood. The Shiloah, by contrast, is identified with the sacred stream so prominent in the myth of the cosmic mountain, the river whose channels "gladden the city of God" (Ps 46:5), the "Fountain of Life" (36:10) of the Temple. Isaiah identifies this aqueduct with the river posited by old folklore in order to set out the contrast between the quiet ways of radical trust and the anxiety and turmoil of political action. The first is the Shiloah; the second is the Euphrates. Both originate in the primal spring of the Garden of Eden (Gen 2:6–14), but the Euphrates becomes a force for chaos, whereas the Shiloah preserves the tranquility and benevolence of paradise. King Ahaz, by choosing alliance with Assyria, has traded the bliss of apolitical existence for the phantom security provided by cooperation with a great power. And so the approach of Assyria will not be gentle, but violent, like the waters of chaos which, in the form of the Euphrates, symbolize the empire. They shall engulf Judah in a flash food, which will "reach up to the neck" (Isa 8:8), that is, nearly drown them. The security that one derives from even the shrewdest and most justified moves in the realm of politics is of a different order from the security of Eden. The assumption in this oracle is that Zion is the result of synergism of divine grace and human effort. Miraculously and gratuitously, YHWH offers Israel a life free of anxiety, but they cannot attain it so long as they yield to the perfectly reasonable anxieties of "normal" life.

In practical terms, what, exactly is Isaiah predicting here? The implication is that the Judean appeal to Tiglath-Pileser III will open the floodgates for an Assyrian waste of the Davidic kingdom. The statement that the waters will "reach up to the neck" (v 8), is, however, ambiguous. It occurs within a context of judgment; the waters execute punishment. And yet, if one takes the clause literally, it holds out the hope of survival, for one does not drown in waters that reach only to the neck. If so literal a reading be admitted, then the oracle sees in the old Zion mythos a grace which has some effect even if it meets rejection in man, but is fully operative only when man embraces it without reservation. In this context, the name of Isaiah's son, who is to accompany his father to meet Ahaz (7:3), is surely significant. "Shear-Yashub" means "a remnant will return." The placement of the noun in the first position may give the name the nuance "*only* a remnant will return" (as in 10:21–23), but, even so, the underlying idea is one of undeserved hope amidst a larger and very much deserved punishment. Human folly may compromise, but it cannot nullify the divine protection that envelops the cosmic center. The tension between God's justice and his mercy in history is never resolved conclusively one way or the other. YHWH holds man accountable, but gives him a chance which his deeds alone have not merited.

Finally, awareness of the background of Isaiah's theology of the Syro-Ephraimite War in the old mythology of the cosmic mountain reveals the depth of the command to the prophet to confront the king "at the end of the conduit of the Upper Pool" (7:3). In a time of siege, such as that in which Ahaz found himself (2 Kgs 16:5), a wise king would wish to inspect his waterworks. Perhaps Ahaz knew of a tradition to the effect that an attack on the old Jebusite water system was central to David's conquest of Jerusalem nearly three centuries earlier (2 Sam 5:8). But to a prophet, the waterworks of the Temple city signify something radically different from what they mean to a king. A king lives in the harsh world of politics; a prophet mediates beween that world and the world of vision and mythopoesis. To the latter, the conduit recalls everything enveloped in the myth of the paradise at the cosmic center—the presence of God, an abundance of grace, the childlike simplicity of existence in the Garden of Eden. Isaiah and Ahaz see the same conduit, but the prophet calls upon the king to interpret it in a radically different way. To bridge the gap between those two worldviews does not seem to have been a possibility. A wise king knows that independence in the case of a tiny state is always a bit of a legal fiction. Tiny states survive to the extent that the superpowers are benevolent or distracted. In fact, for most of the following century, Judah was to live in subjugation to Assyria, until the latter was distracted by the rise of Babylonia, which within a few decades would end Judean "independence" altogether (587 B.C.E.). In this instance, Isaiah agrees that the alliance of petty kingdoms is doomed (Isa 7:7–8), but the seer does not see that the independence which the religious tradition predicates of Judah is not an historical possibility, a form of blindness to which those who dwelt in the earthly Jerusalem were probably especially vulnerable. Isaiah resolves the tension between the heavenly and the earthly Jerusalem by calling upon the king to act in the latter as if he lived in the former.

Isaiah 29:1–8

The complexity and delicacy of this relationship between the promise of God to Jerusalem, on the one hand, and the punishment which he reserves the right to visit upon her, on the other, are most central in the Ariel oracle, also from the book of Isaiah (Isa 29:1–8). The name Ariel is as problematic as it is evocative. The term can be parsed as "the lion of God," and, if this rendering is correct, then Ariel is the ideal designation of the city that symbolizes impregnability guaranteed by YHWH. Note in this connection that the blessing of Jacob calls the tribe of Judah a lion and asserts that the royal sceptre shall never depart from it (Gen 49:8-12). On the other hand, some scholars have noted a similar word in Sumerian, a Mesopotamian tongue, which, although unrelated, has lent a few words to Hebrew. The Sumerian term apparently "referred to the underworld and then to the Temple as the mountain above the underworld."[119] If this speculation is correct, then we have here an explicit connection with the complex of ideas we have been calling the cosmic mountain. It is possible that in the Israelite mind this old non-semitic word was understood to mean "the mountain of God," after a word (*har'ēl*) for the altar-hearth in the Temple (Ezekiel 43:15). If so, this, too, was probably a folk-etymology rather than a scientific understanding of the meaning of the term, for '*ăî'ēl* (or *har'ēl*) could well have signified the altar-hearth without any allusion to cosmic symbolism. My own judgment is that, whatever the historical origin of the word, its suggestion of "the lion of God" and of "the mountain of God" to the Hebrew speaker made it a potent designation of the Temple city, for it is precisely the permanence of the regal, leonine bearing of Jerusalem and the validity of the belief in its inviolability which are at stake in this oracle.

The verse "City where David encamped" (v 1) is equally enigmatic and evocative. Does it refer to David's capture of the Jebusite stronghold (2 Sam 5:6-8), or to his making the city his permanent headquarters and his pitching a tent there for the ark of YHWH (ch. 6)? The first is an image of belligerence, of the fall of Jerusalem; the second, an image of triumph and well-being, of the inauguration and consecration of an eternal capital. And so, the words "City where David encamped" raise the fundamental issue of this oracle. Is it to be one of judgment or one of deliverance? Does it speak of chastisement for a wayward Jerusalem or of an abiding protection for the City of David? One might note that the term "City where David encamped" pointedly recalls an

119   Kaiser, *Isaiah 13-39: A Commentary*, OTL (Philadelphia: Westminster, 1974) 267.

expression discussed earlier in connection with one of the psalms of Zion, "city of the great king" (Ps 48:3)—which, if more than coincidence, signals that the oracle will, like Psalm 48, stress the inviolability of Zion against attack. On the other hand, God's encamping at Jerusalem in Isa 29:3 is clearly hostile in intent. And so the suspenseful ambiguity continues.

In the case of this oracle, the human enemy who will act as the rod of God's anger is probably the Assyrians. The oracle seems to speak to an assault of the emperor Sennacherib upon the Judean capital about 701 B.C.E.[120] The first stanza (Isa 29:1–3) appears on balance to support the interpretation of the poem as an oracle of judgment: God will lay siege to his own place of tabernacling. The second stanza (vv 4–5ab) shows that, as a consequence, the city renowned for its loftiness will suffer a fearful abasement. The mountain that a psalmist termed "fair-crested," where "God had made himself known as a tower of strength" (Ps 48:3, 4) is now brought lower than the ground itself, consigned to the underworld, reduced to less than dust—and by the same God. The mountain on which a victorious emperor recites the divine decree by which he rules and conquers (2:7) is now the source of a squeak with no more vitality in it than there is in the voice of a subterranean ghost (Isa 29:4).

But a ghost is not a nonentity. Just as we feel that the central ambiguity of the Ariel oracle has been resolved, that it definitely is an oracle of judgment rather than one of deliverance, there comes an abrupt reversal of circumstances. The last stanza (vv 5c–8) begins with the words "Suddenly, in an instant" (v 5c), and just as suddenly, the subject changes from the humiliation of Zion to the illusionary quality of the victory of her attackers. When all seems definitively lost, when the mythos of the cosmic mountain appears utterly discredited, then and only then YHWH comes to the deliverance of his city. He answers Ariel as he is to answer Job in

120 On the very problematic nature of this attack and the literature about it, see Childs, *Isaiah and the Assyrian Crisis*, SBT 2/3 (London: SCM, 1967), esp. pp. 53–57, on the Ariel oracle; and Bright, *History*, 298–309.

similar straits: out of a "whirlwind."[121] Redemption comes when it is most needed and most unlikely, after all other sources of hope have been exhausted. In Isa 29:7–8, the nations melt away, their victory a mirage, just as the psalms of Zion speak of the frustration of those who dare wage war against the sacred mountain (e.g., Ps 48:6). The fall of Zion is only a nightmare.

Isa 29:1–8 lends itself easily to the analysis that an original oracle of judgment against Jerusalem has been rewritten so as to apply to Israel's enemies. The edited version is thus the diametric opposite of the original—an oracle of deliverance rather than judgment.[122] It should not be thought that Isaiah held such an allegiance to the mythos of Zion that he could not have pronounced doom upon the Temple city. Instead, the idea of the cosmic mountain was for him a resource to be applied when he deemed it appropriate, not a doctrine in which he continually felt a need to confess faith. Isaiah himself compares the message of God to the methods of planting which a farmer varies according to the crop (28:23–29). What had been appropriate at the time of the Syro-Ephraimite War (734) may not have been appropriate during Sennacherib's siege in 701 B.C.E.

On the other hand, I cannot go so far as to say, as does one contemporary commentator, that the oracle "gives the impression of having been to some extent patched together, and casts an artificial obscurity over what it prophesies."[123] The truth is that the discontinuities within the poem reflect the discontinuity of the religious experience—and perhaps the political experience as well—that it aims to capture. The attributes of absolute justice and absolute mercy in God are in contradiction. Absolute justice means that a sinful Zion will fall; absolute mercy means that the promise of protection will be valid, whatever the sins of the city. In its present form, the Ariel oracle is trying to do justice to each of these two dimensions of the divine personality. In so doing, it

---

121   sĕʻārâ, v 6; Job 38:1.
122   Childs, Isaiah, 57.
123   Kaiser, Isaiah 13–39, 266.

proposes two closely related models for the relationship of myth to historical experience. According to one model, the devastation of mythic security by historical events is only temporary. God will honor his decree. The siege of Jerusalem is a parenthesis in history; YHWH will put an end to this war, as he does in the case of all assaults on Zion (Ps 46:10). According to the second model, the historical challenge is to the mythic complex as a dream is to reality—insubstantial, shadowy, ultimately insignificant. The city under siege is simply a wispy earthly counterpart to the real Jerusalem, the cosmic center that can never fall. Whereas the first model is temporal in nature, the second is more nearly spatial; the Zion that is vulnerable exists in the head of a dreamer. The real Zion is inviolable. One begins to sense here an adumbration of the disengagement of the two tiers of reality, the ideal and the mundane, that will come to characterize the genre of apocalyptic, when it arises a few centuries later. Now if the redactor who has woven together these various ideas and sources has left some ragged seams, it must still be said that the final product is more true to the complexity of experience than any univocal oracle of judgment or oracle of deliverance. The "obscurity" that the comentator remarks lies not in the redactor's literary effort, but in the ways of YHWH, which in the light of Sennacherib's siege, seemed increasingly contradictory. For if the assault on Zion is but a bad dream, it must be noted that it occurs within a culture that tended to view dreams as portents. The Ariel prophecy vindicates the old theology of the inviolability of Jerusalem, but at the price of decreasing confidence. Sennacherib casts a pall upon the old mythos which the redactor's ambiguity captures exquisitely.

Jeremiah 7:1-15

In a little over a hundred years, that nightmare would come true, as the Temple fell to the troops of the neo-Babylonian Empire (587 B.C.E.). In light of Isaiah's counsel at the time of the Syro-Ephraimite War and perhaps also on the occasion of Sennacherib's campaign, we should not be surprised to learn that some in Jerusalem in the days of the Babylonian advance derived confidence from the notion that Mount Zion was invulnerable to any historical onslaught. This becomes clear in the famous "Temple speech" of Jeremiah (Jer 7:1–15).[124] The people whom Jeremiah addresses in this oracle stand in the tradition of the Temple mythos. They rely upon the phrase "the Temple of YHWH" as an incantation to ward off adversity (v 4).[125] The three-fold utterance of these words indicates the mindlessness with which they employ them. The Temple of YHWH has become a string of nonsense-syllables whose mere repetition is supposed to be effective, a mantra bled of meaning. Here we see a denatured form of the old notion of the Temple as the locus of ultimate security. In contrast, Jeremiah asserts the existence of ethical preconditions for Israel's admittance to the central shrine. It is interesting that the verb in the expression "I will let you dwell" in v 7 is of the root (*škn*) that expresses the idea of the presence of the God who sets up his tent (*miškān*) among his people. The term *šĕkînâ,* the (feminine) presence of God, which figures so centrally in Jewish mysticism, derives from the same root. Not only YHWH, but also Israel is a sojourner in the sanctuary, one whose presence is delicate and fragile and not to be taken for granted. In the building, which "bears God's name," (vv 10, 11, 14) that is, which is his personal property, man comes as a guest and not as a proprietor. The decision to allow man to dwell there (vv 3, 7) and the decision to place God's name there (v 12) are God's. The Temple exists and functions in the spiritual universe by his grace alone.

Against the notion that the Temple is automatically immune from threats, Jeremiah adduces the example of Shiloh (vv 12–15),

124 The speech probably dates to 609. See Jer 26:1. On the other hand, 7:1–15 is so Deuteronomistic in idiom and theology that one should hesitate to ascribe it to the historical Jeremiah.

125 In v 4, read *hmh* as a scribe's abbreviation for *hammāqôm hazzeh,* "this sanctuary."

the old shrine whose destruction occurred at the end of the life of the priest Eli and in the youth of the prophet Samuel (1 Samuel 4). This Eli was an ancestor of Abiathar, one of David's two high priests. Unfortunately, Abiathar supported Adonijah in his effort to succeed to the throne of his ailing father, whereas it was Solomon who finally won out, with the support of the other high priest, Zadok (1 Kgs 1:7–8). King Solomon punished Abiathar for his support of the opposition candidate by exiling him to the town of Anathoth (2:26–27). Zadok remained as high priest in the Temple of Jerusalem. But the Elides of Anathoth were yet to be heard from. Jeremiah was "one of the priests who were in Anathoth" (Jer 1:1), in other words, a scion of the old Shilonite priesthood whom Solomon disqualified from service in his Jerusalem Temple. Therefore, when Jeremiah points out that, after all, YHWH destroyed Shiloh and can do the same to Jerusalem, he is executing the revenge of the Elides against the Zadokites.[126] In other words, on the basis of his family history, Jeremiah relativizes the Temple of Jerusalem, rendering it one of at least two such shrines, and thus he tacitly destroys the cosmic dimension which is central to its mythos. And so, to Jeremiah, the Solomonic shrine was a temple, like the one at Shiloh, not *the* Temple, eternal and inviolable, as Isaiah of Jerusalem had thought at the time of Syro-Ephraimite siege. Had Isaiah risen from the dead to repeat his oracle to Ahaz in the days of Jeremiah, it is conceivable that the latter would have branded his predecesor a false prophet, exactly that which he was to brand Hananiah, a prophet who predicted only a short exile for the house of David (Jeremiah 28). The contradiction was possible because prophecy was not systematic theology.

But Jeremiah's Temple sermon is not a sermon against the Temple. In spite of his Shilonite extraction, Jeremiah regards the Temple on Mount Zion as the place that bears YHWH's name (7:10–11) and the locus of the divine presence (vv 10, 15). He

---

126 See Cross, *Canaanite Myth*, 195–215; and Levenson, *Theology*, 129–58.

connects that shrine with the promise of the land to the patriarchs (v 7), a connection that fits nicely with the argument that the holiness of the land is an extension of the holiness of the Temple. In short, one cannot maintain that Jeremiah regards the sanctuary in Jerusalem as extraneous to the relationship with YHWH. The ethical demands which the prophet issues should not be conceived as an alternative to the Temple. What Jeremiah does oppose is the idea that the divine goodness so evident in the Temple is independent of the moral record of those who worship there, in other words, the effort to disengage God's beneficence from man's ethical deeds and to rely, as a consequence, on grace alone. To the complacent cry of his audience that "We are safe" (v 10), the prophet responds by noting that the Temple is not "a den of robbers" (v 11). The grace of God does not mean exemption from the demands of covenant law, from ultimate ethical accountability. Grace and law belong together. In separation, they become parodies of themselves. For Jeremiah, this means that one cannot ascend into the pure existence of the Temple with his impurities intact. He cannot drag his filth into paradise and expect to benefit from paradisical existence. Mount Zion is morally positive. It does not accept the moral debits of those who seek only protection there. Rather, the protection follows naturally from the relationship with God which is appropriate in that place. Such a relationship excludes the practice of the sins prohibited in the Decalogue (v 9).

In light of this moral dimension to life in the Temple, we must protest against the notion that Jeremiah is attacking here the Temple mythos whose nature we have been analyzing throughout Part 2. The fact is that his audience does not adhere to that mythopoetic complex, but to a fragment of it which they have extracted from context. For them, the delicate, highly poetic image of the cosmic mountain has become a matter of doctrine, and the doctrine can be stated in one prosaic sentence: In the Temple one is safe. The Temple does not thrill them and fill them with awe; the vision of it does not transform them. For them, the appropriate response to sight of the Temple is anything but the radical amazement of a pilgrim. Instead, the Temple in their eyes is simply a place like any other, except that there the long arm of moral reckoning will not reach. Hence, they approach Zion in the stance of one about to take possession of what he deserves, not in the stance of one humbly accepting a miraculous gift which no one can deserve. Jeremiah's audience seeks to profit from the Temple without committing themselves to the moral dynamic that animates it.

It seems to me that there is another notion against which Jeremiah is battling in the Temple sermon. Those whom he faults have taken the cosmos out of the cosmic mountain. To them, that glorious vision of a universal center has been degraded into a matter of mere real estate. They do not long in joy and awe for the mountain. Why should they? They are standing on it. The edifice on Mount Zion does not correspond to the gate of heaven; it *is* the gate of heaven. In other words, they have lost the sense of the delicacy of relationship between the higher and lower Jerusalem, and have assumed that the latter always reflects the former perfectly. Hence the emphasis throughout the sermon on the expression "this place," which occurs in no fewer than seven of the fifteen verses. In short, Jeremiah's audience relates to the Temple within the framework of conventional spatiality. It is a place, this place. One cannot imagine a more wooden reading of the mythos of Zion than theirs. Whether Jeremiah would have endorsed the full version of the Temple mythos, from which his audience has detached only a piece for their own benefit, is impossible to say with certainty. The analogy he draws with Shiloh would indicate that he would not. But we must not suppose that it is the idea of the cosmic mountain in its fullness which is attacked in the Temple sermon.

Psalm 24

The moral dimension of the Temple is perhaps the most easily overlooked. In fact, much of biblical scholarship tends to regard the Temple as a source of corruption rather than of a pure and purifying justice. Those whose lives centered upon the Temple are often portrayed, even in recent literature, as elitist, miserly, backward looking, lacking in vision and a passion for justice. One contemporary theologian, for example, goes so far as to characterize the priesthood of the post-exilic era (late sixth century B.C.E.) as "a very exclusive, and even intolerant . . . hierocratic group," whom he identifies with "the ruling classes" who seek "to preserve their position of supremacy."[127] To be sure, Israelite priests were human and not angelic. It is safe to assume that they, like prophets, kings, and ordinary individuals, often pursued their self-interest. What the conventional view of the priesthood does not consider, however, is that there existed an internal critique of the misuse of the Temple, quite apart from the polemic on the part of outsiders. For example, a text like Psalm 24 indicates that, properly conceived, the Temple is a place of electrifying holiness that cannot tolerate injustice.

This psalm, chanted by Jews today on Sunday mornings,[128] opens with a cosmic perspective. The first stanza (vv 1–2) reminds us that the earth rests upon the waters of chaos and owes its endurance to the power of the creator who so established it. This image of God's putting the earth upon a foundation resting over the waters is, once again, a reflection of the idea of the Temple as cosmic capstone, holding back the waters of anti-creation. The term "all that it holds" (v 1; literally, "its fulness") reminds us of the chant of the seraphim in Isaiah's vision in the Temple:

---

127 P. D. Hanson, *The Dawn of Apocalyptic* (Philadelphia: Fortress, 1975) 227, 212.

128 It is also recited as the Torah scroll is being returned to the Ark (except on Sabbath morning). This would imply that the reading of the Torah is analogous to the ascent of the sacred mountain. On the notion of Mount Sinai as an "archetype of the Tabernacle" in the P source, see J. Milgrom, *Studies in Levitical Terminology,* University of California Publications, Near Eastern Studies 14 (Berkeley, London, and Los Angeles: University of California, 1970) 44.

Holy, holy, holy is the Lord of Hosts,
The fulness of the whole earth is his glory (Isa 6:3)

In Isaiah 6, the "fulness of the earth" is God's glory; in Psalm 24, it belongs to God, who is the king of glory. In both instances, the term indicates the cosmic scope of the divine rule exercised from the Temple. Thus, the second stanza of the psalm (vv 3–6) does not change the subject significantly. We have simply moved from a description of the cosmic rooting of the universe to the question of who shall be admitted to the mountain shrine which still incarnates that original creative energy. In this and in the last stanza (vv 7–10), there seems to be an antiphonal structure. One group of worshippers asks the questions, and another answers. It is not readily evident how the roles were divided, who said what, but one can imagine that vv 3, 8a, and 10a were recited by worshippers seeking admission to the Temple complex and that vv 4–6, 8b–9, and 10b–c are the answers of the priests who guarded the gates. Alternatively, it may be that the priests asked the questions by way of examining the congregation to determine whether they indeed met the qualifications for entry, and that the answers were supplied by the congregation to demonstrate their mastery of the requirements. In either case, the issue in the second stanza (vv 3–6) is, what are the ethical characteristics of life within the Temple precincts? What must one be like to reach the top of the sacred mountain? The last stanza (vv 7–10) makes it clear that the presence of God enters the Temple only after the ethical prerequisites of vv 3–6 have been met. It may be that these verses accompanied a procession of some sort, with the Ark, perhaps, symbolizing YHWH. At all events, it must not be missed that the second and third stanzas are parallel. Each records an entrance to the Temple complex, one by visiting worshippers and one by YHWH the king. In light of the first stanza, it is clear that YHWH might have chosen to dwell anywhere. The world is his. His presence in the Temple, as I have argued, does not imply his absence elsewhere. Rather, he intensifies his presence and renders it most dramatic at the cosmic center. It is there that his power and his sovereignty are most vivid, for it is there that we see the palace he founded upon the tamed body of his primal challenger, the seas. Similarly, according to the second stanza (vv 3–6), those who enter there must represent the apex of ethical purity. They must be people of "clean hands and a pure heart" (v 4). In no way could the *cultic* and the *ethical* be more tightly bound together. They are two sides of the same experience. The cult celebrates the glorious victory of God the king, through which he established order in the universe. The ethical tradition, as it appears in Psalm 24, celebrates the order and lawfulness of man, through which he qualifies for entry into the presence of God in the palace he has won. It is significant that in Hebrew the same term (*ṣedeq*) can indicate either victory or righteousness/justice.[129] The Temple represents the victory of God and the ethical ascent of man. The cosmic center is also the moral center.

Psalm 15

Psalm 15 is very similar to Psalm 24, in that it, too, was probably an entrance liturgy for the Temple. In this poem, unlike Psalm 24, the question as to the ethical requirements for ascent to the Temple is asked directly of God, and the answer is more detailed. Those requirements form the body of the poem. The rest of it is structured according to the rhetorical figure known as *inclusio*; that is, the opening and the closing (vv 1 and 5) form an envelope around the larger middle. The expression "shall never be toppled" (*lō' yimmôṭ*, v 5) we have already seen. In Ps 46:6, it predicates the city of God at the time of the dissolution of the created order into watery chaos:

> God is in her midst,
> She shall not be toppled.

It is a term often used to indicate the unshakability of the person

129 The first sense appears, e.g., in Isa 41:2; the second, in Deut 16:20.

who does right.[130] In light of the *inclusio,* however, and the
specific context of Psalm 15, it is clear that here the term draws an
implicit analogy between the mountain and the person qualified
to lodge there. The mountain will not be toppled; one who
practices what it represents will not be toppled. If one looks at
Psalm 15 as he would look at a picture, reading as always from
top to bottom, he sees an interesting scenario. At the very top is a
tent-shrine (v 1b). Beneath it lies the sacred mountain (v 1c).
Then comes a relatively larger section, the arduous prerequisites
for the long climb up (vv 2–5b). Finally, at the very bottom, the
focus shifts to the man, "he who acts thus," and it is asserted that
he already possesses the invincibility of the mountain. In other
words, between him and the shrine above lies the grueling ethical
test, but if he has passed the test, it is as if he already dwells atop
the sacred mountain. The implication is clear: doing justice, living
a clean life, endows one with the invincibility of the cosmic
mountain, whether he is on it in a geographical sense or not. And
if it be appropriate to bring the Temple sermon (Jer 7:1–15) to
bear here, the reverse is also true: one whose life is tainted by
corruption has lost the security of the mountain, even if he is holed
up in the Temple itself. The ascent of Mount Zion is a question of
increasing ethical perfection as well as geography.

This transferral of the qualities of the mountain to the people
fit to abide there is explicit in another psalm:

> [1]A song of ascents
> Those who trust in YHWH are
> Like Mount Zion, which cannot be toppled,
> But endures forever.
> [2]As mountains encompass Jerusalem,
> So does YHWH encompass his people,
> Now and forevermore. (Ps 125:1–2)

Here it is trust in God that renders one inviolable. The idea of
radical trust and its objective correlative, Mount Zion, are here a
bit more disengaged. The commitment to a proper relationship

---

130 E.g., Pss 21:8; 112:6; Prov 10:30.

with YHWH puts one, as it were, on the cosmic mountain. Or, to put the matter differently, Jerusalem is but a visible demonstration of a theological truth, that God surrounds and protects his people. Once again, as in Ps 48:9, one knows by sight in Jerusalem what he knows in a less sensual way elsewhere. The implication of all these texts, considered cumulatively, is that through trusting in God and living accordingly with clean hands, a pure heart, and a tongue free of slander, one can partake of the creative and transforming energy that radiates from the Temple atop Mount Zion. One senses here just how far astray those scholars have gone who draw a hard contrast between ethics and cult, prophecy and priesthood. Texts like Psalms 24 and 15 are evidence that the critique of cult was an essential part of the cult in ancient Israel. The Temple on the mount radiates an electrifying and all-consuming justice.

The charge might be levelled against psalms like these that the moral requirements they exact are too high for any worshipper to attain. Who can honestly claim to have "clean hands and a pure heart," to have lived "without blame," and never to have "wronged his fellow"? Is it not the case, then, that the person who claims admission to the cult is guilty of another sin simply by pleading not guilty to these, the sin of self-righteousness? And if, as Israelite tradition seems to have held rather consistently, it is possible to have sinned without knowing it (Leviticus 4), then of what worth is the claim to innocence which the applicant to the Temple cult makes? If inadvertent sin is possible, how can anyone affirm his innocence?

In point of fact, if one looks at the history of biblical interpretation, this charge of self-righteousness is perhaps the one most frequently levelled against the Hebrew Bible and especially the Psalter, particularly by Christian scholars and preachers eager to contrast this "Old Testament" teaching with the idea in their tradition that a man can be justified in the sight of God only by grace, and not by his own deeds.[131] It is not my intention here to

131   Examples are, C. S. Lewis, *Reflections on the Psalms* (London:

analyze the concept of righteousness in the Hebrew Bible in general. To me, it is obvious that it is different, at the very least in tone and emphasis, from that of the rabbinic literature and of the New Testament. But it must be said that, as regards psalms such as those under discussion, the criticism has missed something essential. As we have seen repeatedly, the ascent of the Temple mount was considered to be something more than simply a change of locale. It was, in fact, a way of entering a different kind of existence, marked by closeness to God, a life at the very center of the cosmos, the point on which the world is balanced, a true paradise. Now, viewed with the eyes of a hard-headed realist, Mount Zion does not appear to be these things at all. How could a mountain so close to the Mediterranean and so far from the Persian Gulf be the center of the inhabited lands? How could a hillock overshadowed by Mount Scopus and the Mount of Olives be termed "fair-crested . . . the utmost peak of Zaphon" (Ps 48:3)? Clearly, the vision of Mount Zion follows not from any empirical view, but from the world of myth and poetry. It is this latter world which stirred the hearts of psalmists as they asked how one might gain admission to the enchanted mountain. Now, just as the cosmic mountain was an idealization of Zion, so was the worshipper fit for admittance there an idealization. What Psalms 24 and 15 ask the worshipper to do at the foot of Mount Zion or at the gate to the Temple complex is to pledge allegiance to the ideal. His own life may have veered from the moral prerequisites of the Temple as much as the earthly Jerusalem fell short of the heavenly. That made no difference: one who would ascend the mountain must start at the bottom. The point is that the ascent into the Temple and participation in the liturgy that took place there were thought to endow the worshipper with a higher self, as it were. The ascent of the sacred mountain thus involved self-transcendence. The self at prayer and sacrifice was different from

Geoffrey Bles, 1958) 9–19; and A. Weiser, *The Psalms* (Philadelphia: Westminster, 1962) 171. It is possible that the negative confessions of the Psalms had a precise juridical context. See L. Delekat, *Asylie und Schutzorakel am Zionheiligtum* (Leiden: Brill, 1967).

the one familiar in ordinary life. And yet, it would be naive to think that one's ordinary dealings would be unaffected by the solemn pledge of allegiance to the moral dimension of the ideal life. The idea of the Temple is static only in that it represents the fixity and permanence of cosmic reality. As it comes into contact with the human will, protean and volatile, it exerts a profound moral dynamic. Zion is a catalyst for moral improvement.

8. YEARNING FOR THE TEMPLE

Given this status of the Temple as the realm of the ideal, including the ideal of ethical dealing, it makes sense that life inside the Temple should often appear as the object of a deep longing. Thus, the poet of the famous twenty-third Psalm concludes his meditation on life under the ultimate protection of YHWH with this hope:

> Only goodness and love shall pursue me,
> All the days of my life,
> And I shall dwell in the Temple of YHWH,
> For days without end. (Ps 23:6)[132]

Another psalmist, perhaps a king, contrasts the turmoil of his life with the security he associates with the Temple. His deepest wish is marked by a passionate longing for the beatific vision:

> One thing only have I asked of YHWH,
> It alone shall I seek:
> To live in the Temple of YHWH,
> All the days of my life,
> To gaze upon the beauty of YHWH,
> And to frequent his palace. (Ps 27:4)

He, too, longs for the beatific vision available in the palace of the God of Israel.

Another poet, the author of Psalm 84, sees the Temple as his

132 Read *wĕyāšabtî* with Targum. Also possible is a revocalization of MT to *wĕšibtî.*

only appropriate home. As was the case with Psalm 15, this poem begins with a mention of the tent-shrine atop the mountain and closes with a reflection on the beatitude of the person whose life is consonant with the deepest meaning of that mountain. Between the opening, which extols the beauty of the divine dwelling, and the closing, which extols the supernal happiness of the man who trusts in God, there is mention of the ethical prerequisite. One must, again, "live without blame" (v 12). Most of the body of Psalm 84, however, is not ethical in character, but expressive of a profound yearning for life in the Temple. The poet longs not for a mystical union with God, but for communion with God in the latter's own abode. The first stanza (vv 2–5) concludes with an assertion of the beatitude of those, perhaps the Korahites or another clan of cultic singers, who are engaged endlessly in the praise of YHWH in his Temple. The psalm itself ends in identical language, except that this time it is the man who trusts in God who is beatified, without mention of his locale. The parallelism suggests that trust in God confers the spiritual status of one who lives in the Temple—the prime desire of the authors of Psalms 23 and 27—and engages there in the praise of YHWH.

The second stanza (Ps 84:6–8) is a vignette of pilgrims as they make their way up the mountains towards Jerusalem and then (in line with the imperatives of Ps 48:13–14) take a tour of the fortifications on Zion itself. The Hebrew of Ps 84:7 is quite garbled; one can only guess at its meaning. If I render it accurately as "They pass through the Valley of Tears,"[133] it implies a kind of natural/spiritual transformation: *natural* in that a valley becomes a mountain, Zion, and *spiritual* in that the ascent somehow enables the worshippers to make the water of tears into springs, changing a symbol of grief into one of fertility. In other words, the road up to the Temple is the objective correlative of an inner spiritual development which is crowned by a vision of God

---

133 *Bākā'* in v 7 should probably be connected with the root *bkh*, "to cry." Cf. *bekeh* in Ezra 10:1.

in his palace on Mount Zion. The physical ascent is also a spiritual ascent. Its motive force is the magnetic attraction exerted upon a person by the object of his love, in this case God manifest in his palace. The centripetal force of that love, which propels the psalmist toward God and Zion, is a thousand times stronger than the centrifugal forces that pull him toward other concerns (v 11).

Whatever its original meaning, the statement of the three psalmists whom we have been examining—that they wish to spend their lives within the Temple—came to be taken as lyrical hyperbole, for the religious traditions recorded in the Hebrew Bible include no parallel to the monasticism that was to develop in the church or, *mutatis mutandis,* in the Buddhist tradition. At any given time, there were a few individuals whose employment, as it were, lay within the Temple, but there did not develop an ideal of religious life that was demarcated from the daily concerns of the masses. The Temple upon Mount Zion was a place of liturgical visitation and the ecstatic experience associated with liturgy, but the worshippers left the Temple afterward to take up again their worldly occupations. In fact, the qualifications for entry prescribed in texts like Ps 15:2–5b relate not to some set of special vows for initiates, but rather to honest dealing in the humdrum of everyday life—telling the truth, abstaining from slander, standing by one's word, lending with compassion, rejecting bribes, etc. The entrance to the ideal lies within a higher way of acting within the realm of ordinary life. The two worlds are not in opposition. Purity and justice within the lower one opens the gates to the upper one. Or, to be more precise, one who strives toward purity and justice in the lower world already stands within the higher world.

9. THE SURVIVAL OF
THE TEMPLE IN JUDAISM

The Second Temple, the one initiated at the end of the sixth century B.C.E., after the Babylonian Exile, was destroyed by the

Romans in 70 C.E. One might think that the whole discussion of this Part is, to Jews at least, of historical interest only, as the institution that we have been probing no longer exists. The truth is, however, that the Temple and Mount Zion retain a central role in the rabbinic tradition until this very day. How an institution destroyed two millennia ago can continue to live is the last issue for our consideration in the discussion of Zion as the mountain of the Temple.

We should note at the outset that Jewish tradition did not accept the finality of the destruction of the Temple and the absence of the redemption of which it was taken to be a symbol. On the contrary, the Jewish liturgy gives eloquent testimony to the longing for the reconstruction of the shrine and its city. The longing for the Temple was, as we have seen, a prominent theme in biblical times. It was only rendered more intense by the absence of the physical object of this passionate desire. Three times a day the practicing Jew voices his longing in these words:

> Find favor, O Lord our God, in your people Israel and in their prayer, and restore the Temple service to the innermost chamber of your House. May you accept Israel's burnt offerings and prayer with love and grace, and may the service of your people Israel be ever pleasing to you. May our eyes see your return to Zion in mercy. Blessed are you, O Lord, who restores your presence to Zion!

Throughout history, there have always been some Jews who wish to see not only God's presence, but also that of his people Israel restored to Zion even before the end of time. And thus it is appropriate that the movement for the restoration of Jewish sovereignty should have acquired the name *Zionism,* after the mountain tied so closely to the fortunes of the people Israel. However much Zionism may resemble a typical modern nationalism with the unfortunate consequences for outsiders that such movements entail, we should still not overlook Martin Buber's point that "this national concept was named after a place and not, like the others, after a people, which indicates that it is not so much a question of a particular people as such but of its association with a particular land, its native land."[134] For the modern Zionist the ancient association of the people of Israel and the land of Israel has been rejoined. This return to the land was possible because for the most part, the Jewish tradition did not spiritualize the concept of Zion/Jerusalem/the land of Israel to the extent that it ceased to have any reference to real history. On the contrary, however much the holy mountain, city, and land may have become the subject of liturgy and poetry and the object of spiritual yearning, they still retain their literal place. They have not been emasculated by typology, made into mere signs of some other reality, spiritual, psychological, or whatever. The earthly Jerusalem remains linked somehow to the heavenly Jerusalem. The latter has not been allowed to float off into the ether. In this instance, history and myth, the temporal and the timeless, remain in a vibrant conjunction.

Even in modern Israel, the Judaism practiced is not that of the Hebrew Bible, but the continuation of its rabbinic successor, which fashioned a tradition that could deal with a world without a Temple, Jewish sovereignty, or, increasingly, a homeland. In rabbinic religion, strangely enough, the Temple lives on, and not just as the object of longing. Prayer, for example, is seen as the replacement for the sacrifices. Or, to be more precise, prayer is seen as a form of sacrifice, the only form of it available in the present, unredeemed world. This association of prayer and sacrifice appears already in the Hebrew Bible:

> Let my prayer be counted as incense in your presence,
> My upraised hands as the evening sacrifice. (Ps 141:2)

A verse such as this should not be thought to disparage the spiritual value of sacrifice in any way. On the contrary, were sacrifice of no value, the author would hardly wish his prayer counted as sacrifice.[135] Instead, in the biblical period, sacrifice

---

134 M. Buber, *On Zion* (New York: Schocken, 1973) xvii.
135 On prayer as a form of sacrifice in Judaism, see Heschel, *Man's*

was a known and respected entity, in terms of which personal prayer could be justified. The historical tragedy is that the justification became complete only when sacrifice became impossible because of the Romans. The end of the Temple evoked a whole series of dislocations in Judaism. Just as prayer replaces sacrifice, so does the synagogue succeed the Temple, the rabbi inherits the authority of the priest, and the family's table replaces the altar.[136] "Rabbi Yochanan and Rabbi Eleazar both used to say," reads the Talmud, "'So long as the Temple stood, the altar made atonement for Israel. Now a man's table makes atonement for him.'"[137] In other words, the Jewish home acquires the centrality that had defined the Temple in Jerusalem. The daily and yearly rhythm of prayer and celebration at home becomes the focus of the old/new religion, the Temple religion without the Temple. Domesticity acquires cosmic significance, and profane life, life "outside the sanctuary," becomes the medium for the sanctifying presence of God.

This survival of Judaism after the destruction of its Temple and the loss of the land of Israel is the most remarkable feature of Jewish history. No people ever placed greater importance upon their land than did the Jews of ancient times, and yet no ancient people other than they has survived the loss of their land. The reason is that the land and the Temple, which are really one, always possessed a significance beyond what one sees if he examines only their mundane reality—in a word, a *cosmic* significance. Since the land was more than a territory, and since the Temple was more than a building, the loss of both did not mean death. The land was no longer available, but the covenant whose observance grounded Israel's tenure in it remained in force. The earthly Temple lay in ruins, but YHWH remained enthroned in some sense in its celestial archetype, which the initiate were still

Quest for God (New York: Scribner's, 1954) 70-72.

136 But see the biblical adumbration of this shift explored in Levenson, "From Temple to Synagogue: 1 Kings 8."

137 *b. Ber.* 55a.

able to approach through ecstatic experience.[138] It would be a mistake to regard these dislocations and transformations as a spiritualization of mundane realities recently terminated. Rather, land, Temple, and sovereignty were never strictly mundane in character. They had always been perceived mythically as well as historically, and it is this spiritualization of them while they yet stood which has enabled the Jews to survive, and even at times to thrive, despite dispersion to the ends of the earth.

The survival of the Temple in Jewish consciousness, not only as a promise for the future, but as a contemporary reality, appears most explicitly in a passage from Maimonides, the great legist and philosopher of the twelfth century C.E. Maimonides lists nine names that the Hebrew Bible gives for the future life which the rabbis termed the *world-to-come*.[139] The first among these names is "the mountain of the Lord," and the others are of a similar cast: "his sacred place," "the sacred way," "the courts of the Lord," "the beauty of the Lord," "the tent of the Lord," "the palace of the Lord," "the Temple of the Lord," and "the gate of the Lord."[140] Maimonides saw all this Temple terminology as parabolic language by which to convey some sense of the higher reality which the rabbis saw as the destiny of the righteous after the travails of this world. This identification of the Temple and the world-to-come was quite predictable, in fact inevitable. We have already seen that Mount Zion was identified in biblical times with the

138 The Temple tour of biblical times is an ancestor of the tour of the heavens prominent in apocalyptic literature and in kabbalistic mysticism. The pivotal text is Ezekiel 40–42, which is an inspection of the Temple effected by visionary transport (40:1–2). See Levenson, *Theology*, 7–24. Since the heavenly and the earthly Temple were in some sense one, the absence or contamination of the latter could only increase the importance of the former, especially to the priesthood, whose very identity was in jeopardy once the mundane antitype was no longer available.

139 On the notions of afterlife that do appear (despite common opinion) already in the Hebrew Bible, see L. J. Greenspoon, "The Origins of the Idea of the Resurrection of the Dead," in *Traditions in Transformation*, ed. Halpern and Levenson, 247–321.

140 Maimonides, *Mishneh Torah, Teshuvah*, 8:4.

primordial paradise known as the Garden of Eden. The rabbis termed the coming era the "Garden of Eden"; they saw protology as a prefigurement of eschatology, as did their biblical predecessors. Now, since both Mount Zion and the coming era were identified with the Garden of Eden, and since the reconstruction of the Temple on Zion was central to the vision of that future age, it was quite logical to see the names and epithets of the Temple as references to the era of bliss to follow the present. What is interesting is that Maimonides sees this Temple/world-to-come as a present reality and not simply a future state:

> That which the rabbis called "the world-to-come" was not called thus because it is not in existence now, and this world is perishing, and so the world-to-come will follow it. Rather, it is in existence now, as the Bible says, "which you have made," etc. They called it "the world-to-come" only because that type of life comes to a man after the life of this world, in which we exist in body and soul.[141]

Here, Maimonides interprets the Temple/world-to-come as having a spatial rather than an exclusively temporal relationship to this world. It is not that the world-to-come only follows the present world in time; both exist now. The question for the Jew then becomes what it was already in Psalms 15 and 24: How does one climb that mountain? What must one do to move from profane space to sacred space, from this world to the world-to-come? The question is a large one in rabbinic theology. It will be enlightening to examine two Talmudic passages, quoted in the Sabbath liturgy, which address it directly:

> "A psalm. A song for the Sabbath Day." It [Psalm 92] is a psalm and a song for the era to come, for the day which will be entirely Sabbath, for eternal life.[142]

In this Mishnah, the Sabbath is seen as a proleptic glimpse of the eternal life of the coming age. In other words, eternal life is not

---

141 Maimonides, *Mishneh Torah, Teshuvah,* 8:8. The biblical quote here is Ps 31:20.
142 *m. Tam.* 7:4.

simply ordinary life prolonged indefinitely, like the life of Tennyson's Tithonus, but differs from it qualitatively. And the quality of eternal life the Jew can experience even now in the form of the Sabbath. Those who observe the Sabbath experience an earnest of the coming redemption. They climb the cosmic mountain weekly. Again, the rabbinic thinking simply makes a logical connection among elements implicit and linked only impressionistically in the Hebrew Bible. If the Temple is both a protological and an eschatological reality, and if the creation of the world and the construction of the Temple are parallel events, then the completion of the eschatological Temple coincides with the eschatological Sabbath, of which the present Sabbath is a prefigurement. But it is not the only such foretaste of the world-to-come:

> Anyone who studies Jewish law (*hălākôt*) everyday is assured that he is a member of the world-to-come.[143]

This statement sees the *mitsvah* of the study of Torah as a way to move from the lower to the higher realms within the limitations of present human existence. Like the Sabbath, the study of Torah is a taste of the ideal life, the portal to the ideal world, which is somehow available, at least in part, now. The destruction of the Temple did not close the gates of heaven to those who walk the path of Sinai up to the world of which Zion is the symbol.

---

143 *b. Meg.* 28b.

3

The Manifold Relationships between Sinai and Zion

3

1. ZION AS THE HEIR TO SINAI

In Section 1 of Part 2, we saw that Mount Zion fell heir to the legacy of Mount Sinai. Zion became the prime locus of theophany, the home of YHWH, the seat of his government, from which he promulgated decrees and at which Israel renewed her partnership in covenant with him. The assumption by Zion of the themes of Sinai was so thoroughgoing that even the location of the latter came to be forgotten. Zion became *the* mountain of Israel. In light of this transfer of traditions, one might be tempted to characterize the relationship of the two mountains as one of chronological succession. The early traditions emphasize Sinai; the latter ones, those of David's time and after, emphasize Zion. Such a classification, however, is simplistic, for if Zion had absorbed the traditions of Sinai *in toto,* we should have a much less secure idea of the importance of the latter in the consciousness of ancient Israel than we do, in fact, have. For the truth is, a quick reading of the Hebrew Bible leaves one with a larger awareness of Sinai than Zion. The notion of a Mosaic revelation at Sinai endured. It shaped new literature, even hundreds of years after the historical Moses (if such there was) had died, literature such as Deuteronomy, which is cast as the last testament of the leader. In fact, tradition came to canonize the Mosaic moment, as it did not canonize the Davidic-Solomonic. "There has never arisen another prophet like Moses," we read at the end of Deuteronomy (34:10), "whom YHWH knew face to face." In other words, all prophecy after the great hero of Sinai is of a lower order,[1] and this presumably includes the oracle in which Nathan prophesies the

1 On this, see the stimulating study by J. Blenkinsopp, *Prophecy and Canon,* University of Notre Dame Center for the Study of Judaism and Christianity in Antiquity 3 (Notre Dame and London: University of Notre Dame, 1977), esp. pp. 80–95.

house of David and the house of YHWH, which David's son will build (2 Sam 7:8–16). God's continuing availability is at Zion, not Sinai, but the canonical division of the Pentateuch from the rest of the Hebrew Bible, adumbrated in Deut 34:10, insures that the heir will be eternally subordinate to the testator, Zion to Sinai, David to Moses. By limiting the concept of Torah proper to the Pentateuch, the canonical process speaks more directly to an Israel on the move, its promises of land and rest as yet unrealized, than to the Israel of the Zionistic traditions, which is "planted" in the land, secure, inviolable (e.g., 2 Sam 7:10).[2] The presence is the presence of Zion, but the voice is the voice of Sinai.

In sum, the relationship of the two great mountains of Israelite tradition is more complex than the transfer of traditions might suggest. The relationship is more than chronological.

2. SINAI AND ZION, NORTH AND SOUTH

In the scholarly literature, the chronological factor—based upon the observation that Zion absorbed Sinai traditions—has received little attention. The most prevalent account of the relationship speaks, instead, in geographical terms: Sinai survived in the north, Zion displaced it in the south.

In the generation of David's grandson Rehoboam, about the year 922 B.C.E., the kingdom dissolved into two states, a northern one termed "Israel" or "Ephraim" or "Joseph," and a southern one, "Judah." The taxonomy is confusing, for as we shall see, "Israel" survived even in Judah as a term for the entire people bifurcated politically by the events of 922. The kingdom of Israel survived until 722 B.C.E., when the neo-Assyrian Empire destroyed it. Judah survived as a monarchy until the neo-Babylonian capture of Jerusalem in about 587 B.C.E. Unlike the events of 722, those of 587 did not cause the victim to disappear from

2 See J. A. Sanders, *Torah and Canon* (Philadelphia: Fortress, 1972), esp. pp. 47–48.

history. On the contrary, the Judean community retained a distinctive identity, both in the land of Israel and in the various lands of its dispersion. Ultimately, outsiders came to refer to all Israelites as Judeans, or "Jews."

One of the most enduring positions in biblical scholarship in our century has been one that sees in the dichotomy of Israel and Judah a theological, and not simply a geographical or political categorization. Many scholars have, on linguistic and other grounds, attributed a northern origin to Deuteronomy.[3] This, in turn, suggests that the Sinaitic covenant traditions so prominent in that book retained their vitality in the north, rather than in the community centered in Jerusalem. The continued activity of old northern shrines, with roots in the periods of the Patriarchs (Genesis 12-50) or the Conquest (Joshua), is often cited as the locus in which the Sinaitic traditions remained alive. For example, in Amos 5:4-6, the prophet of the eighth century B.C.E. who preached in the north (Israel, Joseph), testifies indirectly to continued activity at the ancient cultic centers of Bethel and Gilgal. The assumption of most modern scholarship is that these shrines functioned as alternative repositories for traditions suppressed or ignored in the great southern shrine at Jerusalem, in which the Zion traditions found their home.

The attitudes towards monarchy are also widely held to reflect the geographical dichotomy. In Judah, one dynasty, the house of David, reigned from about 1000 B.C.E. all the way until the destruction of the state in 587 B.C.E. In Israel, by contrast, we find a succession of individual kings of various ancestries usually designated by a prophetic oracle. The longest dynasty lasted for only four generations and a little less than a century. This is taken to indicate a resistance in the north to the sort of royal theology that underlay the longevity of the house of David in the south. The north was allegedly more conservative. It held fast to the

3   On this and the general question of a northern theology, see the bibliography in E. W. Nicholson, *Deuteronomy and Tradition* (Oxford: Blackwell, 1967) 58 n. 1.

older traditions, which the Davidic theology had displaced in Judah. We see an instance of this unmonarchical or antimonarchical thinking in the Law of the King in Deuteronomy 17:14–20. This is a passage that does, indeed, accept kingship, even dynastic kingship of a sort (v 20). But it sees the institution as foreign to Israel's true nature; it is something that Israel, not God, initiates, an imitation of the Gentiles (v 14). In fact, the Law of the King places limits upon the royal office which no king worthy of the name could ever embrace. He may have only a few horses (v 16), in other words, a small cavalry, and his ability to seal alliances through marriage is impeded by the prohibition upon his having many wives. The prohibition upon his acquiring vast amounts of gold and silver (v 17) limits his ability to centralize wealth in his own hands. Finally, only one positive action is prescribed for him, the copying of the Deuteronomic law at the dictation of, or at least in the presence of the priesthood. He is subordinate to them (v 18). His kingship seems to be conditional upon his observance of the stipulations of covenant (vv 19–20). All of this is very distant from the grandeur of the reign of the house of David, eternally enthroned with God upon Mount Zion, their kingship, like his, rooted in cosmic symbolism. With kingship as it was known in the north, transient and subject to prophetic designation, however, the Deuteronomic Law of the King seems much more compatible. In fact, the only anthology of oracles stemming from a native northern prophet, the book of Hosea, offers a comparably negative view of kingship.[4] Therefore, the majority of scholars attributes a northern origin not only to Deuteronomy, but also to the theology of monarchy it exemplifies. Since that theology derives from the Sinaitic covenant, which was often held to be incompatible with human kingship, these scholars view the continuing Sinai traditions as localized in the kingdom of Israel, just as the Zion traditions and the Davidic covenant were localized in Judah.

4 Hos 5:1; 8:10; 10:3–4; 13:10–11.

Although it is the priests, in Deuteronomy indistinguishable from the Levites, who are the custodians of the instruction (Torah) that binds the king (v 18), his designation comes presumably through a prophet. In fact, Deuteronomy affirms the continuation of Mosaic authority through the prophetic office. If Deut 17:20 shows awareness of a continuing monarchy, Deut 18:15-19, especially v 18, offers a counterpoint in which Mosaic authority also continues. The voice of Sinai will be heard in the land, the mountain itself having lost significance. If Zion has come into the legacy of Sinai, David must still put up with the executors of Moses' will, the prophets. But was the continuing Mosaic office a reality in Judah? Those scholars who speak of a northern theology doubt it. They tend to note that between the court prophets of David's reign and the rise of classical prophecy late in the eighth century, there lies a gap of over two hundred years, in which the south seems to have been bereft of the prophetic word. In the north, by contrast, we see the survival of prophecy in a way that would have made the author of Deut 18:15-19 proud. Not only was there the tradition of the prophetic designation of kings, but also the memorable careers of Elijah and Elisha, which extended throughout the second half of the ninth century (1 Kings 17-2 Kings 13). Those careers were marked by a passion for Israel's ancient covenant law and an almost reactionary resistance to the new social and political order, which the prophets deemed unjust (e.g., 1 Kings 21). The connection with the Sinaitic experience is explicit in 1 Kings 19 in which Elijah attempts to duplicate the master's experience at Horeb/Sinai. The brunt of the social criticism of Elijah and Elisha fell upon the kings. In fact, it was these two prophets who brought down Israel's longest dynasty (v 16). This perception of the prophets as the bearers of the Mosaic commission, or, to put it differently, of the Sinaitic covenant-mediator as a prophet, appears nowhere more clearly than in the book of another northern prophet, Hosea:

> It was through a prophet that YHWH brought Israel up from Egypt,
> And through a prophet they were preserved. (Hos 12:14)

In summary, the traditions of Sinai, whose classic statement is the book of Deuteronomy, can be seen to reflect the experience of the north. Of course, a passion for social justice animates the classical prophets of Judah as well, when they emerge a century later. But here the scholars tend to note that Isaiah and Micah, however much they may predict catastrophe for the sins of Judah, still hold out a hope for restoration afterwards to which the Davidic material is central.[5] Their Sinai is limited by Zion. Only in the north did the Sinaitic covenant traditions endure without such limitation.

What shall we make of this effort of scholars to see the Sinai traditions as northern, and the Zion as southern? It is my contention that the nuances the scholars detect are real, but that they cannot be so easily linked to the political bifurcation of the nation. Their basis is not geography. Let us begin with the effort to see the northern sanctuaries as the bearers of an ongoing Sinaitic tradition at variance with the traditions of the royal shrine of Jerusalem. Amos 5:4–5 does indeed testify to the survival of activity at the ancient sanctuaries at Bethel and Gilgal, but the prophet denounces this activity and pronounces the doom of YHWH upon it. Hosea, too, attacks the ancient shrines with caustic invective, including these two.[6] How likely is it, then, that these shrines served to perpetuate prophetic authority and the Mosaic/Sinaitic traditions upon which it is based in at least some of the literature? One could rejoin that when the shrines became corrupt, the prophets assumed a critical posture towards them. But this could just as easily have happened in Judah. There is no prophet who regarded Jerusalem as *more* depraved than Amos and Hosea regarded Bethel and Gilgal. Furthermore, Amos 5:5 mentions Beer-sheba, a holy city to the *south* of Jerusalem, in the same breath with these two cult centers. This indicates the survival in Judah of cultic activity apart from that at the royal

5   E.g., Alt, "Die Heimat des Deuteronomiums," in *Kleine Schriften* (Munich: Beck'sche, 1953) 2:167.

6   E.g., Hos 8:11–14; 9:15; 10:5.

Temple. In other words, one cannot assume, as many scholars tend to do, that a non-Jerusalemite or anti-Jerusalemite *Tendenz* suggests a northern origin. The fact is that there existed a plurality of shrines in the south throughout the Davidic monarchy.[7] The Deuteronomic program of centralization (Deuteronomy 12) was late and it failed. There is no basis for the assumption that alienation from the royal theology celebrated upon Mount Zion was peculiarly northern.[8]

The same point can be made about the putative northern view of kingship. I grant that Deut 17:14–20 shows a skepticism about monarchy that one does not detect in the royal psalms. But are we to believe that such skepticism was never found among those closer to the Davidic court, but only among those far from it? If David faced rebellion, even from his own son (2 Samuel 13–20), are we to believe that no southern circles continued to harbor doubts about the divine right of the dynasty? If so, then the kings of his line benefitted from a measure of consensus unparalleled in any known society. Surely, if there are Soviets who criticize communism, Israelis who criticize Zionism, and Roman Catholics who criticize church dogma, then it is naive to imagine that the Davidic court managed to hoodwink *all* sectors of its populace into unquestioning acceptance of its theology for hundreds of years. That intense critique of the kings was not abhorrent to all southerners is apparent from the very fact that we have literature like Deuteronomy and Hosea at all, for all the northern literature comes to us through Judean hands. Some of those hands did indeed redact the northern material in accordance with their

7 See R. Brinker, *The Influence of Sanctuaries in Early Israel* (Manchester: Manchester University, 1946), esp. pp. 136–78; Y. Aharoni, "Arad: Its Inscriptions and Temple," *BA* 31 (1968) 18–32; and "The Horned Altar of Beer-sheba," *BA* 37 (1974) 2–6.

8 It is interesting to note a counterstatement to those who see a northern origin for Deuteronomy and its theology in the works of Aage Bentzen and Gerhard von Rad. See A. Bentzen, *Die Josianische Reform* (Copenhagen: Haase, 1926); and von Rad, *Studies in Deuteronomy*, SBT 9 (London: SCM, 1953). Both tend to speak of country Levites as the source of Deuteronomy.

southern orientation (e.g., Hos 3:5). But the fact that they accepted that antimonarchical literature as scripture and were able to juxtapose their Davidic theology to it without feeling an intolerable degree of contradiction shows that the two positions were not so distant as they may seem to us.

Now, if the supposedly northern theology met approval among some circles in the south, why do we call it northern at all? Again, there is a rejoinder. It might be argued that the northern traditions migrated southward only after the destruction of the kingdom of Israel (722 B.C.E.),[9] an event that terrified Judeans into rethinking their view of the monarchy and of prophecy. But there are two salient problems with this rejoinder. First, passages like Hos 3:5, with their pro-Davidic affinity amidst an antimonarchical book, suggest that the Judean redactors of northern traditions were not so terrified and did not so rethink their theology. Instead, they joined two positions whose contradiction may appear greater to us than to them. One cannot assume that the "northern" materials were accepted only because of sudden loss of faith on the part of Judeans in their native traditions. We shall soon see that even in demonstrably southern literature, the Mosaic/Sinaitic and the Davidic/Zionistic orientations could coexist peacefully. Not that they always did, but that they could. The second problem with the idea that southern acceptance of northern traditions came only late and after a jolt to the Davidic theology is the simple fact that there is plentiful evidence for the survival of that theology throughout the period between 722 and 587 B.C.E., when Judah fell, and even after.[10] In fact, the Davidic theology is the origin of Jewish messianism and the christology of the church. Our conclusion must be that despite the royal cultus, or better, alongside the royal cultus, the material that the scholarly consensus sees as northern existed in Judah. There is no reason to believe that this entailed a late and radical change.

9 See Nicholson, *Deuteronomy*, 94.

10 See Cross, *Canaanite Myth and Hebrew Epic* (Cambridge: Harvard University, 1973) 241–85.

I have argued above that there is no basis to think that a theology ostensibly at variance with that of the royal cultus of Jerusalem could not have existed in Judah. But can we go farther and find evidence that the traditions of Sinai, as known to us from sources generally considered northern, flourished in the south? In this connection, a study by Walter Beyerlin is most enlightening. Beyerlin sought to show that the main influence upon the oracles of the eighth century Judean prophet Micah was the cultic tradition of Sinai. In this connection, Mic 6:1-8, a prophetic lawsuit by YHWH against Israel for breach of the Sinaitic covenant, is most revealing. Beyerlin observed that this oracle closely resembles a number of passages which recount the theophany at Sinai.[11] Here, as there, YHWH marches forth from his abode and descends upon the earth (vv 3-4). Moreover, as in the case of Psalm 81, the Mican oracle presents a lawsuit against Israel, one in which her sin is that of idolatry (vv 2, 7), abandoning her lord in covenant to chase promiscuously after his rivals. In short, just as the Mican theophany recalls that of Sinai, so does the sin remind us of the moral dynamics of the covenant believed to have been sealed there. One can, of course, argue that these traditions are not distinctively Sinaitic at all. The theophany resembles that of Psalm 97 very closely, a psalm that is explicitly one of Zion (v 8), and the Sinaitic resonance of the accusation is also at home in the Temple at Jerusalem, which, I argued, has inherited the legacy of Sinai anyway. The retort is accurate, but it concedes a point essential to the scholarly consensus here under attack, the point that a firm line between the traditions of Sinai and those of Zion cannot be drawn, so that a geographical separation is not only unnecessary, but artificial. If Micah's Sinai came to him through the medium of Zion, its authenticity has been in no measure compromised by the process. And if Sinai

11 W. Beyerlin, *Die Kulttraditionen Israels in der Verkündigung des Propheten Micah*, FRLANT 62 (Göttingen: Vandenhoeck and Ruprecht, 1959) 35. He compares passages such as Psalms 97; 18; 63; and Exod 19:18.

continued to speak in Judah through Zion, then Zion has not eradicated or supplanted Sinai.

Another point Beyerlin studied was the use of the name "Israel" in oracles that date to Micah himself. It will be recalled that this name designates both the ancient twelve tribe league and the later kingdom established in the north after the schism. The great covenant/law texts of the Pentateuch employ the term only in the former sense, even though they date, for the most part, from a period long after the primal unity of the nation had perished. By the concept of a Mosaic speaking voice, the Deuteronomic and Priestly authors sought to restore the ancient situation and, conversely, to downplay the significance of the division into two kingdoms. Of course, the royal theology of Jerusalem moves in the opposite direction: it attributes cosmic significance to the founding of Jerusalem and of the house of David. It is Zion and Judah who have the most cause to rejoice in YHWH, they for whose benefit his judgments are rendered (Ps 97:8). Thus, the Judean royal theology shares with the Pentateuchal traditions of Sinai a distaste for the schism—but for a radically different reason: David alone bears the promise. One would expect a book imbued with the southern perspective, such as Micah, to reflect this notion that Judah is the heir of a promise of cosmic scope which he does not share with the tribes of the north, his rebellious brothers (Ps 78:67–68). It is interesting, therefore, that Beyerlin found that in Micah's preaching, Israel refers only to the ancient tribal confederation.[12] In fact, Mic 1:5 propounds the analogy by which Jerusalem is to Judah as the northern capital Samaria is to Israel/Jacob. Just as Samaria shall be turned into "a heap of ruins" (v 6), so shall Jerusalem. Just as the northern capital shall be made into "ground for planting vines," so shall the Temple mount be made into "a shrine in the woods" (3:12).[13] It was this prediction of doom for Jerusalem for which Micah was still remembered a century later, when Jeremiah proclaimed a similar

12 Beyerlin, *Kulttraditionen*, 11–28.
13 In Mic 3:12, it is probably best to read *lĕbāmat* with LXX.

message (Jer 26:18). There is thus nothing distinctively northern about the belief that all the tribes stand equally under the judgment of God.

The stipulations of the Sinaitic covenant, Beyerlin found, underlie Micah's social criticism. In fact, specific laws can be heard beneath the prophet's poetry. Consider, for example, his accusation of the rulers in light of the laws of the Book of the Covenant. Micah's passionate indictment of them for bribery (3:9–12) seems to echo closely the covenant stipulation of Exod 23:6–8. In each case, we see the notion of the perversion of justice at the hands of a leadership that accepts bribes. It is interesting that it is this violation of old covenant law which Micah sees as the mechanism for building Zion/Jerusalem (Mic 3:10) and, in turn, the cause of their downfall (v 12). A similar concern for the rights of the simple country folk can be seen elsewhere in his oracles, for example in 2:1–2, a denunciation of land-fraud that recalls Lev 19:13 and Deut 27:17. We have already seen in Micah's first oracle (1:2–7) an attack upon idolatry and a connection of it with harlotry, whose Sinaitic resonance is unmistakable. In other passages of his as well, covenant law can be detected, as in his polemic against sorcery (5:11), which recalls a law in the Book of the Covenant (Exod 22:17), and his unmitigated opposition to cultic imagery (Mic 5:12–13), which recalls the Decalogic prohibition upon iconography (Exod 20:4–5) and other injunctions of a similar cast (e.g., Deut 27:15). Beyerlin adduces many other examples.[14] Cumulatively, what they show is that the traditions of Sinai, specifically of the Mosaic covenant, survived in their full vitality in Judah. They were not banished into the kingdom of Israel or displaced by the Zion/David traditions.

But is Micah's Sinaitic material at least limited by a commitment to Davidic theology, as those who dichotomize north and south are inclined to believe? After all, we do find in the book of Micah a moving messianic prophecy (Mic 5:1–5), which sees, in

14 Beyerlin, *Kulttraditionen*, 55–62. Note also the Sinaitic connotations he attributes to the verb *higgîd* (Mic 6:8) in Micah's *rîb* (p. 51).

Bethlehem, David's ancestral city, the emergence of the deliverer of Israel from Assyria. Scholars are divided as to the composition and authorship of this oracle. The book of Micah has undergone a complicated process of redaction extending at least into the Babylonian Exile (sixth century B.C.E.). The hand of an exilic author can be seen without ambiguity, for example, in the passage that follows the messianic oracle, in which we hear of the life of the Israelite remnant in its dispersion (5:6-8). V 2b, here the allusion to the return of the lost remnant, may be a similar exilic interpolation into an older oracle, or it may be original to the oracle, which is therefore entirely exilic. There is no need to enter into the complicated technical argument involving the date of Mic 5:1-5.[15] I regard its core as original to the poetry of the eighth century Judean prophet for two reasons. First, the emphasis upon Bethlehem rather than Jerusalem as the ancestral city of the coming ruler, a point not made elsewhere in the Hebrew Bible, would seem to imply the continued vitality of the relations among clans in Judah, and it fits nicely with the designation of Micah as a Judean from rural Moreshet, not from the capital Jerusalem.[16] The second reason for seeing a Mican kernel to the messianic oracle is the anxiety it shows about the possibility of an Assyrian invasion (Mic 5:4a-5b). This fits quite nicely with the situation in Judah in the decades after Assyria had eliminated her neighbor to the north in ca. 722 B.C.E. In that case, the survivors who return in v 2b would be a remnant of the kingdom of Israel. If we date the oracle much later, as in the exilic period, when Assyria had

---

15 I accept Beyerlin's argument that vv 4b-5a are a later interpolation, which is inconsistent with the prediction of the one coming king (*Kulttraditionen*, p. 79). In fact, the last two cola of v 5b are an attempt to resume v 4a after the intrusion. On the whole problem, see O. Eissfeldt, *The Old Testament: An Introduction* (New York and Evanston: Harper and Row, 1965) 410-11.

16 Mic 1:1 and Jer 26:18. See K. Elliger, "Die Heimat des Propheten Micha," in *Kleine Schriften*, Theologische Bücherei 32 (Munich: Kaiser, 1966) 9-71.

already fallen, then we must see the references to that empire as formulaic or symbolic. This seems much less likely.

If we follow the school of thought that dates the messianic oracle of Mic 5:1–5 after the prophet's time, then we can say conclusively that Micah's Sinaitic commitments were in no way compromised by an allegiance to Davidic theology. In that case, Micah would exhibit only those (Sinaitic) traditions character- istic of the north, which, since they appear in a southern prophet unalloyed, could then no longer be termed northern. Hence, the north-south dichotomy would fall. If, as I am inclined to do, we attribute the messianic oracle to the prophet in whose book it is placed, then the situation is more complicated. The least we could say, in that event, is that the Sinaitic and the Davidic (if not Zionisitic) theologies can coexist. The Davidic surely did not displace the Sinaitic in Micah, where the latter is still dominant, as Beyerlin emphasizes.[17] But was the Sinaitic heard differently because of the presence of a Davidic oracle of deliverance? There is, to be sure, a logical contradiction between the prediction that "Zion shall be plowed as a field/And Jerusalem shall become a heap of ruins" (3:12) and the assurance that a Davidic ruler "will deliver us from Assyria/If it invades our country." (5:5b). But we have no evidence that Micah's audience recognized the logical contradiction and therefore relied upon his Davidic promise for insurance against his Sinaitic threat of destruction. In other words, there is no empirical basis upon which to assert that the Davidic theology blunted the impact of Micah's covenantal preaching. In fact, it may be the case that each of the two streams of tradition came to the fore alone, in a different period of the prophet's career. One should note that Assyrian aggression against Judah in the late eighth century came in more than one wave.[18] V 2a, which seems to allude to suffering in Israel that ends only with the messianic birth, may well indicate that the

17 Beyerlin, *Kulttraditionen*, 87.
18 See Bright, *A History of Israel*, 3rd ed. (Philadelphia: Westminster, 1981) 269–88, 298–309.

Davidic prophecy followed the humiliation of Zion predicted earlier, as in 3:12. In that case, the Messianic oracle would offer hope for Israel *after* the curses of covenant have been actualized. Promise does not avert punishment, but follows it, offering new hope, a second chance. We must conclude that, whatever we may think the logical implications of Micah's Davidic promise to be, neither he nor his audience seems to have felt them to be a hedge upon his Sinaitic preaching. On the contrary, the portrayal of the messianic figure as a humble shepherd from Bethlehem, rather than as a king from Jerusalem, who is to "govern" Israel rather than to reign over her, may represent a Sinaitic tempering of the Davidic theology. Such moderation may have been characteristic of the religion of the Judean countryside, which was Micah's home and context. If so, then the operative contrast is *social* rather than geographical. It pits city against countryside, rather than Judah (south) against Israel (north).

One of the major differences between Israel and Judah, according to the regnant theory, is that kingship in the former was dependent upon prophetic designation, whereas, in the latter, the principle of dynastic succession prevailed. Hence, the rapid turnover of monarchs in the north and the longevity of the house of David in the south. Once again, we must ask whether the difference appeared as great to ancient Israelites as it does to modern western scholars. For David was also designated by a prophet; that is the burden of the oracles in 2 Samuel 7 and Psalm 89. The difference is that those oracles implicate David's descendents no less than he. But is that much of a difference? In ancient Israelite thinking, a man's household was an extension of himself, if not in the legal system, then in the eyes of God. Thus, Joshua, speaking in the name of YHWH, orders that the entire household of Achan, including his sons and daughters, be stoned for the sin of Achan alone (Josh 7:24–25). The man and his descendents are not differentiated.[19] Similarly, a prophet in the Exile can predict

19 It is this old idea of family guilt, which appears in the Decalogue itself (Exod 20:5), that calls forth the protest of Ezekiel 18. See the discussion of

the return of David (Ezek 34:23), about four centuries after the king's death. Is it David himself or simply a Davidid, a member of his household or dynasty, whose advent is envisioned here? The question is probably meaningless. The prophet's mind does not make the distinction. And so, it is most likely the case that the dynastic oracles in 2 Samuel 7, Psalm 89, and elsewhere do not break with tradition so radically as we initially think. They simply make explicit the applicability to the sons of the election of the father. There is, furthermore, strong evidence that each Davidic king saw himself exactly this way, as the person elected when David was. For example, perhaps the most extravagant of all royal psalms puts these words in the mouth of the monarch:

> ⁶Of me, he says, "I have installed my king,
> On Zion, my sacred mountain."
> ⁷Let me recite YHWH's decree:
> "You are my son," he said to me,
> "This day I have become your father." (Ps 2:6–7)

Although Psalm 2, unlike most of the poems in the first two books of the Psalter, is not ascribed to David, the king refers to Nathan's words to David[20] as if they were spoken to *him*. It is not only David who is adopted into divine sonship, but each Davidic king to follow. In other words, the prophetic designation of David was reenacted in every generation. No southern king lacked the putatively northern trait of selection by YHWH. Of course, it is only the firstborn son of the reigning Davidid who will be eligible for prophetic designation. In this sense, the dynastic theology is indeed different from the kind of prophetic designation in which the spirit falls where it listeth. Some ancient Israelites may have taken offense at the dynastic limitation upon the freedom of the spirit. But we have no evidence that they did. One cannot assume that criticism of the house of David implies rejection of its claim to

this aspect of Hebrew psychology in Johnson, *The One and the Many in the Israelite Conception of God,* 2nd ed. (Cardiff: University of Wales, 1961).

20 2 Sam 7:14; Ps 89:27.

divine election. The book of Micah savages the kings and predicts the fall of Zion.

Those who wish to portray whatever difference there is between kingship by prophetic designation and kingship by dynastic succession in the terms of a north-south dichotomy pay insufficient attention to the fact that one dynasty reigned in the kingdom of Israel for half of the life of the state. The house of Jehu held the throne for five generations, for a period of about one hundred years, from the middle of the ninth century B.C.E. to the middle of the eighth. Thus, its reign endured more years than the combined total of the houses of Lancaster and of York in England. We are fortunate that a passage has survived in which we see the reaction of a northern official to a prophetic oracle predicting that God will turn upon this dynasty with a sword. In Amos 7:10–17, the priest of a northern state-sanctuary, Amaziah, expels Amos for having predicted the death of the king and the exile of the northern kingdom. If only Amos were a northerner, and Amaziah a Judean, this encounter would be a great boon to the attempt to categorize theological differences according to the political split. In that event, Amos would stand for the northern tradition of prophetic authority, before which even kings must yield, while Amaziah would represent the southern royal theology which does not tolerate prophetic critique and which places temple and dynasty outside the jurisdiction of the covenant curse.

The problem is that the roles are the opposite. Amos is from Tekoa, in the Judean wilderness (1:1), and Amaziah is the priest of the northern shrine at Bethel (7:10). It is the southerner who asserts prophetic authority, and the northerner who resists in the name of the royal temple and the royal palace. Amos' attitude toward Jeroboam II, last major monarch from the line of Jehu, can perhaps be explained as a corollary of the Judean belief in the election of the house of David: it is not dynasty in general that Judah endorsed, but only her own. Jeroboam, and in fact the entire northern kingdom, would then be usurpers and schismatics in rebellion against the promise of David. The position Amaziah enunciates, however, is more problematic. If we retain the north-south dichotomy, we are obliged to say that some northerners fell away from the pure Sinaitic traditions of the old league in favor of a high royalism foreign to those traditions. Such is apparently the case. But if we concede that a royal theology can be found in the north, then we have, in fact, conceded that the differences in the understanding of kingship are to be explained sociologically, not geographically. The likelihood is that royal officers, whether in Jerusalem or Bethel, found it beneficial to espouse the palace position. The alternative theology, more conservative and more critical of the palace, held sway in the provinces, from which Micah, for example, originated. In short, the distinctions are real, but their basis lies in institutional history, not in political geography. The difference between city and countryside and between royal priest and independent prophet applied in both kingdoms.

The element of royal theology in Amaziah's words suggests that the house of Jehu, like that of David, may have based its entitlement to the throne upon a dynastic oracle like that of Nathan in 2 Sam 7:8–16. In fact, we have such an oracle in some form in Kings:

> YHWH said to Jehu: Because you have acted well and done what is right in my eyes and carried out everything that I desired against the House of Ahab, four generations of your descendants shall sit upon the throne of Israel. (2 Kgs 10:30)

This verse insures that, for the next four generations, God will designate the Jehuidic monarchs exactly as he designates their Davidic neighbors, through the ancestor rather than through the

21 See Ahlström, "Solomon, the Chosen One," *HR* 8 (1968) 93–100, esp. pp. 95–97; and T. G. G. Thornton, "Charismatic Kingship in Israel and Judah," *JTS* 14 (1963) 1–11. Note also that Psalm 80, a northern poem (v 3), exhibits royal adoption language (vv 16, 18).

The curious tendency of scholars to invert the canonical judgment by treating Israel as normative and Judah as deviant owes much to an unreflective identification of Israel with Protestantism, and Judah, with its inviolable monarchy, centralized authority, and high liturgy, with Roman

individual as a *novus homo*.[21] The only difference between this anonymous word of God and the oracle of 2 Samuel 7 and Psalm 89 is the term of the dynastic appointment. David's is eternal; Jehu's is to last four more generations. This limitation, however, is a rather awkward *vaticinium ex eventu,* a "prophesy after the event." As 2 Kgs 10:30 would have it, God is so pleased with Jehu's eradication of the house of Ahab (the Omrides) that he promises him a dynasty, but so displeased with it that he limits the dynasty to a total of five generations. The oracle obviously shows awareness of the end of the Jehuids at the assassination of Zechariah, son of Jeroboam II (2 Kgs 15:8–12), four generations after this speech of God is supposed to have been heard. The nature of the promise suggests that originally it was not limited in time. Jehu was rewarded for cleaning out the syncretistic house of Ahab. It is his zeal for YHWH that earns him a dynasty. This theme of the grant of a dynasty, or at least of continued existence of the clan, as a reward for loyalty to YHWH appears in several other cases in the Bible, for example, those of Noah, Abraham, Caleb,[22] and, most importantly, Phinehas the priest, whose zeal in killing Baalistic idolators wins him "an eternal covenant of priesthood" in Num 25:10–12. The mention of an eternal covenant recalls the promise to David. In fact, the promise to Phinehas is a fine example of the same type of covenant that guaranteed the throne to the house of David, the covenant of grant. As Moshe Weinfeld, who pioneered research in this area, puts it:

> As in other grants so also here the grant is given for showing one's zeal and devotion for his master; and like the other grants so also the gift of priesthood is given in perpetuity.[23]

Catholicism.

22   Gen 6:9; 9:1–17; 17:1–14 (see also 26:5); Num 14:24. On the origins and nature of these dynastic promises, see J. D. Levenson, "On the Promise to the Rechabites," *CBQ* 38 (1976) 508–14.

23   Weinfeld, "The Covenant of Grant in the Old Testament and in the Ancient Near East," *JAOS* 90 (1970) 201.

Now the zeal of Jehu was no less than that of Phinehas. It was he who "eradicated the Baal from Israel" (2 Kgs 10:28). The likelihood is that he, too, was rewarded by an eternal covenant, in this case, a royal dynastic covenant of the same order as the grant to David. Hence, the anger of Amaziah at Amos' prediction that Jeroboam would die a violent death and, more importantly, that Israel would go into exile, the royal grant of the house of Jehu thus terminated (Amos 7:10–11). When the prophecy of doom came true, it became convenient to modify the eternal covenant so as to reflect the fact that Jehu's dynasty lasted four generations, and it is just such an adjustment that we see in the *vaticinium ex eventu* of 2 Kgs 10:30.[24] In any event, a southern redactor would have found an eternal grant to a non-Davidic dynasty an embarrassment to his own royal theology. It is also possible, then, that the Judean redaction of this northern history accounts for the peculiar limitation in that verse. After all, it is odd that the passage as it stands mentions that Jehu "eradicated the Baal" (v 28), but also maintained the golden calves that, in the Judean mind, constituted the arch-sin of the kingdom of Israel (v 29). It is most probable that Jehu was granted his dynasty for his zealous YHWHistic purism, so that either the calves were not seen as inconsistent with this,[25] or he did not patronize them at all. At all events, if I am right that the original form of the dynastic oracle to Jehu did not entail a temporal limitation, then the notion that the underlying shape of the Davidic theology is unique to Judah has been disproven. Just as the Sinaitic material, with its lack of a

24 That an "eternal covenant" could come to be reinterpreted as limited in duration in the light of new historical events is clear from 1 Sam 2:27–36, in which the eternal priesthood (v 30) of Eli is transferred to the "faithful priest" (v 35) to come, most likely Zadok. See Levenson, *Theology of the Program of Restoration of Ezekiel* 40–48, HSM 10 (Missoula: Scholars, 1976) 147. The covenant with David was not immune to this sort of change either. In the Exile, after the house has fallen, Second Isaiah applies messianic language to the Median liberator Cyrus (e.g., Isa 45:1) and transfers the Davidic covenant graces to all Israel (55:3).

25 See Cross, *Canaanite Myth*, 73–75.

theology of dynastic kingship, was no more northern than southern, so was the dynastic promise, although better attested in the south, in no way alien to the north.

3. COVENANT RENEWAL
ON THE COSMIC MOUNTAIN

In the previous section, we have seen that both the Sinaitic/
Mosaic and the Zionistic/Davidic complexes of tradition retained
their vitality in Judah, although only the former seems to have
thrived in the kingdom of Israel. It is not impossible, of course,
that there were Davidic loyalists in the north even after the
schism, but we have no convincing evidence for their existence. In
any event, the lack of importance of the traditions of Zion and
David in Israel cannot be cited as an indication of the submer-
gence of the Sinaitic material in Judah. The two complexes were
quite capable of coexistence without tension. The florescence of
one need not imply the diminishment of the other.

If, in fact, Zion inherited the legacy of Sinai, then even the term
"coexistence" is too weak to describe aspects of this relationship.
To be sure, some elements of the developing Zion traditions, such
as the centrality of the dynasty to the divine economy, can be said
to have "coexisted" with the old covenant traditions which lacked
this royalist feature. Other aspects of Zion, however, were nothing more than the continuation of the Sinaitic experience on a
new mountain. For example, in Part 1, we saw that one feature of
the traditions of Sinai was the renewal of covenant, which often
included an indictment of the people for breach of covenant. It
was this feature which we saw as underlying Psalm 81.[26] Another
psalm, Psalm 50, locates the same idea on Mount Zion. Like Mic
6:1–8, this psalm is a rîb, a divine lawsuit against Israel for breach
of covenant. In it, God invokes the olden gods, heaven and earth,
as witnesses to the trial of his people for violation of the pact

26 P. 80.

whose consummation these two have witnessed (Ps 50:4, 6). The defendant is explicitly characterized as "those who make a covenant with me," God's "loyal servants" (v 5). The charge against them is that they are hypocritical in their liturgies of covenant renewal (v 16), since they ignore the commandments between man and his neighbor and apply themselves only to the sacrificial cultus. But given the universal scope of God's domain (vv 10–12), the sacrifices his partners in covenant offer him must not be interpreted as having a material effect—as if he needed the food and the drink (v 13)—but rather as the medium to communicate gratitude to him (vv 14, 23). So far the poem sounds only the notes of Sinaitic covenant: law, loyalty, witnesses, sacrifice. Vv 1–3, however, make it clear that this drama took place in the Temple upon Mount Zion, which is described in its classic cosmic terms. God summons not only Israel (v 5), but the entire world (v 1) to the proceedings; he shines forth from his cosmic capital, "Zion, perfect in beauty" (v 2). In short, the renewal of the Sinaitic covenant has become a liturgy of the Temple of Jerusalem. It is not that the two traditions simply occupy the same building. Rather, that shrine does not have a cult of its own, but has become a locus for the continuing traditions of the old Israelite tribal league. The voice of Sinai is heard on Zion. The critique of cult, which we found to be characteristic of the cult in Israel, here assumes the shape of a *rîb*. Thus, there is nothing peculiarly prophetic about Jeremiah's attack on the misuse of the Temple (Jer 7:1–15). On the contrary, the insight that the cultus might be misused was known to its practitioners. The Temple liturgy itself kept that insight alive.

It would not be correct to regard this translation of Sinaitic traditions to Zion as an indication that the earlier material survived the development of the Temple mythos without alteration. Instead, the Zion traditions in Psalm 50 have changed the resonance of the covenant *rîb* in a subtle but remarkable way. Their presence enhances the universalistic dimension of the covenant and tempers its inherent particularism. God summons not only Israel, his ally, and heaven and earth, the witnesses to their pact, but also the entire world, "from the rising to the setting sun" (v 1). The cosmos turns its attention to Zion, its most perfect spot. The Zion material in vv 1-3 thus serves to highlight the cosmic implications of Sinai. All the world is asked to witness the old theophany, with its fire and storm (v 3), its significance no longer a matter of only Israelite interest. To be sure, the notion that the whole world is YHWH's possession is not unique to the Temple traditions. "Now, then, if you will obey me faithfully and keep my covenant, you shall be my treasured possession among all peoples," reads a classic Sinaitic text, "for all the world is mine" (Exod 19:5). But Psalm 50 goes further, focusing the attention of "all the world" upon Israel and her covenant. This universalistic focus, then, sets the stage for the critique of the misinterpretation of the sacrifical cultus, for if "every animal in the forest is [God's]," if he "know[s] every bird of the mountains" and cares for "everything that moves in the fields" (vv 10-11), then how absurd must be the idea that Israel's sacrifices assuage his hunger and slake his thirst. In Psalm 50, in other words, the functions of the Sinaitic and the Zionistic traditions are the reverse of what we found them to be in Jer 7:1-15. In the prophetic speech, the covenant, especially the stipulations of the Decalogue (v 9), serves to critique the misinterpretation of the Temple according to which the ethical status of the worshippers is not important to the question of whether they live or die. In Psalm 50, the Temple tradition, with its emphasis upon the cosmic import of Mount Zion, serves to critique a misinterpretation of the Sinaitic covenant, in which the sacrifices it mandates are seen as having a material effect upon the lord in covenant. That lord, the psalm tells us, is the lord of the cosmos as well. He does not hunger for the flesh and thirst for the blood of the animals that Israel offers in obedience to the stipulations of Sinai. In Jeremiah's Temple speech, Sinai undermines the tendency in the Zion traditions to an otherworldliness evasive of responsibility, just as the transcendental dimension of the Zionistic element in Psalm 50 undermines the tendency in the covenant to view God as a this-worldly party with whom one can deal, *quid pro quo*. In Jeremiah 7, Sinai demolishes the hubris of Zion; in Psalm 50, Zion demolishes the hubris of Sinai. The traditions correct each other. Each is fulfilled only in the presence of the other. The whole is greater than the sum of its parts.

4. MOSES AND DAVID

One element often associated with Mount Zion is not found in Psalm 50, the king from the house of David. Could he, too, have been integrated into the legacy of Sinai, or was the dynastic grant to David doomed to do no more than to coexist with the old treaty tradition, if that?[27] Some scholars have argued that the integration was a reality. Cleus Schedl, for example, maintains that the messianic promise in the Hebrew Bible is simply the realization of a covenant blessing. In other words, Israel's observance of the stipulations of Sinai will bring about the rule of the ideal Davidid.[28] In a similar vein, Roland de Vaux noticed that anointment was not only the means of inauguration of Israelite kings, but also a rite of initiation into vassalage.[29] The implication is clear: the messianic hope, *sensu stricto*, the hope in the anointed king (*māšîaḥ*) of the house of David, is ultimately to be located within the tradition of Israel as the vassal of YHWH, that is, the tradition of Sinai. Finally, another researcher, Klaus Seybold, sees in the very fact that 2 Samuel 7 speaks of the election of David in covenantal language a firm indication of continuity with the Sinaitic material. He speaks of an "integration" of the two covenant traditions.[30]

27 See Levenson, "The Davidic Covenant and its Modern Interpreters," *CBQ* 40 (1978), esp. pp. 207-15.
28 C. Schedl, "Die heilsgeschichtliche Funktion der propheten," *BK* 19 (1964) 9-12.
29 De Vaux, "Le roi d'Israel, vassel de YHWH," in *Mélanges Eugene Tisserant* (Vatican City: Biblioteca Apostolica Vaticana, 1964) 1:119.
30 K. Seybold, *Das davidischen Königtum im Zeugnis der Propheten,*

The difficulty with Schedl's argument is that the messianic oracles in the Hebrew Bible tend to be phrased in such way as to stress the unexpected dimension of the advent of the new king:

> The people that walked in darkness
> Have seen a brilliant light;
> On those who dwelt in the land of the shadow of death,
> Light has dawned! (Isa 9:1)

One does not sense in these oracles that the messianic reign comes as something deserved, as a divine response to human righteousness. On the contrary, the prophets who deliver messianic promises are the same prophets who savage Israel for her wickedness. Seybold's observation about the covenantal context of the Davidic promise is equally weak, for, as we saw in Part 2,[31] the Sinaitic and Davidic covenants, at least as the latter appears in 2 Samuel 7 and Psalm 89, are of radically different types. The former is a *treaty*; the latter is a *grant*. Since covenant was not a unitary concept in ancient Israel, the use of the term should not be taken to indicate an integrative movement. The same criticism applies, *mutatis mutandis,* to de Vaux's argument. Anointing may have signified the Davidid's inauguration into fealty, but this need not imply that the backdrop to the ceremony is the Sinaitic/Mosaic concept of the vassalage of all Israel. The Davidic covenant chooses as vassal an Israelite, therefore, someone bound by Sinaitic norms, but the relationship does not have to be seen as directly involving Israel. It takes the form of a special alliance of YHWH and David.

There are texts in which the Davidic covenant is explicitly related, even subordinated to the Sinaitic. One thinks, for example, of Solomon's prayer at the dedication of his Temple:

> [24]"You kept the promise you made to your servant, my father David, fulfilling with deeds the promises you uttered, as it is now the case. [25]And now, YHWH God of Israel, keep the promise you made to your

FRLANT 107 (Göttingen: Vandenhoeck and Ruprecht, 1972) 44.
31 Pp. 98–101.

servant, my father David, when you said to him: You will not lack a man sitting before me on the throne of Israel, but only if your descendents guard their ways, walking before me as you have done. (1 Kgs 8:24–25).[32]

The allusion in v 25 is to the dynastic promise of Nathan to David in 2 Sam 7:8–16. The part about the house of YHWH has now been fulfilled (1 Kgs 8:24); only the other half of Nathan's prediction, the part about the house of David, is outstanding. What is interesting here is that the clause beginning with the words "but only if" departs radically from Nathan's oracle in that it makes the continuation of the Davidic dynasty conditional upon observance of certain stipulations. The royal family of Judah will wield the sceptre only so long as their deeds show that they deserve it. This is precisely the theology that 2 Sam 7:14–16 and Ps 89:31–38 explicitly and univocally negate. The subordination of the Davidic covenant to the Sinaitic in 1 Kgs 8:25, therefore, must be seen as a reinterpretation of the pristine Davidic covenantal material, a reinterpretation that reflects the growing canonical status of the Sinaitic traditions that will become the Pentateuch. 1 Kgs 8:25 is the vengeance of Moses upon David, of the "kingdom of priests" upon the hubris of the political state, for it resolves the clash between the two covenants in favor of the Mosaic one. The entitlement of the house of David is no longer indefeasible; it is contingent upon the observance of *mitsvot*. The ultimate implication of the alteration of the promise to David in 1 Kgs 8:25 becomes manifest in the work of the Chronicler, who changes "walking before me" to "walking in my Torah" (2 Chr 6:16). David has come to Canossa.

There is a school of interpretation, very different from that of Schedl, de Vaux, and Seybold,[33] which emphasizes this notion of

32 On the exilic dating of this part of 1 Kings 8, see Levenson, "From Temple to Synagogue," in *Traditions in Transformation,* ed. B. Halpern and Levenson (Winona Lake: Eisenbrauns, 1981) 142–66.

33 Similar to the thinking of these three is A. H. J. Gunneweg, "Sinaibund und Davidsbund," *VT* 10 (1960) 335–41.

a clash between the Sinaitic and Davidic covenants. John Bright, for example, in his *History of Israel,* writes that "the covenant with David inevitably tended to crowd the Sinaitic Covenant and its stipulations into the background, thereby setting up a tension between the two." Thus, the Davidic covenant could encourage Israel "to hallow the state in the name of God and to suppose that the aims of the state and the aims of religion must necessarily coincide."[34] For example, in the time of Jeremiah, "the people were [so] entrenched in the confidence that Temple, city, and nation were eternally secure in YHWH's covenant with David" that they became spiritually complacent.[35] In support of this, Bright cites three verses, Jer 5:12; 7:4; and 14:13. We shall return to these citations. The idea that the Davidic material implies the total identification of the state with the will of God appears in more pungent form in the thinking of George Mendenhall. "As in other pagan states" Mendenhall writes, "the very idea that one could appeal to God against the decision or acts of the one to whom God had delegated final authority was a logical and political absurdity, which only the prophetic movement persisted in. . . ."[36] The difference in thrusts between the Mosaic and the Davidic covenants is nicely stated by Walter Brueggemann. Whereas the former "is radically concerned for *justice,*" the latter "is more concerned for *order.*"[37] The two covenants thus stand in diametric opposition. One had to give way, and since the Davidic could marshal political support, it was the Sinaitic which waned

---

34   Bright, *History,* 227 . Bright sees "the autumn festival" as the occasion for this crowding out of the Sinaitic covenant by the Davidic.

35   Bright, *History,* 326. Bright's certainty about the negative impact of the Davidic upon the Sinaitic covenant is diminished in his later book, *Covenant and Promise* (Philadelphia: Westminster, 1976), in which he notes that "to be sure, we cannot document this as we should like; but it was almost certainly the case" (p. 73).

36   Mendenhall, *The Tenth Generation* (Baltimore and London: Johns Hopkins, 1973) 87.

37   W. A. Brueggemann, "The Epistemological Crisis in Israel's Two Histories (Jer 9:22–23)," in *Israelite Wisdom,* Terrien Festschrift, ed. J. G. Gammie et al. (Missoula: Scholars, 1978) 86 (his italics).

in Judah. E. W. Nicholson goes so far as to write that "the Davidic covenant traditions eventually took precedence over the older Sinaitic tradition and developed it in such a manner as to alter its normative form and reduce it to a secondary position.
..."[38]

There is much of value in the thinking of the school that focuses upon the disjuncture of the two covenant traditions.[39] As we saw at length in Parts 1 and 2, the two derive from different Near Eastern antecedents, and, as we saw above, they can come into conflict, as in 1 Kings 8. On the other hand, it is an overstatement to present them as always standing in sharp and irreconcilable antithesis. We have already noted that Davidic circles were quite capable of accepting and redacting literature that had originally no place for David but a central place for Moses, for example, the book of Hosea. There may be a tension in the final product of such redaction, but the tension was tolerable to the proponents of Judean royalism. Not always did one covenant yield to the other. Furthermore, it is important to remember that the Davidic covenant as presented in both 2 Sam 7:14 and Ps 89:31–38 would seem to presuppose obligation by the Sinaitic pact. If the king disobeys the *mitsvot*, he will be punished. No statement of the Davidic covenant identifies the state with the will of God or exempts the king from punishment. In fact, a Hittite grant, which both de Vaux and Weinfeld adduce as a parallel to the Davidic covenant, specifically states that a sinning king will be executed. The only qualification is that the throne will not be alienated from his line.[40] To be sure, this qualification does limit the application of the curse of the Sinaitic covenant that

---

38 Nicholson, *Deuteronomy*, 93.

39 A similar thrust can be seen in L. Rost, "Sinaibund und Davidsbund," *TLZ* 72 (1947) 129–34; M. Sekine, "Davidsbund und Sinaibund bei Jeremiah," *VT* 9 (1959) 47–57; and R. E. Clements, *Abraham and David*, SBT 2/5 (London: SCM, 1967), esp. pp. 54, 68.

40 De Vaux, "Le roi," 125; Weinfeld, "Covenant of Grant," 189. The grant is that to Ulmi-Teshub of Dattasa. See D. J. McCarthy, *Treaty and Covenant*, 2nd ed., AnBib 21A (Rome: Pontifical Biblical Institute, 1978)

> YHWH will drive you and your king whom you will set up over you to a nation you and your fathers have not known, and there you shall serve other gods, of wood and stone. (Deut 28:36)

If David's throne is secure forever, as 2 Samuel 7 and Psalm 89 stipulate, then YHWH's punishment cannot include the overthrow and exile of the royal house of Judah. In Matitiahu Tsevat's metaphor, ". . . if the existence of the confederacy, which is the body, is conditional, kingship, which is an organ, cannot be unconditional."[41] This contradiction should not, however, be emphasized to the point of claiming, as Bright and Mendenhall do, that the Davidic covenant implies the infallibility of the king and his possession of ultimate authority. Any king who imagines otherwise—and we have no record of any who did—would be sure to feel the "rod" and the "lashes" of which 2 Sam 7:14 and Ps 89:33 warn. Nor is there any evidence that the Judean masses misinterpreted the Davidic covenant to mean that they were exempt from the stipulations of Sinai and the punishment of God. Of the three verses in Jeremiah that Bright cites in support of the existence of this interpretation, not one even mentions the covenant with David. Jer 7:4 attacks the people for relying on the mindless incantation, "the Temple of YHWH, the Temple of YHWH, the Temple of YHWH." I argued in Part 2 that Jeremiah's barbs are directed against a degradation of the Zion mythos which emptied the cosmic mountain of its fundamental ethical character,[42] but one cannot assume that the Davidic covenant, which is not at issue here, was similarly reinterpreted by the iniquitous Judeans of Jeremiah's or any other time. Not only Zion, but also the kings who ruled from it were celebrated as sources of justice (e.g., 2 Sam 8:15). In fact, one of the most daringly mythological of the royal psalms, one ascribed variously

302-5.

41 M. Tsevat, "Studies in the Book of Samuel, III," *HUCA* 34 (1963) 73. On this, see also Levenson, "Who Inserted the Book of the Torah," *HTR* 68 (1975) 223-27.

42 Pp. 167-68.

both to David and to Solomon, sees the king's justice as a manifestation of God's (Ps 72:1-2, 12-14).

This concern for justice, especially justice for the poor, was
characteristic of the Judean concept of kingship, just as it was
characteristic of the Mesopotamian and Canaanite concepts
before.[43] It cannot be seen as the result of Sinaitic influence.
Brueggemann's antithesis between justice and order is foreign to
Israel's patterns of thought. Only a just order is perdurable. In
fact, the king's calling is to guarantee the order of justice against
all predation and perversion. The global empire that the psalmist
wishes for him (v 8) is thus a dominion of justice. The concept of
justice of our century cannot, perhaps, tolerate imperialism. The
ancient one could. Of course, nothing in the royal theology denies
that cosmic order may not be visible in the dealings of men. It is
the duty of the king, however, to make it visible, and the glory of
the kings who are esteemed was that they strove to do so. They
became archetypes of success.

Finally, the idea that appears in Bright, Mendenhall, and
especially Brueggemann that the Davidic crowded out the
Sinaitic covenant is belied by the relative number of references to
the two. Only a handful of passages mention the Davidic covenant
or its salient ideas, and only two, 2 Samuel 7 and Psalm 89,
expound it with clarity and detail. Awareness of the Sinaitic
covenant, by contrast, appears in most of the books of the Hebrew
Bible. The block from Exodus 19 until the close of 2 Kings is
saturated with it. These proportions would be quite odd if the
Davidic replaced the Sinaitic as the focus of attention. The most

---

43   E.g., see the Code of Hammurabi, king of Babylon about the
eighteenth century B.C.E., translated by T. J. Meek, *ANET,* 163-80. In his
prologue, Hammurabi sees as central to his divine commission the obligation
to insure "that the strong ... not oppress the weak" (p. 164). A Canaanite
example can be found in the Ugaritic "Legend of King Keret," translated by
H. L. Ginsberg in *ANET,* 142-49. Cf. Ps 82:2-4. On the specific event
underlying the king's proclamation of justice in Mesopotamia and Israel, see
Weinfeld, *Deuteronomy and the Deuteronomic School* (Oxford: Clarendon)
153-55. See also Fensham, "Widow, Orphan, and the Poor in Ancient Near
Eastern Legal and Wisdom Literature," *JNES* 21 (1962) 129-39.

one can reasonably argue is that the courtiers in Jerusalem paid more attention to the Davidic materials than to the Mosaic. Even this is exceedingly difficult to ascertain, since the two blocks overlap so much on practical points, such as the need for justice and compassion for the poor. In any event, the point at issue in the Davidic convenantal texts, namely, which family has a valid entitlement to the throne, is not likely to have engaged the minds of ordinary Judeans continually, as it would an attendant upon the king in Jerusalem. There is plentful evidence for royal participation in, and patronage of, the Sinai cult on Zion.[44] After all, the city becomes the religious capital only when David moved the ancient Ark of the Covenant there (2 Samuel 6). But there is no evidence for a royal cultus independent of the traditions of the old Israelite league. Israel's deafness to the voice of Sinai cannot be blamed on Zion or on the theology of kingship so often associated with it.

If the Davidic covenant never displaced the Sinaitic in the Hebrew Bible, it did, in a sense, in the New Testament. The emerging church adopted Paul's position that the messiah of their belief brought exemption from the law of Moses.[45] Faith in the messianic identity of Jesus, son of David (Matt 1:1–17), enables the Christian to experience the grace of God without a commitment to this law (Galatians 3). It is not that the law is bad or primitive; on the contrary, it is "holy and just and good" (Rom 7:12). But in the new situation in which the Davidic promise has been fulfilled, the law has expired. It comes to be relegated to the status of an *Old* Testament. The effect of this messianic suspension of Sinai is to render the relationship between the two dispensations, the old and the new, immensely problematic, for it endows the religion of the church with a shape very different from that of the religion of the Hebrew Bible and of Rabbinic Judaism. In other words, the Christian Bible includes within it a book of an

44 See Levenson, *Theology of the Program,* 55–107.
45 Cf. J. C. Rylaarsdam, "Jewish-Christian Relationship: The Two Covenants and the Dilemmas of Christology," *JES* 9 (1972) 249–70.

alien religion.[46] The resulting tension, which has plagued the church from the beginning, is at times so intense that voices in the church have been heard to question the status of the Old Testament as Christian scripture.

In Judaism, which adheres to both the Mosaic covenant and the messianic expectation, the relationship between Moses and David, Sinai and Zion, remains pluriform. In the Talmud and midrash, as in the Hebrew Bible, no single statement of the relationship suffices. On the one hand, one finds sayings of the rabbis which make the fulfillment of the Davidic promise conditional upon Israel's obedience. The messiah would come "Today, if you will heed his voice," the prophet Elijah tells Rabbi Joshua ben Levi, quoting Ps 95:7. Here, David is again subordinated to Moses, and the restoration of Zion, an essential component of Jewish messianic expectation, is subordinated to the righteousness of the Jews, as yet unrealized. Against this homogenization and harmonization of the traditions, one can cite, from the same page of the Talmud,[47] the statement of Rabbi Yochanan that "the Son of David will come only in a generation which is entirely blameless or entirely wicked." Rabbi Yochanan's second possibility preserves for David a measure of autonomy over against Moses, although it does not detach the two traditions definitively and absolutely, as Paul did. It is impossible to give a consistent, systematic account of the relationship of these items in a tradition in which statements so contradictory are not only preserved, but venerated. What can be said, however, is that the survival of these two ancient traditions endows the Jew with the obligation to become an active partner, in the redemption not only of his people, but of the world, to live in a simultaneous and indissoluble awareness of commandment and of promise. The two poles of Sinai and Zion thus delineate an entry not only into the Jewish Bible, but also into Jewish life.

---

46 See A. H. J. Gunneweg, *Understanding the Old Testament,* OTL (Philadelphia: Westminster, 1978), esp. pp. 142–72.

47 *b. Sanh.* 98a.

INDEX OF CITATIONS

Genesis

1–11	40
1:1–2:4a	41, 144
1:2	133
1:31	143
2:1–2	143
2:3	143
2:4	118
2:4b–14	129–31
2:4b–3:24	128
2:6–14	159
4:1	78
6–8	134–35
6–9	57, 152
9	100 n. 20
11:31	41
12:1–3	11
12:6	6 n. 8
14:18	93
15	45
17	45, 100 n. 20
17:1–4	82
22	147–48
22:2	94
22:14	94, 95, 141
33:20	112
49:5	10 n. 16
49:8–12	162

Exodus

3:1	16 n. 3, 21
3:1–6	20
3:14	22
5:2	22
5:3	22
6:2	58
13:16	79
15:11	59–60, 63, 68

15:17	112, 136
16:1	20
17:6	16
19	89, 90
19:1	16
19:3b–8	24–25, 26 n. 10, 30–32, 37, 40
19:4	41
19:5	208
19:5–6	72
19:6	71
19:8	85
19:16–22	15
19:21	95 n. 11
20:2	32, 83
20:3	59, 65, 150 n. 109
20:2–3	80 n. 78
20:4–5	197
20:5	200 n. 19
20:22–23:33	18, 48–49
20:25	96
20:11	144
21:12	46 n. 34
21:18–19	46, 52
21:34	7 n. 10
22:17	197
22:19	65
22:20	46, 52
22:21	11 n. 21
23:6	11 n. 21
23:6–8	197
23:12	144 n. 102
24:4	50
25:9	140
25:31–40	132 n. 78
25:40	140
25:31–39	20–21

25–30	128
33:6	16
34:12–16	66
34:27	50
37:17–24	132 n. 78
39:32	143
39:43	143
40:9	143

Leviticus

2	71 n. 70
3	132
4	174
11	52, 121
11:45	52
17–26	18
19:10	11 n. 21
19:13	197
19:17–18	46
19:18	51, 53
20:22–26	120
21:21–23	127–28
22:12–16	128
23	121
25:3–7	143
26	35
26:7–8	80 n. 79

Numbers

6:9–20	128
7:89	123 n. 59
10:29–33	21
14	100 n. 20
15:37–41	82–84, 121
15:39	29 n. 15
25	100 n. 20
25:10–12	204

Deuteronomy

4:7	138
4:9–10	18
4:9–19	150 n. 109
4:10	17
4:15	16
4:15–16	95 n. 10
4:24	20
4:39	59–60
5:1–4	81
5:6–7	80 n. 78
5:14	144 n. 102
6:4–9	82–84
7:6–8	76
7:7	120
10:12–15	77
11:13–21	82–84
12	193
12:2	36
12:5	125
12–26	18
13	68
13:2–19	65–66
14	52
14:2	52
14:21	52
16	146
16:13	144
16:20	172 n. 129
17:14–20	190–91, 193
18:15–19	191
26:5	40
27:15	197
27:17	197
27:19	11 n. 21
28	35
28:7	80 n. 79
28:36	214
30:19–20	81
31:10–13	34
32	55 n. 48
33:2	91
33:8	126
33:10	126
34:5–12	6
34:10	90, 187–88

Joshua

			115, 213
7:24–25	200	8:15	214
10	93	12:20	96
15:63	93	13–20	193
19:28	93	24	94
22:19	136	24:15–25	95
24	40	1 Kings	
24:1–28	32–36, 37	1	131
24:6–7	38	1:7–8	167
24:24	39	1:33–45	131 n. 74

Judges

		1:50–53	96 n. 13
3:15	71 n. 70	2:10	105
5:4–5	20	2:26–27	167
6:22–24	95	2:28–31	96 n. 13
8	74	5–7	148
8:22–23	73	5:17–19	96
9:37	115	6:1	105–6
9:39	119 n. 52	6:19–28	123

1 Samuel

		6:38	143
2:27–36	205 n. 24	7:13–14	120
3:1–18	123 n. 59	7:23–26	138–39
3:3	96	7:49	21
4	167	8	213
8	74	8:2	144
8:7	73	8:24–25	210–11
15	98	8:28–29	125
16:7	147	8:31–55	144

2 Samuel

		15:4	101
5:1–3	74	18	37 n. 24, 90, 110
5:6–7	93–94		n. 38
5:6–8	162	19	90, 191
5:7	92	19:8	16 n. 3
5:8	160	19:11–12	89
5:9	95	21	191
6	162, 216	22	57–58
6:17	96	2 Kings	
7	98, 156, 157, 200–ֿ	8:19	101
	201, 204, 209,	10:28	205
	210, 214, 215	10:30	203, 204, 205
7:8–16	188, 203, 211	15:8–12	204
7:14	99 n. 16, 155 n.	15:37	157

16:5   157, 160

16:7   158

22–23   35

Isaiah

2:2–4   126 n. 66, 131

6   71, 125–26

6:1–8   122–24

6:3   141, 170–71

7–8   130, 156–61

8:18   91

9:1   210

10:21–23   160

14:12–15   124, 128

28:23–29   164

29:1–8   161–65

30:15   153

40:18–19   150

41:2   172 n. 129

44   69

45:1   205 n. 24

51:9–11   139 n. 91

51:16   137

55:3   205 n. 24

57:13   136

66:1   144–45

Jeremiah

1:1   167

5:12   212

7:1–15   165–69, 173, 207, 208, 209

7:4   212, 214

10:2–10   67–68

14:13   212

17:12   133

26:1   166 n. 124

26:18   197

28   167

46:10   129

Ezekiel

1:28   150

5:5   115–16, 119

16:14   129

18   200 n. 19

28:2–5   128–29

28:11–15   128

34:23   105, 201

38:12   115–17, 118, 119 n. 52

40–42   182 n. 138

40–48   49 n. 41

43:2   133

43:13–17   139

43:15   162

Hosea

1:6   76

1:9   76

2   110 n. 38

2:15–25   77–79

3:5   194

5:1   190 n. 4

7:10–13   72

8:10   190 n. 4

8:11–14   192 n. 6

9:15   192 n. 6

10:3–4   190 n. 4

10:5   192 n. 6

12:14   191

13:10–11   190 n. 4

Amos

1:1   202

5:4–5   192

5:4–6   189

7:10–11   205

7:10–17   202

Micah

1:2–7   197

1:5–6   196

2:1–2   197

3:9–12   197

3:12   196, 199

4:1–5   126 n. 66, 131

5:1–5   197–98, 199

5:5b	199
5:6–8	198
5:11	197
5:12–13	197
6:1–8	54–55, 195, 206

Zechariah

2:11	137 n. 89

Malachi

1:7–9	71
2:6–7	126
2:14	76

Psalms

2	70, 154–56, 157
2:6–7	201
2:7	163
11:4	140
14	61 n. 54
15	172–76, 177, 183
15:2–5b	178
21:8	172 n. 130
23	177
23:6	176
24	169–72, 174–76, 183
27	177
27:4	176
30	96 n. 12
36:8–10	132–33
36:10	159
42–83	61 n. 54
46	151–54, 156
46:5	159
46:6	172
46:7	155
46:10	165
48	145–51
48:1–2	112
48:2–3	136
48:3	124, 163, 175
48:4	163
48:6	164

48:9	174
48:13–14	177
50	206–9
50:2	118, 129
50:2–3	91
53	61 n. 54
65:8	153 n. 113
68	19, 20
68:8–9	91
72	215
74:12–17	139 n. 91
76:3	92, 155
78	146
78:67–68	196
78:69–70	106
80	203 n. 21
81	80, 195, 206
82	61–62, 112
84	176–78
85:5–8	58
89	98–99, 157, 200–201, 204, 210, 211, 214, 215
89:9–11	139 n. 91
89:26	108
89:27	112, 155 n. 115
89:31–38	213
89:114	139 n. 91
90:2	152
92	183
93	109, 139
95:3	61
95:7	217
97	90, 195
97:8	196
110:1–2	155–56
112:6	172 n. 130
115	110
115:4–8	109
125:1–2	173
132:13–14	144

	141:2	180
	145:18	138
Job		
	38:1	164
Proverbs		
	10:30	172 n. 130
	24:32	149
Lamentations		
	2:15	129
Daniel		
	2:44	85
	6:11	125
Ezra		
	3:6	71
	10:1	177 n. 133
1 Chronicles		
	11:5	91
	17:21	10
	22:9	144, 145
	28:2–3	96
	28:11–19	140
2 Chronicles		
	3:1	94, 141
	6:16	211
	13:11	132
	28:17	157

INDEX OF AUTHORS

Aharoni, Y., 193 n. 7

Ahlström, G. W., 123 n. 58, 203 n. 21

Albrektson, B., 69 n. 69

Albright, W. F., 19 n. 6, 120 n. 53, 139 n. 92

Alfrink, B., 124 n. 62, 146 n. 105

Alt, A., 45–48, 49, 192 n. 5

Alter, R., 8 n. 13

Anderson, B. W., 3

Auerbach, E., 147–48

Barr, J., 25 n. 10

Baltzer, D., 25 n. 10, 26, 29 n. 16 & 17, 37 n. 25, 82 n. 82

Begrich, J., 126 n. 65

Bentzen, A., 193 n. 8

Beyerlin, W., 25 n. 10, 195–99

Bickerman, E., 26 n. 11

Blenkinsopp, J., 142 n. 100, 187 n. 1

Bolling, R. G., 117 n. 46

Bright, J., 16 n. 2, 163 n. 120, 199 n. 18, 212, 214–15

Brinker, R., 193 n. 7

Brueggemann, W. A., 212, 215

Buber, M., 33 n. 22, 179–80

Budde, K., 61 n. 55

Burrows, E., 134 n. 85, 142

Busink, Th. A., 120 n. 53

Cassuto, M. D., 142 n. 100

Childs, B., 25 n. 10, 30 n. 19, 50 n. 42, 52 n. 45, 103, 124 n. 62, 163 n. 120, 164

Clements, R. E., 122 n. 57, 139 n. 92, 213 n. 39

Clifford, R. J., 17 n. 4, 109 n. 36, 111–13, 124, 130, 151

Coote, R. B., 89 n. 1

Cross, F. M., 19 n. 6, 59 n. 50, 89 n. 1, 91 n. 2, 101 n. 21, 109 n. 35, 139 n. 91, 153, 167 n. 126, 194 n. 10, 205 n. 25

Dahood, M., 153

Davies, G. H., 107 n. 30

Delekat, L., 174 n. 131

Eichrodt, W., 2

Eissfeldt, O., 198 n. 15

Eliade, M., 103, 114, 115 n. 44, 122, 124, 127, 136

Eilliger, 198 n. 16

Ezra, A. Ibn, 6 n. 8, 82 n. 85, 155

Fackenheim, E. L., 5 n. 6, 8 n. 14

Farmer, H. H., 63, 65

Fensham, F. C., 11 n. 22, 215 n. 43

Finkelstein, J. J., 10 n. 17

Finley, M. J., 104 n. 28

Fishbane, M. A., 119 n. 52

Fontenrose, J. E., 102 n. 22

Frankfort, H., 73 n. 71, 108 n. 33, 156 n. 116

Freedman, D. N., 19 n. 6

Gaster, T. H., 117 n. 47

Gordon, C. H., 60 n. 51

Greenspoon, L. J., 182 n. 139

Gray, J., 93 n. 5

Gunkel, H., 107 n. 30, 129 n. 70

Gunneweg, A. H. J., 211 n. 33, 217 n. 46

Halpern, B., 74 n. 72
Hanson, P. D., 170
Haran, M., 122 n. 57
Harvey, J., 55 n. 48
Harvey, V. A., 69 n. 68
Hayes, J. H., 7 n. 11
Heidel, A., 64 n. 61, 109 n. 35
Hertz, J. H., 5 n. 6, 6, 7 n. 12
Heschel, A. J., 145, 180 n. 135
Hillers, D. R., 27 n. 12, 54 n. 46
Hooke, S. H., 134 n. 85
Huffmon, H. B., 44 n. 30, 55 n. 48

Jacobson, T., 119 n. 52
Jellinek, A., 118 n. 48
Johnson, A. R., 156 n. 116, 200 n. 19
Joshua ben Korhah, Rabbi, 84
Joshua ben Levi, Rabbi, 217
Judah the Patriarch, Rabbi, 2

Kaiser, O., 109 n. 35, 130 n. 72, 162, 164
Kapelrud, A. S., 94 n. 140
Kaufmann, Y., 11 n. 20, 40, 56, 67–68, 107 n. 31, 108–11
Kenyon, K., 92 n. 3
Kraeling, E. G., 76 n. 73
Kraus, H. -J., 80 n. 80
Kristensen, W. B., 114 n. 43
Kutsch, E., 25 n. 10

Labushchagne, C. J., 64 n. 58 & 59, 69
Lauterbach, J. Z., 85 n. 88
Levenson, J., 49 n 41, 50 n. 43, 68 n. 66, 98 n. 15, 99 n. 17 & 18, 100 n. 20, 109 n. 37, 125 n. 64, 128 n. 69, 140 n. 94, 141 n. 97, 144 n. 101
Lewis, C. S., 174 n. 131

Maimonides, M., 182–83

Margoliot, M., 67 n. 65
McCarthy, D. J., 25 n. 10, 26 n. 11, 21, 35–36, 98 n. 15, 213 n. 40
Mendenhall, G. E., 26, 37, 41, 48–49, 212, 214–15
Meyers, C. L., 21 n. 7, 132 n. 78
Miles, J. A., 8 n. 15
Milgrom, J., 170 n. 128
Miller, P. D., 91 n. 2
Moran, W. L., 28 n. 14, 31 n. 20, 77 n. 74
Morenz, S., 119 n. 52
Morgenstern, J., 61 n. 53, 129 n. 71
Mowinckel, S., 80 n. 80
Muilenburg, J., 26 n. 10

Newman, M., 25 n. 10
Nicholson, E. W., 189 n. 3, 194 n. 9, 213

Oded, B., 157 n. 117
Otto, R., 16

Patai, R., 133, 134 n. 82, 140 n. 93
Paul, S. M., 47 n. 37
Perlitt, L., 25 n. 10

Rashbam, 7, 82 n. 85
Rad, G. von, 40 n. 26, 44 n. 31, 81 n. 81, 193 n. 8
Rashi, 10 n. 16, 60
Ringgren, H., 109 n. 37
Roberts, J. J. M., 69 n. 69
Robinson, A., 124 n. 63
Rogerson, J. W., 102 n. 23, 104, 107 n. 30
Rost, L., 213 n. 39
Rylaarsdam, J. C., 216 n. 45

Saggs, H. W. F., 10 n. 19, 45 n. 32, 108 n. 33, 109 n. 37

Sanders, J. A., 188 n. 2
Sarna, N. M., 6 n. 9, 121 n. 54
Schedl, C., 209–11
Schmidt, H., 134 n. 84
Schmitt, G., 36 n. 24
Sekine, M., 213 n. 39
Seybold, K., 209–11
Shanks, H., 92 n. 3
Simon bar Yohai, Rabbi, 141
Speiser, E. A., 5, 130 n. 72, 131
Sperling, D., 117 n. 47

Talmon, S., 23 n. 9, 115–16, 120
Terrien, S., 117 n. 47
Thompson, T. L., 10 n. 18
Thornton, T. G. G., 203 n. 21
Thureau-Dangin, R., 140 n. 94
Tigay, J., 71 n. 70
Tillich, P., 142
Tsevat, M., 214

Urbach, E. A., 82 n. 83, 85 n. 89

Vaux, R. de, 74 n. 72, 80 n. 77, 94 n. 9, 96 n. 13, 209–11, 213
Voegelin, E., 122 n, 55

Weinfeld, M., 5, 17 n. 5, 46 n. 34, 48 n. 38, 55 n. 47, 66, 100 n. 19, 140 n. 94, 142 n. 100, 204, 213, 215 n. 43
Weiser, A., 174 n. 131
Weisman, Z., 22–23
Wellhausen, J., 2, 36 n. 23
Wensinck, A. J., 116 n. 45
Widengren, G., 132 n. 77
Wolff, H. W., 78 n. 75 & 76
Wright, G. E., 42–43, 55 n. 48, 105 n. 29, 107 n. 31, 120 n. 53
Yadin, Y., 94 n. 7
Yochanan, Rabbi, 217

Zimmerli, W., 119 n. 51, 145 n. 103